A SLAUGHTERED
LAMB

A SLAUGHTERED
LAMB

REVELATION AND THE APOCALYPTIC
RESPONSE TO EVIL AND SUFFERING

GREGORY
STEVENSON

Abilene Christian University Press

A SLAUGHTERED LAMB
Revelation and the Apocalyptic Response to Evil and Suffering

ACU
PRESS

Copyright 2013 by Gregory Stevenson

ISBN 978-0-89112-424-5

Printed in the United States of America

Cover design by Thinkpen Design, LLC
Interior text design by Sandy Armstrong

For information contact:
Abilene Christian University Press
1626 Campus Court
Abilene, Texas 79601

1-877-816-4455 toll free
www.abilenechristianuniversitypress.com

13 14 15 16 17 18 / 7 6 5 4 3 2 1

To Nicholas, Alexandra, and Isabella,
who constantly inspire me.

I pray this book will inspire you
as you seek to be faithful witnesses.

ACKNOWLEDGMENTS

The writing of a book is a community project and so there are several people I would like to thank for their various contributions. John Barton, Mike Cope, John Mark Hicks, and Rubel Shelly read portions of the manuscript and offered insightful and helpful suggestions. I also thank Mike Cope for his tireless and repeated encouragements to "finish the book." I would like to thank Carl Holladay and Luke Johnson for their always helpful advice at various stages of this project. I thank Patti Bowman for her encouragement and generosity. I am grateful to my colleagues and to the administration of Rochester College for their support and to the students in my Revelation classes whose questions and comments have helped me refine some of my thinking in this book. Above all I want to thank my family for their patience and support throughout this project and to thank God for revealing himself through the slaughtered Lamb.

CONTENTS

PART ONE
ORIENTATION

INTRODUCTION

1

Revelation is a dangerous book. Its heavy use of symbolism, controversial imagery, and foreign genre (apocalyptic) creates a combustible mixture that often explodes into misinterpretation and abuse. Historically, Revelation has played a role in the perpetuation of violence, the justification of warfare and genocide, the stoking of vengeful fantasies, and the creation of a militant and arrogant perversion of Christianity that trades in self-glorification. Such irresponsible interpretations of the book are indeed dangerous, yet we should not therefore deceive ourselves into thinking that more responsible interpretations carry any less of an edge. Even when handled faithfully, the book of Revelation remains dangerous because it does not allow Christians to be comfortable in this world. Revelation challenges our worldviews, demands allegiance to God alone, and calls for a life of radical obedience and service. It does provide comfort to those who suffer, yet does so paradoxically by encouraging them to continue in the same behavior (faithful witness) that generated their suffering in the first place. In a world like that of our twenty-first century culture where "the good life" is defined as prosperity and comfort, where tolerance is the highest value, where suffering is an evil to be avoided and eradicated at all costs, where the kingdom of God is often made indistinguishable from the kingdom of the world, Revelation is a dangerous book indeed.

Some Christians, through their mishandling of the book, have made it dangerous in ways it ought not to be. Others have so domesticated the book of Revelation by making it into little more than an assurance of Christian victory in the face of oppression that they have removed its bite. Reading Revelation as a guide for faith means not just that we seek to avoid the abuses of the past, but that we allow it to be dangerous to us today by challenging our thinking, calling us to account, and questioning our allegiances. Revelation is dangerous because it calls upon us to conform our lives to the pattern of the Christ—a pattern defined as a life of faithfulness beset by suffering and opposition. Yes, Revelation is a dangerous book, but perhaps a book that holds no danger to us at all is not a book worth reading.

The Relevance of Revelation

No book of the Bible generates such opposite extremes of fanaticism and antagonism as the book of Revelation. The former group reads the book as a prophetic blueprint for the return of Christ, which is invariably dependent on current events, and so embraces Revelation as an indispensable guide to living in the last days. For the latter group, Revelation's dense symbolism and problematic narrative render the book, at best, open to frequent misinterpretation and, at worst, incomprehensible. For them it is a book with little relevance for Christian faith in the twenty-first century. Between these two poles of fanatical attachment and outright rejection lies the curious combination of intrigue and indifference. Most Christians are simultaneously drawn to and repelled by the book of Revelation, much like a child who covers his eyes during a scary movie yet cannot help but spread his fingers enough to allow selective peaking. They are compelled by the book's images of hope, its suggestion of a grand plan for creation, and the comfort of its eschatological vision, yet find the demonic locusts, obscure references, and complex system of symbolic enumeration to be an impediment to clear communication. They suspect there may be theological value concealed within the book, but are not convinced it's worth the effort to uncover. For them, Revelation lacks the narrative clarity of the Gospels, the theological depth of Romans, and the practical application of James. They find its relevance to be in doubt, while giving lip service to the book's message by watering down John's twenty-two dense chapters to simple motivational platitudes like "We win!"

What all of these popular responses to the book of Revelation have in common is a tendency to reduce Revelation's theological message to assurances of Christian victory based in the threat/promise of individual judgment and reward. Unfortunately, this creates the perception that Revelation is primarily about the end of time and one's ultimate and personal destination. I suggest, however, that Revelation is one of the most relevant books in Scripture for the *daily* living out of the Christian faith in the twenty-first century. One reason is because Revelation addresses a highly contemporary issue—the maintaining of Christian faithfulness in a world saturated with evil and suffering. We live in a world where, despite rapid and astounding medical advancements, diseases ravage human lives. A quick perusal of cable news shows opens our eyes to evil and suffering on a global scale: genocide, famine, tsunamis, terrorism, military suppression, and heartbreaking levels of poverty. The growing epidemic of violence in American schools alerts us to the frightening reality that we live in a world where parents send their children off to school in the morning with no guarantee they will be coming home. We live in a world where accounts of murder, rape, and child abuse occupy more time on the evening news than the sports and weather combined. How can one take seriously the words of the old hymn "This Is My Father's World" when so much evidence points to the contrary? How does one maintain faithful witness to Christ in a culture that embraces materialism as lifestyle, wealth and power as the ultimate good, pornography as harmless sexual expression, gambling as a form of government revenue, and the idolization of celebrity figures?

The book of Revelation is apocalyptic literature and one of the functions of apocalyptic literature is to alter perceptions of reality. Because most people's perceptions of reality are intertwined with their experiences of evil and suffering, it is not surprising that apocalyptic writings regularly explore these topics. In particular, the book of Revelation addresses the challenge of living a life patterned after the witness of Christ in a world that opposes such witness whether through active opposition or through more subtle and deceptive forms. As such, Revelation's engagement of the topics of evil and suffering evoke numerous questions that have abiding relevance for any who seek to live a life of faithful Christian witness. Why do Christians suffer? Why does God allow suffering as a component of his creation? What is the nature of evil and what is God doing about it? What is a Christian's responsibility in the face of evil and suffering? How does one maintain a belief in the sovereignty and justice of God in a world beset by injustice?

From John's opening assertion that he is their "companion in the affliction" (1:9; my translation) to the book's concluding imagery of a holy city where there no longer exists "mourning nor crying nor pain" (21:4),[1] Revelation presents a narrative that from beginning to end engages the topic of human suffering. Likewise, though Revelation employs the terminology of "evil" sparingly,[2] the book contains highly provocative images of evil, including a seven-headed red dragon bent on war, two ferocious and blasphemous beasts, and a "great whore" who is intoxicated from drinking the blood of the saints. With such imagery and more, John constructs a narrative world of symbols in which he reinterprets his readers' experiences of evil and suffering in the light of divine revelation.

Thinking about Evil and Suffering

Writing a book on Revelation is a daunting task due to its pervasive use of symbolism and volatile history of interpretation. Adding the topics of evil and suffering to the mix creates a whole other level of complexity because modern thought on these topics is equally varied and debated.

It is not my intention to provide a comprehensive discussion of evil and suffering as such an enterprise would be well beyond the scope of any single book. My focus is on the message of Revelation as it relates to evil and suffering and so I primarily limit my observations to a *theological* exploration of these concepts, knowing full well that they acquire new complexities and raise new questions when explored from a philosophical, social-scientific, or medical perspective.

Although I will explore some introductory aspects of the broader social and philosophical debates on evil and suffering as a means of laying a foundation, most of my analysis of Revelation operates with a definition of evil derived from the text itself. In Revelation John envisions evil as that which stands in *opposition* to the kingdom of God. As such, Revelation more commonly engages evil and suffering as they relate to one's choices or allegiances in the world rather than to experiences some call "natural evils" (natural disasters, disease, etc.). I believe that the message of Revelation can speak to experiences of suffering that go beyond this more narrow focus, yet most of my introductory comments on evil and suffering and my analysis of Revelation follow John's lead. Although a more detailed discussion of evil and suffering occurs in the next chapter, it is important to highlight here two foundational principles for my approach to these topics.

First is *acceptance of the reality of evil* (and, by extension, "good" as well). Talking about evil as a reality is problematic because evil is an abstract concept that is difficult to define or quantify. A definition of evil that functions well in one context may be ill-suited to another. If one identifies an act of harm willingly perpetrated on another as "evil," does one consider pinching someone on the arm to be the same "evil" as an act of murder? Further complicating the matter is the movement within Western culture to downplay or even deny evil. For some the concept of evil belongs to the realms of mythology and superstition, not to the grounded world of human rationality. This causes them to locate the origin of human destructiveness in natural and social processes. The result is a shifting of blame away from personal responsibility and choice. "Evil" becomes merely the unintended result of irregular brain chemistry, genetic anomalies, dysfunctional family situations, or environmental pressures. Others view "good" and "evil" as the language of manipulation. They are simply terms used to induce guilt, to motivate others or ourselves towards or away from certain behaviors, or to justify positions or actions by demonizing the opposition while declaring ourselves to be on the side of the angels. "Good" and "evil" have no intrinsic reality. All that matters is power—who has it (and who doesn't) and how they use it.

When I write of the "reality" of evil, I mean by it that evil has validity as a category of human experience and is *helpful* language that allows us to conceptualize certain experiences that are otherwise disorienting at best or incomprehensible at worst. Any attempt to mitigate evil as a category of human experience robs us of a valuable component of human expression. There are acts so vile that no other language does them justice, that no other explanation (biological, social, environmental) helps us make sense of them. When a child is tortured, raped, and murdered, we could discuss at length the perpetrator's abusive childhood or chemical imbalances in his brain, but ultimately we possess no better terminology in the English language to capture the soul-rending offensiveness of such acts than "evil."

From a theological perspective, we could take this a step further as the concepts of good and evil have a particular validity within the Judeo-Christian worldview where they are ultimately rooted in the *imago dei* (the image of God). As beings created in the image of God, we conceptualize "goodness" in terms of conformity to that image. (In the case of Revelation, goodness—or more accurately "faithfulness"—becomes conformity to the pattern of the Christ.) Evil, by contrast, becomes a violation of that image, whether conceived of as an active and substantive opposing force or, in a more Augustinian sense, as the lack of being or goodness.

In accepting the validity of evil as a category of human experience, however, one must guard against "the myth of pure evil" as it relates to human agency. The myth of pure evil refers to the tendency to operate with stereotypical conceptions of unadulterated evil in which the evil figure has always been evil, inflicts harm solely for pleasure, and represents "the other, the enemy, the outsider," while the victim is always and completely innocent and good.[3] Within this myth evil is always obvious and easily identifiable. One danger of buying into this myth is that it blinds us to the seductive, deceptive, and often ordinary manifestations of evil. During the trial of Nazi Adolf Eichmann, Hannah Arendt commented on the extreme ordinariness of his appearance with the phrase "the banality of evil."[4] This man, guilty of horrible atrocities that defy imagination, looked no different than you or I. He did not stride into court with horns and a tail, with demonic eyes and fire spewing from his mouth. We encounter this banality of evil every time a person appears on the evening news to comment that their neighbor could not have committed the horrible crimes of which he was accused because he was "a nice guy." A second danger of the myth of pure evil is that it blinds us to our own potential complicity in evil. Evil becomes something that is done to us, never something we ourselves perpetrate. We are always the innocent victims. When used to immunize ourselves against any responsibility for evil, this perspective becomes a dangerous self-deception.

Acceptance of the validity of evil as a category of human experience must be further tempered by the recognition that human beings are notoriously fallible when it comes to identifying evil. The issue is one of interpretation. Human beings often fail to recognize accurately the evil within others and within themselves. According to the myth of pure evil, evil is obvious and unambiguous. The reality, though, is that people are often blind to the evil that is in their midst, while at other times they misidentify evil due to the same personal, cultural, political, and social influences that affect all interpretation. Furthermore, good and evil may coexist within the same person or situation. These mitigating factors, however, do not negate the validity of evil as a concept. Just as accepting the reality of evil should not blind us to the difficulties of always recognizing evil accurately, so too should an awareness of those difficulties not lead to a denial of that reality.

A second principle guiding my analysis is a *rejection of the unwarranted equating of evil and suffering*. One single page of *USA Today* several years ago contained four separate stories of human tragedy. A nurse in New Jersey admitted killing twenty-nine patients in a critical care unit; a pilot died when his ultralight aircraft crashed; a teenage boy lost his leg in a shark attack; and Dennis Rader, the "BTK" serial killer, made an appearance in court and recounted some of his murderous acts. Each of these events involved human suffering, but are they all evil? Many people view evil and suffering synonymously. They believe that suffering of any sort cannot be compatible with the will of a benevolent Creator who wants only good for human beings. God wants us to be "happy," we assume, and in the Western world we define happiness as the absence of suffering. Suffering assaults our sense of entitlement to happiness so that any intrusion of suffering into our lives becomes a violation of God's design and thus must be categorized as evil.

Human suffering is always unpleasant, often heartbreaking, and sometimes horrific, yet one must be careful to distinguish between the act of suffering itself and evil. Precision is important in this regard. At its most basic level, suffering is the experience of pain—whether that pain is physical, emotional, psychological, or spiritual. Pain, by itself, has no intrinsic moral value. It functions as a warning signal that something is wrong. As such, pain is potentially beneficial. When a disc ruptured in my back, the pain I experienced was a blessing to me because it alerted me to the need to seek immediate medical attention. Without that pain to prompt me to action, I would have received serious and permanent nerve damage. Such suffering was unpleasant, but it was not evil.

Luke Johnson writes of the need "to distinguish between the *experiential* aspects of suffering and its *moral* dimensions."[5] The unwarranted equating of suffering with evil is a result of assuming that the level of one's dislike for an experience translates into moral evaluation. When viewed as an experience of pain, suffering is neither good nor evil *in and of itself.* Evil, however, possesses a distinct and inflexible moral valence that suffering lacks. Whereas suffering can be good, evil, by definition, cannot. If we are to think precisely about evil and suffering, we must maintain a distinction between that which is merely tragic and that which is evil. Of the stories in *USA Today* mentioned above, the loss of a limb in an animal attack and the loss of life in a plane crash are heartbreaking tragedies, but from a moral perspective they are in a whole different category than the actions of a man like Dennis Rader who stated in regard to a twenty-four-year-old mother of three, as though describing a trip to the market, "I got her a glass of water, comforted her a little bit and then went ahead and tied her up and put a bag over her head and strangled her."[6]

As a significant human experience, suffering interacts with our moral sensibilities in many ways. Suffering may be the result of a benevolent action—such as if I slap the hand of my young child as she reaches up to touch a hot stove—or may itself result in activity we would term "good." One who witnesses on the news widespread devastation in an area hit by a natural disaster may choose to devote time and money to relief efforts. A young child who endures and survives heart surgery may grow up to become a pediatric cardiologist, to use his or her suffering as an impetus for the healing of others. Conversely, suffering may result from evil actions or result in evil itself, as in the case of the abused who becomes the abuser. There is, however, something about extreme suffering that assaults our sense of justice, that declares, "This is not the way it should be," and so leads us to see such suffering as a violation of God's will for his creation. Although it is important to recognize conceptually that the mere act of suffering has no intrinsic moral value—that it is neither good nor evil in itself—in reality the two concepts of evil and suffering are so frequently interconnected that it can be difficult to speak of one without the other. At times the line between evil and the suffering connected to it can be so thin that drawing any practical and meaningful distinction between them becomes an exercise in futility.

For the purposes of theological reflection, however, it is important to maintain a distinction between the experience of suffering and the moral evaluation of that suffering itself as evil. Unnecessarily equating evil and suffering creates a web of distortion that extends into several aspects of Christian thought. When all suffering becomes characterized as evil, the goodness of God comes into question as one struggles to reconcile scriptural declarations of God's goodness with the image of a God who creates human beings with the capacity to suffer, who creates a world with the potential for suffering, and who at times generates human suffering, be it through a collapsing sea or a devastating plague (Ex. 14:26-28; 24:15). Furthermore, it precludes the possibility that some suffering may function positively within God's creation. It is the Christian witness that suffering may lead to righteousness, maturity, and a deeper faith (Heb. 12:11; Jas. 1:2-4; 1 Pet. 1:6-7). It is the Christian witness, as Johnson notes, that "suffering freely accepted as a service for the life of others can reveal the highest degree of participation in the Spirit of God."[7] To declare that all suffering is evil is to deny the very pattern of Christ in which the *choice* of suffering provides not only redemption but a pattern to be imitated by those who bear his name.

Experience and Interpretation

No interpretation occurs in a vacuum, but is always affected by a variety of social, cultural, and personal factors. Gender, race, economic situation, political persuasion, cultural influences, religious background, and a myriad of other influences all impact how one interprets the world around them. In particular one's experiences of evil and suffering tend to be deeply personal and, as such, they shape one's thinking in many ways. A person's encounters with evil and suffering influence how they think about the world, about justice, and about God.

My wife and I have had very different experiences with evil and suffering. For me, evil has always been an abstraction. I have seen the face of evil on the evening news, read about it in newspapers and books, but though I recognize its appearance, I have always stood at arm's length from evil. I have never been the victim of a great injustice or the recipient of an act of violence. I have never truly experienced evil first-hand. Much the same is true of suffering. Compared to many others, I have lived a relatively easy life. I have experienced the suffering that comes with the normal processes of life, but have mostly been spared the kind of harsh, soul-wrenching affliction that turns a person's life upside down. Mostly, my experience of genuine hardship has come through witnessing the lives of others. I have never lacked for food or basic needs, but I have seen hunger in the faces of children in small villages in Syria. I have witnessed destitution in the eyes of a woman with no arms and legs left on a blanket to beg at the Damascus Gate in Jerusalem. I have encountered the human faces of oppression while traveling in the West Bank with a group of Palestinian students and coming to a checkpoint where I was allowed to pass, but they could not. Nevertheless, my thinking on evil and suffering has been shaped more by an academic worldview than by personal experience.

I quickly realized, though, that my wife had a different experience of the world than did I when, on our first date, I asked her why she came to America, expecting her to talk about her father's job opportunities or the desire to be closer to family members. Instead she uttered one word: "freedom." My wife, Saysavad, was born in Laos, a country in Southeast Asia between Vietnam and Thailand. In the mid to late seventies, with the country under communist control, her father, who worked for the Americans, was forced to flee the country, leaving behind a wife with seven children. She and her family endured many hardships under communist rule. Her oldest sister had been taken away and forced to join the communist army, and because her father had worked for the Americans and then fled the country, her family was kept under constant surveillance by communist soldiers. She experienced the indoctrination of hatred and racism in school where, instead of learning to read and write, her lessons were filled with teachings on why she should hate Americans.

She unknowingly walked with her mother through a minefield on their way to find the communist camp where her sister had been taken in order to retrieve her temporarily under a pretense. With her sister in tow, they escaped in the middle of the night. During the day they hid in the jungle from patrolling soldiers, aware that if discovered they would be shot on sight. When her infant sister began to cry, Saysavad watched helplessly as one of the leaders of their group prepared to kill her sister with the butt of his rifle in order to avoid discovery. Only the quick thinking of another calmed the baby down and spared her life. Upon their arrival in Thailand, she watched as her mother narrowly escaped being killed by a man upset that she did not have the proper currency to pay for their escape. The following two years spent in a refugee camp were a time of poverty, hardship, and fear. Rape, murder, and theft were not uncommon occurrences in the camp. Before the age of thirteen, she had narrowly escaped kidnapping attempts on two occasions, acts which if successful would likely have led to her forced entry into the sex slave trade.

Her life experiences could not be more different than mine. As a result, we each understand the world in different ways and thus respond to the culture around us differently. On an intellectual level, I understand the concept of evil, I usually recognize injustice when I see it, and my heart aches for those who encounter great hardship and loss. Yet, because I have not experienced personally the worst things that the world has to offer, my default conception of the world around me is that it is a place of relative safety, a place which is essentially just if not always fair, and a place where I feel comfortable. My Christian faith tells me that the world is opposed to me and yet I have never really experienced it that way. This level of comfort I have with the world around me makes it easy for me to accommodate myself to the surrounding culture, to make compromises in my faith in order to maintain my comfortable position. I view the society in which I live as more of a friend than an enemy. If I do not maintain constant vigilance, I can easily find myself lured in by the siren song of my culture and forget that the world can be a treacherous place.

My wife responds to the world very differently. She obsessively locks our doors, becomes nervous when the children travel beyond an assigned perimeter, and is far less willing to trust authority at face value than am I. She believes strongly in the reality of Satan and in the power of evil to assault us on a daily basis. If I forget to lock the doors at night, to me that is a minor oversight; to her, it is on a level with failing to secure nuclear launch codes. Sometimes I find such reasoning bizarre—but then again I have never been hunted by people with rifles. If I need God to hold my feet to the fire, to remind me that the world and my faith do not always coexist comfortably, she needs God to provide a sense of protection and an assurance that there is justice in this world.

My point is that she and I are a part of the same family, live in the same house, sit next to each other in church, and yet experience the same world that surrounds us in very different ways. Every Sunday churches are filled with people who see the world in similarly varied fashion. Churches are not monolithic. They do not embody a single way of responding to the world, but a multiplicity of responses based on their members' assorted experiences. The same is true of the seven churches in western Asia Minor to which the book of Revelation was addressed.

Too often interpreters of Revelation tend to view ancient congregations more as conceptual entities than as flesh and blood communities of complex individuals and so have treated these churches monolithically as though they are all dealing with a single, overriding issue across the board—whether that issue is deemed to be persecution or, more recently, cultural compromise. The book of Revelation represents a spectrum of experiences ranging from those who perceive the Roman world as a source of opposition and oppression to those who fit comfortably within that world and deem it compatible with Christian faith. This issue will be addressed in more depth in Chapter Four, but for now I only make the point that restricting the message of Revelation by viewing it as a response to a *single* type of situation (whether persecution or compromise) is to suggest that John's audience had a unified experience of Roman culture, which they did not. Furthermore, recognizing that John's audience would have had varied experiences with Roman culture holds significant implications for our understanding of how Revelation would have communicated to its audience.

The language of Revelation accommodates more than one perspective. One who perceives Roman culture as an oppressive force would interpret the language and symbolism of Revelation differently than would one who has made successful accommodations with Roman culture. For the first group, John's depiction of Roman power as a demonic beast mirrors their own perception and grants comfort through an awareness that God understands the nature of the forces arrayed against them. For the latter group, the same image serves as a shock to the system. It forces their eyes open to the true nature of the empire with which they have compromised themselves.

In the same way, a person's own experiences with evil and suffering today affect how that person interprets Revelation. David Barr is an adept interpreter of Revelation, but one who finds the book's images of violence to be "repulsive and morally inadequate."[8] The violent imagery, he says, lends credence to the view that power, not love, is the supreme value in the universe. Consequently, he proposes a reading of Revelation that neutralizes the violent imagery by subverting it in the interest of love. He correspondingly reinterprets any hint of divine violence in the narrative by assigning all judgment to the actions of evil people turned against themselves.[9] Barr admits, however, that his interpretation of the violent imagery of Revelation has much to do with the fact that he reads the book "from the perspective of an educated Western person in a secure social and economic situation."[10]

By contrast Allan Boesak reads Revelation from the perspective of one who has been "arrested, threatened, imprisoned in solitary confinement . . . tear-gassed in churches, faced with horrors I had never dreamed of, seeing our children die on the streets."[11] As one representing the experiences of black church members in South Africa during apartheid, Boesak contends that for these people Revelation "is an exciting, inspiring, and marvelous book" whose images of violence provide comfort in the belief that God will act in justice to redeem his people from oppression.[12] Boesak writes: "People who do not know what oppression and suffering is react strangely to the language of the Bible. The truth is that God *is* the God of the poor and the oppressed.... Because they are powerless, God will take up their cause and redeem them from oppression and violence. The oppressed do not see any dichotomy between God's love and God's justice."[13]

Both of these readings have value as the symbolic nature of Revelation's language allows for diversity of interpretation. As I will argue later, one reason John may have chosen to communicate through the apocalyptic genre is because apocalyptic symbolism is capable of speaking both to the comfortable and to the afflicted simultaneously. Nor is it the case, however, that one's experiences of evil and suffering alone determine how one reads Revelation. I, like David Barr, am an educated Westerner in a secure social and economic environment; yet, though I find much that is useful in Barr's analysis, I sympathize more closely with Boesak's reading of Revelation. In part this may owe to the fact that Barr admittedly writes as a "secular critic" with no theological tradition, while I, like Boesak, write from within a community of faith. In other words, experience with evil and suffering is merely one factor among many that influence interpretation. Yet for a book like Revelation, which is full to the brim with imagery and language of oppression and affliction, it is a factor that greatly impacts how one hears that language.

From Creation to New Creation

The apocalyptic genre typically communicates through narrative and Revelation is no exception. The story that John shares is the story of God's plan for his creation. Revelation provides one of the grandest, most all-encompassing narratives in Scripture, one that extends backwards to the Garden of Eden and forwards to God's new creation. Yet this story is not a generalized narrative of God's plan or a prophetic glimpse into the future for the purpose of granting later generations of Christians secret knowledge into historical events or end-time scenarios. Rather, Revelation's narrative is generated by the distinct historical circumstances of John's audience in the first-century Roman Empire. One function of Revelation's narrative is to encourage John's audience to understand *their* place within the larger scheme, to interpret the culture in which *they* live and the experiences that *they* face in light of God's larger plan for his creation.

In this sense, Revelation's primary focus is not the future, but the present. The future-oriented language of Revelation actually functions to illuminate the present. If a person receives a diagnosis of a terminal disease, that knowledge of their future sparks a reevaluation of their current situation. Priorities shift, things that had been important cease to be so, and plans that had been pushed into the indefinite future take on new urgency. Likewise, John's visions of the future similarly motivate his readers to take stock of their current situation and to evaluate their present choices based on that knowledge. These visions cast the present into sharper focus by situating the story of *their* (and our) Christian existence within God's larger story.

John describes his writing as "prophecy" (Rev. 1:3; 22:18-19), but by this he does not mean foretelling the future. John does not see himself as an ancestor of Nostradamus, but as a descendant of Ezekiel. John's work of prophecy stands in continuity with the great prophets of the Hebrew Bible. In its Old Testament usage, a "prophet" is a spokesperson for God, one who receives a message from a divine source and then faithfully passes that message on. It is the reception of a divine message that makes one a prophet, not the temporal orientation of that message. The message itself may or may not deal with the future. When a prophet's message does address the future, however, it is always in service to the present.

Another important feature of John's conception of prophecy is that prophecy for him is all about Christ. In Revelation 19:10, John says, "For the testimony of Jesus is the spirit of prophecy." This statement can be taken at least two ways, which are not mutually exclusive. One way to read this statement is that prophecy witnesses *about* Jesus, that it points to the role of Jesus in the plan of God as worked out in history. A second way to read John's statement is that the message of Jesus and the pattern of his life are the power that animates prophetic witness. In this second sense it is Jesus's own witness through his life and teachings that form the essence of prophecy. Although both ideas find representation, it is the second way of reading that best fits the message of Revelation, given John's consistent focus on the witness of Jesus as the model for the faithful witness to which he calls his own readers. Regardless, with this statement, John reveals that the essence of prophecy is not predictions of the future but the witness of Christ. By calling his work "prophecy" and then defining such prophecy as the "testimony of Jesus," John discloses that Revelation is a book that is primarily about Jesus Christ. Contrary to Martin Luther's derogatory assessment of Revelation as a book in which "Christ is neither taught nor known in it," Revelation presents a narrative vision in which Christ represents the focal point of God's divine plan for his creation.[14]

The dominant image for Christ in Revelation is that of a slaughtered Lamb and it is this image that best represents the divine response to evil and suffering. We encounter in this provocative image one who chose to join humanity in suffering, to identify with creation rather than stand above it. It is precisely through his suffering that Jesus achieves victory over evil and death and in doing so provides the model for his followers. Jesus is the preeminent faithful witness (Rev. 1:5). The paradox is that his faithful witness both leads to his death and is the source of his victory over death. As such, he provides the model in Revelation for Christian victory—not victory *from* suffering but *through* suffering. Commentators often point out that a central question posed by Revelation is "Who rules in this world?" An equally vital question is "Who is a faithful witness?" Revelation's narrative, which encompasses God's story from creation to new creation, reveals what it means to be a faithful witness after the pattern of Christ's own witness, whether in the first century or in the twenty-first century.

Before exploring how John addresses the issues of evil and suffering within the framework of Revelation's narrative, however, we must first reflect on the current state of thought on these topics, a discussion to which we turn in the next chapter.

2

FAITH AND THE "PROBLEM" OF EVIL AND SUFFERING

In the film *Shadowlands*, C. S. Lewis (played by Anthony Hopkins) gives a recurring lecture on the topic of suffering. He eloquently informs his audience that God allows them to suffer for a reason and that Christian faith involves accepting pain along with blessing. This lecture of his remains firmly grounded in dispassionate intellectualism until the day his wife dies. Now that suffering has intruded personally into his life, Lewis has difficulty accepting it and it becomes a challenge to his faith. He admits, "I've come up against experience. . . . Experience is a brutal teacher." The dilemma faced by the character of C. S. Lewis in this film is shared by all who have found their sheltered claims of faith requiring reevaluation in the light of their experience.

Faith and experience often stand in tension. Classic Christian faith asserts that God is all-powerful, just, benevolent, and good. From those fundamental assertions, we naturally draw assumptions about how the world should be. A world under the sovereign rule of such a deity should be a place where the righteous prosper, where justice prevails, where evil holds no sway, and where incomprehensible suffering has no place. Experience shatters those assumptions. It presents us with a world of injustice, inequity, violence, and unimaginable tragedy. The Christian constantly resides within this tension between how the world ought to be and how it is.

Although a world in which this tension does not exist, in which God's sovereign rule is clear and evident to all, may be the desire of many Christians, this tension between faith and experience is valuable. Scripture itself maintains this tension. It acknowledges that the world does not conform to a utopian vision of justice and righteousness and yet it holds out hope for such a vision. Even as it asserts the justice and sovereignty of God, it depicts a world that actively seeks to thwart God's will. The dialogue between Job and his three friends is a classic example of this tension. Every attempt by his friends to reconcile Job's faith with his experiences in a coherent explanation fails to convince Job. Even when God himself weighs in, God gives no explanation for Job's suffering. God provides no self-justification for his actions or inaction. Job suffers; God is faithful and just. Both are asserted as true. God calls Job to live faithfully within the tension, not to resolve it.

Likewise, mature Christian faith embraces this tension. Although a popular (and not always incorrect) opinion about Christians suggests that they look at the world through rose-colored glasses and so refuse to accept the world as it is, mature Christian faith actually requires an honest appraisal of the world. Luke Johnson writes: "It is important to state that *faith* itself incorporates this perception, for some critics make a 'realistic' perception of the world (one that sees all its evil and suffering) the very antithesis of faith."[1] Embracing the tension between faith and experience serves a vital corrective function. Experience keeps faith grounded by forcing the Christian to make his or her faith intelligible and functional within the context of real world struggles with evil and suffering. Faith, for its part, instructs the Christian that his or her experience of the world must be interpreted and engaged within the larger spiritual context of God's involvement with his creation. Yet there are times when the dissonance between faith and experience becomes so strong that one's experience can undercut or distort one's faith or that faith struggles to come to grips with experience. This tension between faith and experience is much like a rubber band. A rubber band is only functional when kept in proper tension. Too little tension and the rubber band is useless; too much and it snaps.

The relationship between faith and experience is so interconnected that one affects the other. How one experiences the world affects how one views God and vice versa. When the tension becomes too extreme, something has to give. The inability to reconcile faith and experience is sometimes termed a "faith crisis." The perceived crisis may arise from a naïve or distorted faith that fails to make sense of an experience and so requires alteration or refinement, or it may be one's interpretation of an experience that is in need of refinement. Part of the value of an apocalyptic response to a crisis of faith is that apocalyptic seeks to clarify *both* faith and experience.

If the faith crisis arises from an inaccurate conception of God or from a naïve view of the world, this tension can lead to a healthy reevaluation. As a freshman in college at Harding University, I met a sophomore student named John. John was a Missions major who was planning to spend his life in a foreign country ministering to those in need. I was an eighteen-year-old kid who had never traveled more than two states away from my birthplace, so that kind of commitment was incomprehensible to me. John embodied for me the kind of sacrificial Christian spirit to which I could only hope to aspire. At that time, my understanding of both God and the world was such that I believed all who devoted their lives in service to God would find blessing and protection. I had a mechanistic view of God whereby faith was a *quid pro quo* transaction. Over the summer, I went home and John got married. Upon my return to school, I learned that about two weeks after his wedding, John, his wife, and some friends went down to a local river to swim. While swimming, John drowned.

Upon learning this, the world no longer made sense to me and God no longer made sense to me. I had believed in a world with certain rules and in a God who operated within those rules. One such rule was that a young, newly married Christian devoting his life to mission work did not drown in front of his new wife. The problem, however, was that my conception of how God and the world worked was faulty. This experience forced me to a deeper and more mature faith involving a realization that God cannot be confined to the rules I establish for him and an acceptance that the world often plays by no rules at all.[2]

Other times experiences of evil and suffering can generate a distorted view of God. C. S. Lewis, following the death of his wife, writes of the challenge facing him: "Not that I am (I think) in much danger of ceasing to believe in God. The real danger is of coming to believe such dreadful things about Him."[3] When experience and faith come into conflict, it is often faith that proves more malleable. We look around us at a world that is violent, unjust, and full of suffering and we may say, "What has gone wrong with the world?," but what is often lurking in the back of our minds is the nagging thought, "What has gone wrong with God?" Because extreme suffering challenges the belief in a God who is good and powerful, such experiences lead to a reevaluation of the nature and disposition of God. In the early 1990s a devastating cyclone struck Florida causing massive damage. A subsequent newspaper headline, a paraphrase of a statement made by one of the victims, was quite telling: "God Must Be Very Angry."[4] Following the tsunami that struck Indonesia in 2004, the Detroit *Free Press* carried the headline: "Where was God?"[5] In light of such experiences, the only way for many to make sense of God is to conclude that God is angry, indifferent, unable to prevent such atrocities, or not even there.

No better example exists of the challenge that evil and suffering presents for faith than the Holocaust. The atrocities committed at Auschwitz and other concentration camps assault our religious sensibilities because they defy theological explanation. Jean Améry, an Auschwitz survivor, writes, "What happened, happened. But *that* it happened cannot be so easily accepted."[6] For the Jew or Christian, *that* it happened cannot be easily accepted because it undercuts the notion of a God who punishes evil and protects the innocent. As Frederick

Sontag states, "If we believe God can or will save us from such danger, this conviction will have to rest on evidence other than a holocaust."[7] For some, like Richard Rubinstein, the evidence of Auschwitz sounds the death knell for the traditional view of God. He writes, "I could not possibly believe in such a God . . . after Auschwitz."[8] Others who do not share Rubinstein's extreme skepticism nonetheless acknowledge that to speak of the love and benevolence of God after Auschwitz is a task that requires careful articulation. The famous quote by Irving Greenberg best represents this view: "No statement, theological or otherwise, should be made that would not be credible in the presence of burning children."[9] This is the challenge for Christian faith in a post-Holocaust world—to speak intelligibly and credibly about God in the presence of burning children. It is this challenge of reconciling faith with such experiences that leads theologians to take up the task of theodicy.

Theodicy

A "theodicy" (a combination of two Greek words meaning "the justice of God") is the attempt to reconcile the existence of evil with belief in a benevolent and omnipotent God, essentially a response to "the problem of evil." The problem of evil presupposes two fundamental beliefs: belief in the goodness and omnipotence of God and belief in the reality of evil. Without both, no problem exists. In essence, theodicists attempt to explain the relationship between the nature of God and the nature of the world. Their primary focus is the existence of evil, yet many theodicists define evil broadly enough to incorporate various forms of human suffering within its purview by describing natural disasters, devastating illnesses, and the like as "natural evils." Thus for many the problem is really the problem of evil *and* suffering.

The goal of this section is to provide a brief sketch of some modern approaches to theodicy in order to illustrate the variety of attempts to reconcile experience and faith, while also exposing some common threads among them. This is neither a detailed nor comprehensive description of any approach, but provides an overview of modern attempts to wrestle with these issues and lays the groundwork for raising the question of whether Revelation can or should be considered a theodicy.

Before surveying specific approaches, it is important to stress that, although earlier Christians struggled with many of these same issues, the modern approach to theodicy owes its origins to the seventeenth-century development known as the Enlightenment. Prior to the Enlightenment, Christian faith accepted evil as a component of human existence and thus the focus was on how to live faithfully in the light of such reality. With the growing Enlightenment perception of the world as a rational and highly ordered place, the need to make Christian faith intelligible within that world became critical. In particular, the existence of evil and the presence of human suffering required explanation because, for many, they did not make rational sense in light of the Christian belief in a God who rules the world with goodness and power. Out of this concern grew the modern task of theodicy. As a way of illustrating the varied approaches to theodicy, I briefly survey five modern examples.

1) Soul-Making Theodicy. A soul-making theodicy explains the existence of evil and suffering as a necessary component of creation in order to provide the proper environment for being fully human. Humanity requires an environment of hardship and challenge so as to develop properly in relationship with God and in relation to creation.[10] A world in which humanity coexists with evil and suffering provides the necessary crucible and so furthers the purposes of God. A soul-making theodicy requires eschatology for its fulfillment because this process of growth is never completed in this life.[11]

2) Free Will Theodicy. With free will theodicy, God also allows for a world in which evil and suffering are possible because such a world serves a greater purpose. God created a world characterized primarily by freedom. Though the world initially contained no evil, by granting humanity free will, God accepted the risk that they would choose evil and the suffering resulting from such choice.[12] Although God has the power to abolish evil, his love, which requires that humanity possess free will in order to enter into true communion with him, dictates that he restrain himself from doing so. Free will theodicies primarily address "moral evil," which involves the element of choice, more so than "natural evil."

3) Warfare Theodicy. Whereas soul-making and free will theodicies posit a God whose allowance of evil and suffering are an expression of his sovereignty in that they ultimately serve his will, warfare theodicy asserts that God is constrained in his expression of sovereignty. Gregory Boyd, a proponent of warfare theodicy, argues that Christian faith must accept that sometimes evil occurs because God is "unable to prevent" it.[13] In similarity to free will theodicy, Boyd suggests that God limits himself in order to allow for free will. This granting of free will extended even to the angels who used it to rebel against God with Satan as their leader.[14] Thus the stage was set for continual conflict between Satan and his forces of evil over against God and all who follow him. God does not will or allow evil, but battles against evil in a context where God is limited by his own creative act.

4) Process Theodicy. A process theodicy takes the limitations on God's sovereignty to a greater extreme by denying God's omnipotence altogether. Essentially God does not do away with evil because he cannot. David Griffin argues that when God created the world, there were pre-existent powers with which God had to contend.[15] Thus, creation is about God struggling to achieve order out of chaos. Griffin holds God "ultimately responsible" for the evil that is in the world because of his decision to create, yet says God should not be blamed for evil because human beings choose whether to side with God or with the forces of chaos.[16] A process theodicy does not accept the self-limitation of God that characterizes free-will theodicies, instead viewing the limitation of God's power as a genuine lack of omnipotence. In essence God is doing the best he can as he continues working to bring order out of chaos.

5) Protest Theodicy. Whereas process theodicy embraces the goodness of God while sacrificing his omnipotence, protest theodicy embraces the omnipotence of God while questioning his goodness. This approach despairs of any viable solution to the problem of evil that leaves God fully justified. Evil and suffering cannot be explained away as part of some larger divine plan. Because God is omnipotent, he must bear responsibility for the state of the world. For some protest theodicists, the very existence of evil and suffering challenges classic notions of God's goodness. Consequently, a protest theodicy "puts God on trial" for his "wasteful complicity in evil."[17] Protest theodicy also rejects approaches that look to some eschatological happy ending to justify present suffering because the cost paid is deemed too high.[18] Because of its emphasis that "no matter what happens, God is going to be much less than perfectly justified," protest theodicy may essentially be termed "anti-theodicy."[19]

The Problem of Theodicy

Human beings crave explanation. We are most secure when everything makes sense, when we can concoct rational answers for life's questions. This is especially true within a scientific worldview that prizes reason above all else. It has been said that the goal of science is the destruction of mystery. The scientific mind views mystery and uncertainty as an enemy to be conquered. Science seeks to shine a bright light into all corners of the universe and of life in order to illuminate what is hidden. Yet one of the most pervasive and enduring mysteries of life is that of evil. For all their efforts, science and rationality have consistently failed to eradicate evil or to provide a comprehensive explanation for its origin and activity. The existence and persistence of evil exposes the limitations of the scientific project. Evil resists quantification. It defies expectation. It does not fit neatly within a rational worldview because evil is not rational. The theodicies described above are all attempts by theologians and philosophers to create a rational and comprehensive solution to the "problem of evil."

An increasing number of theologians and philosophers, however, are beginning to question the whole enterprise. They suggest that accepting the problem of evil as classically stated is itself problematic, that seeking a systematic and rational explanation for evil (and suffering) fails to do justice both to the witness of Scripture and to human experience. The major critiques of the modern approach to theodicy fall along several lines.

First, one of the difficulties of providing a comprehensive explanation of evil is that of definition. Theodicists and other writers on evil do not operate with a consistent definition of their subject. Some equate evil with victimization resulting from the intentional infliction of harm, while others equate it more broadly with destructiveness.[20] N. T. Wright defines evil as "the absence or deprivation of good," essentially a type of spiritual "black hole."[21] Others identify it as the use or non-use of power.[22] Debates rage over whether evil derives from personal choice or social influence[23] or whether it is a metaphysical reality that has substance outside of humanity or comes wholly from within human beings as a sort of "permanent and indestructible negative possibility of being human."[24] Some include natural disasters or traffic accidents within their conception of evil; others do not. Some view grief, loss, and pain as a manifestation of evil; others do not. What is clear is that evil resists easy categorization.

This lack of clarity and consistency in definition should inspire caution when dealing with any theodicy that purports to offer a systematic and comprehensive explanation for all evil. Since the classic articulation of the problem of evil questions the goodness and/or omnipotence of God in light of the existence of evil, the way one defines "evil" determines the extent to which it poses a problem as well as the nature of the solution. With no consistent definition of evil there can be no consistent agreement on the nature of the problem. Consequently, any theodicy, rather than offering a comprehensive explanation for evil, functions, at best, as a partial answer.

Second, early Christians did not view evil and suffering as a problem to be solved but as an inescapable component of life to be endured in faith. Their focus was not on explaining the origins of evil but on witnessing faithfully in the face of evil, even as they yearned in hope for its eventual resolution. For them sharing in the sufferings of Christ gave their faith meaning rather than calling into question the goodness of God. In our post-Enlightenment world, however, "no source of atheism is presented so insistently or so dramatically as the existence of suffering."[25] The problem of evil arose from the assumption that evil and suffering are rationally incompatible with the Christian doctrine of God. The modern approach to theodicy, then, as an attempt to defend God by demonstrating the rationality of faith in the face of evil/suffering, is largely a recent enterprise. Arthur McGill asserts that "the belief in the intolerable evil of suffering and the single-minded quest to avoid suffering are peculiarly our own, with roots in our time. It was not the orientation of the New Testament nor of most of the Christian tradition."[26] Although McGill may slightly overstate his case, his assertion of differing attitudes towards evil and suffering is certainly valid. Whereas early Christians accepted the tension between faith and their experiences of evil and suffering as an integral component of their Christian journey, modern theodicists (and many Christians) seek to eradicate that tension.

Although the roots of modern theodicies are thoroughly grounded in the Enlightenment emphasis on reason and science that has dominated the modern Western world, the West is gradually pulling away from those roots. At the center of this movement is the rejection of the modern claim that reason is the sole avenue to truth and a new willingness to embrace mystery. There is a growing level of comfort in many circles with the belief that not all of life's mysteries can be reduced to rational explanations. Rational apologetics (attempts to defend the faith through reason), like theodicies, are losing popularity in favor of embodied apologetics (attempts to defend the faith by living out the Christian witness). The development of the modern form of theodicy made sense in a post-Enlightenment world where reason reigned supreme, but that approach becomes less persuasive in a world that increasingly rejects the ultimacy of reason. In line with their first-century ancestors, Christians in the twenty-first century may need to become more accepting of the tension between faith and experience and learn to embrace that tension as a potential source for the strengthening rather than the weakening of their faith.

Third, attempts to account for evil and suffering within a systematic and rational framework are attempts to explain the unexplainable. When a mother sits beside a hospital bed watching her young daughter slowly die before her eyes, no rational explanation will suffice. Neither could anyone gaze upon the burning bodies of children at Auschwitz and produce a viable justification for it. Sometimes suffering just is, despite all efforts to force it to fit within a comprehensible pattern. A theodicy that does not allow for the often inexplicable nature of evil and suffering falters because "it requires us to be articulate in the face of the unspeakable."[27] This does not mean, as some claim, that suffering is categorically "useless," serving no greater purpose, and incapable of functioning within a larger divine plan.[28] What it means is that we must allow for experiences that are beyond *our* ability to explain and learn to accept our own rational limitations. Sontag, thinking of Auschwitz, states, "A holocaust returns a sense of mystery to life that is never to be dispelled."[29]

Twenty-first-century Christians, conditioned by unparalleled advancements in science and technology that herald human achievement and knowledge, do not have a good track record of being comfortable with mystery. Our false confidence in human ingenuity can deceive us into thinking that we can discern the mind of God if only we try hard enough. Yet Scripture asserts that God's ways are unknowable and that his thoughts are beyond human comprehension (Is. 55:8-9). When faced with inexplicable evil and suffering, we can only confess that we do not understand but God does. But such a confession bothers some who believe that Christian faith is not valid unless it can provide a rational justification for the existence of evil and suffering. For the atheist, secularist, or thoroughgoing rationalist, an appeal to mystery is unpersuasive and a cop-out. They view appealing to the greater wisdom of God whenever faced with questions that cannot be answered as turning a blind eye to reality.

An acknowledgment, however, of the relationship between the created and the Creator is a fundamental component of faith within Jewish and Christian tradition. To confess God as Creator is to admit that we operate with an inferior perspective, that we glimpse truth only in part, and that the ways of God are not our ways. It is a harsh blow to our rational sensibilities to admit that God may not value clear and definitive answers as we do.[30] Whereas science may be about the destruction of mystery, there is a sense in which Christian faith is about the perpetuation of mystery because it rests on the awareness that we are not God and that we cannot fully comprehend God's thoughts and ways of working in the world.

Faith involves living in tension. Mature Christian faith does not turn a blind eye to reality, but faces it squarely. When a roof collapsed during a wedding reception in Israel, killing twenty-three and wounding hundreds more, the father of the bride was asked to explain the tragedy. He replied, "I am a religious man. That is why I do not ask God why." I cannot agree. Though there may be no answer forthcoming, the asking of "why" is a response of faith. This is the essence of lament. Lament psalmists pour out their anger, frustration, and doubt to God. They ask God "why" but they do so within a relationship of trust. There is a reason why so many lament psalms end in praise, even when the psalmist has received no resolution for his crisis and no answers to his pleas. Lament is all about living faithfully in tension. It grows out of an acknowledgment that the world is not as it ought to be, that our suffering is often incomprehensible to us, and that the willingness to express that is part of a genuine and honest relationship with God. Thus, lament psalms often end in praise because the psalmists recognize that God is the Creator while they are the created and that God cares for his creation and is actively working within it to accomplish his will even when that will may be out of their conceptual grasp.

A fourth critique is that theodicies often deal in the abstract rather than in the specific.[31] Although much can be gained by reflecting on evil and suffering at the theoretical level, human encounters with evil and suffering are neither theoretical nor abstract. They are personal and specific. A theodicy that operates only on the theoretical level runs the risk of generating a generic, one-size-fits-all explanation that fails to do justice to real life experience. Theoretical explanations for why evil exists provide no comfort to the parents whose child has been abducted and murdered nor do well-meaning but horribly misguided attempts by Christians to grant meaning to the event by assuring the parents that "all things work together for good" or that God "needed another angel in heaven." Those parents may eventually discern some meaning in the event, but such awareness can come only from living through it. Meaning grows from within the experience, not by being forced upon it from without. Abstract reflection on evil and suffering has a place, but must remain sensitive to its own limitations. It can provide a general framework within which one may analyze one's own experiences, but, as McGill notes, "abstract reason can give us only abstract meanings, and these unfortunately are too general to connect with the specificity of our suffering."[32]

Stanley Hauerwas argues that theoretical approaches to theodicy often prioritize accommodations to worldly expectations over being an alternative to worldly expectations. He says they grow out of the desire "to show why those with the right beliefs do not always win in worldly terms."[33] The assumption is that Christian faith ought to result in a life of blessing and comfort. When this fails to materialize, Christian suffering then becomes an indictment of God for not living up to his perceived responsibilities. This mindset derives from buying into the theoretical description of God as "good," a description so vague as to allow us to define God in terms of what we think of as "good"—our own comfort and success. Yet, Hauerwas suggests that God has not called his people merely to enjoy the comforts of creation, but to be a people who by their faithful witness show the world another way of being.[34]

Is Revelation a Theodicy?

On one level, the answer to the question of whether the book of Revelation is a theodicy is "yes" in that it addresses the relationship between the faith of its audience and their interactions with evil and suffering while asserting that the actions of God in the world are just. Concerns about the justice of God in the light of troubling and horrific encounters with evil by his people are part and parcel of many ancient apocalyptic writings. The writings of 4 Ezra and 2 Baruch, for instance, utilize the destruction of Jerusalem and the subsequent enslavement of God's people by the Babylonians in the sixth century BC as a symbolic backdrop for engaging the struggles of the Jewish people following their own violent conflict with Rome in the first century AD that likewise ended in the destruction of their city. A prominent theme in each of these writings is the justice of God's actions relative to these events. Revelation could thus be considered a theodicy to the same extent that other ancient prophetic and apocalyptic writings may be termed such.

Revelation, however, is distinctly not a theodicy in the modern sense. Though Revelation may deal some of the same cards as do modern theodicies, it is not playing quite the same game. Revelation does not share their post-Enlightenment view of the world nor its desire to sacrifice divine revelation to human reason; it betrays no interest in the "problem of evil" as classically rendered; it attempts no systematic explanation for evil and suffering; and it is specific and contextual in its treatment rather than abstract and theoretical.

As mentioned previously, the Enlightenment heavily influenced philosophical and theological reflection on evil and suffering to the point that belief in an omnipotent and benevolent God was attacked as *irrational* in light of the horrible atrocities and gratuitous suffering that characterize the world. The problem of evil was thus defined as a problem of rationality and so attempts to solve it were conducted mainly as rational endeavors designed to make God's nature and actions intelligible within a modern worldview. John, the author of Revelation, does not share that mentality. Governing his writing is an apocalyptic worldview which prioritizes divine revelation over human reason. Over against a modern view that tries to shape God's perspective so that it fits comfortably within our own, John writes as one who believes that the revelation of God must transform us in line with God's perspective.

Consequently, the book of Revelation shows little interest in some of the fundamental questions that consume modern discussions of evil and suffering. Revelation offers no explanation for the origin of evil nor does it attempt to defend the omnipotence of God over against evil. Revelation assumes that evil and suffering are a part of human existence and that their presence does not nullify God's sovereignty. Revelation begins with the foundational assumptions that God is on his throne and that evil exists. For John, evil is not a problem to be solved as much as it is a reality to be countered by the faithful witness of God's people who model their own witness on that of Jesus. Revelation's primary response to evil and suffering finds embodiment in the image of the slaughtered Lamb. By means of the dual horizons of the incarnation (12:2) and the crucifixion (5:9), Revelation reveals a God who deals with human suffering by joining us in it and who counsels the faithful to stand up to evil not with force of arms but with the power of faithful witness—even to the point of death (2:10).

Revelation's engagement with the topics of evil and suffering is specific and situational rather than abstract and theoretical. John's concern is not the conceptual problem of evil, but the painfully real problem of religious, political, and economic oppression in first-century western Asia Minor. His concern is not a justification for the peaceful coexistence of divine power and divine goodness in the face of evil, but the coexistence of Christian faith and endurance in the face of evil. Though Revelation's theological horizon extends from creation to new creation, that broad framework serves as a backdrop for assuring the seven churches comprising Revelation's recipients that the challenges and struggles they face, whether physical or spiritual, have not gone unnoticed by the God who is actively at work within creation and actively at work within their own lives.

Because John's aim is to comfort and challenge the seven churches rather than to provide a systematic statement on the nature of evil, his definition of evil is specific and contextual. John writes to churches in which some believers are experiencing hardship, pressure, and suffering that John traces to the policies, procedures, and environment of the Roman Empire and in which other believers have put their faith in jeopardy by unwarranted compromise within that environment. For John, Rome and the religious and economic culture that thrives under its guidance stand in adversarial relationship to faithful Christian existence. Consequently, John defines evil primarily as that which stands in opposition to the will of God. His use of dualism and the warfare metaphor reinforce this perception. John constructs his narrative world with dualistic categories that identify opposing sides: Satan over against God, the beasts over against the Lamb, Babylon over against Mt. Zion. Even heaven and earth are symbolically in opposition. Throughout Revelation those who align themselves with Satan and with the beast are consistently associated with the earth, while those who align themselves with God and with the Lamb are consistently associated with heaven. When Revelation uses the phrase "the inhabitants of the earth," it is never a reference to all humanity, but always a symbolic code word for the followers of the beast.

In Revelation, these two opposing sides are at war. The beast does battle against the two witnesses of God (11:7). Satan and his angels go to war against Michael and his angels (12:7-9), and upon failing to achieve victory, declare war on those who hold to the testimony of Jesus (12:17). The beast, likewise, makes war against the saints (13:7), against the Lamb (17:14), and against the rider on the white horse (19:19) who, in turn makes war against the beast and the kings of the earth (19:11). The name "Satan" derives from a term which means "to oppose." As leader of the hostile forces in Revelation, Satan embodies the book's perception of evil as opposition to God. Whether the issue is Christian false teachers

(2:2) or a troubled relationship with the neighboring Jewish community (2:9), these various forms of opposition to God and his people are cast in terms that evoke evil. John describes the false apostles at Ephesus as "evildoers" (2:2) and characterizes the apparently antagonistic Jewish community at Smyrna as "a synagogue of Satan" (2:9). Even the poverty experienced by some of the churches (2:9) is linked to the oppressive and unjust economic policies of the Roman Empire (18:11-20).

Suffering in Revelation is mostly connected to opposition as well. When Revelation addresses suffering, it is typically not the generalized and pervasive suffering of life, but the suffering that stems from opposition to God and to his will. In Revelation faithful witness does not lead to a life of comfort and blessing but to affliction and even death (2:3, 10, 13; 11:7). If we are to understand Revelation's apocalyptic response to evil and suffering, we must then understand these categories in their context of opposition and we must learn to think about faithful witness in that same context. For in Revelation faith is not something that guarantees immunity from hardship and trial; rather, faith grants the strength to endure hardship and trial, to stand firm in the face of opposition, and to come out victorious on the other end.

3

THE PROBLEM OF REVELATION AND EVIL

In the previous chapter I argued that our modern obsession with a narrowly defined rationalism and its relationship to evil should not be projected back onto John, the author of Revelation. The flip side of that coin, however, is that we cannot ignore that we inhabit a different conceptual world than did John and the early Christians. When we read Revelation, we do so within a post-Enlightenment, post-Holocaust, post-9/11 world and the impact of those paradigm shifting events on our views of evil and on our interpretations of Revelation must be faced. The dissonance between John's presuppositions—his definition of evil, his apocalyptic worldview, his openness to divine revelation— and the presuppositions that often accompany a post-Enlightenment and post-Holocaust world can create quite a challenge for reading Revelation, particularly in its depiction of evil and its representation of the divine response to evil. In this chapter, I describe some of these problems that Revelation's treatment of evil presents for interpreters and then offer some general reflections by way of response.

Problems with Revelation's Depiction of Evil

Some interpreters of Revelation find fault with the way John tells his story. The symbolism he employs and his method of establishing opposition between groups create, in their estimation, unhealthy attitudes towards others. Among the charges leveled against Revelation are demonization and misogyny.

Demonization

In addressing the opposition that in some cases exists and in other cases ought to exist between his audience and the larger Roman system, John employs dualism. He categorizes the experiences of his audience into two opposing factions: the beast and the Lamb, Babylon and Mt. Zion, etc. One potential danger of dualistic language is that it can easily lead to an "us vs. them" mentality whereby one side characterizes the other as the epitome of evil and casts it in demonic terms. A contemporary example is the common tendency among certain groups to attach to each new president of an opposing political party, be it Democrat or Republican, the label of "antichrist." In any ideological conflict, demonization often afflicts both sides of the aisle, as in the case of militant Islamic leaders declaring America to be "The Great Satan," while many Americans, still reeling from the devastation of 9/11, characterize militant Islam as the face of evil in the twenty-first century. The function of such demonization for a particular group is to create incentives to hate and fight against their enemy by convincing themselves that God is on their side and that their enemy is God's enemy, thus ensuring the confidence of victory.[1]

John does employ demonization in Revelation, such as when he depicts Roman imperial authority as a demonic beast that rises out of the abyss and aligns itself with Satan. Many scholars object to Revelation's use of demonization because of the effect it can have on present-day Christian attitudes towards other groups. Steven Friesen, for example, laments that Revelation's rhetoric has been used to foster "Christian hostility toward Jews, Christian imperialism, and Christian sectarian violence."[2] In particular, he describes Revelation's identification of the synagogues at Smyrna and Philadelphia as being "a synagogue of Satan" (Rev. 2:9; 3:9) as a "volatile form of vilification" that he refuses to defend.[3] Friesen states that such language is "extremely distasteful nowadays" because it facilitates anti-Semitism and outright rejection of Judaism by Christians.[4]

Another unfortunate outgrowth of demonization in Revelation is its role in intensifying apocalyptic fanaticism. For certain groups who are already predisposed to an "us vs. them" mentality, Revelation's depiction of the demonic nature of the enemy can heighten both their perception that they are oppressed by anti-divine forces and their resolve to wage righteous (and often violent) battle against them. Certainly the 1993 tragedy in Waco, Texas, where nearly a hundred members of the Branch Davidians perished along with a handful of federal agents illustrates the point. David Koresh used the book of Revelation as a script for how events were to unfold. He instructed his followers that they would play a prominent role in the battle of Armageddon, the sign of which would be the arrival of the antichrist come to make war upon them. When the Bureau of Alcohol, Tobacco, and Firearms invaded their compound, it looked to them like the beast of Revelation come to declare war on God's faithful. That act played into their apocalyptic imagination and led to disaster.

Misogyny

Revelation employs a variety of female images, including Jezebel (2:20), the pregnant woman clothed with the sun (12:1-2), the bride of Christ (19:7), and the Whore of Babylon (17:1-18). Some scholars object to how John portrays this feminine imagery. Tina Pippin concludes that all representations of women in Revelation are deficient in that the females function as victims in one form or another.[5] The ones of most concern to her, however, are those like Jezebel and the Whore of Babylon that link female imagery with evil. Pippin argues that the Whore of Babylon represents for John "the embodiment of evil," and that his association of the Whore of Babylon with the beast of Revelation is symptomatic of the book's larger attitude towards women.[6] She finds that women in Revelation are "used or abused" and "disempowered in every way," thus leading to her assessment that the book of Revelation "is not a safe place for women."[7] In her view, Revelation is not only misogynist itself, but also provides the "roots of misogyny in the history of the Christian church."[8]

Problems with Revelation's Response to Evil

In addition to Revelation's depiction of evil, the book's responses to evil prove equally troubling to some interpreters whose accusations relate to the use or misuse of power and an inappropriate fixation on violence.

Abuse of Power

The God depicted in Revelation is one of great power. He is the "Almighty" who reigns from a heavenly throne and issues forth devastating judgments. At issue here is how God uses that power and how the righteous respond to it. David Barr finds fault with interpretations of Revelation that have God responding to evil by actively executing judgment on the ungodly and destroying enemy forces in battle. If God responds to evil with unassailable power, Barr contends, then any worship directed towards him by repentant enemies is forced and thus a form of coercion. If God uses force to coerce obedience and compliance to his will, then that is merely the Inquisition writ large.[9] What troubles Barr is that having God defeat evil through a display of power means that "power—not love or goodness or truth—is the ultimate value of the universe."[10] In a similar vein, Greg Carey interprets the worship directed towards God by the nations in Revelation as that of a conquered people offering obeisance purely out of fear and thus forms one example of "Revelation's morbid fascination with vengeance."[11] This obsession with vengeance surfaces also in the glee expressed over the downfall of God's enemies (Rev. 16:5-6; 19:1-3). Carey questions how anyone who experienced outrage over the rejoicing that occurred among certain anti-American groups in the aftermath of 9/11 could, in turn, defend such rejoicing over the devastation of others in Revelation.[12]

In Revelation the faithfulness of the saints in the face of evil results in their glorification and reward. For D. H. Lawrence, that glorification becomes problematic in many popular interpretations of Revelation because of how it relates to power. Lawrence reads Revelation over against the societal patterns of his own time and determines that it feeds vengeful wish-fulfillment fantasies of the poor and uneducated who are envious of the powerful. Lawrence's own intellectual bigotry with regard to Revelation bleeds through when he describes it as "the work of a second-rate mind" that appeals mainly "to second-rate minds."[13] These "second-rate minds," the uneducated and the poor, desire out of jealousy to bring their enemies down to destruction while raising themselves up in glory.[14] Lawrence writes that Christian victory as depicted in Revelation would result in "a millennium of pseudo-humble saints, and gruesome to contemplate."[15] Revelation represents "the Christianity of self-glorification," which is, in Lawrence's estimation, nothing more than "an expression of the frustrated desire to reign here and now."[16] He writes: "For Revelation, be it said once and for all, is the revelation of the undying will-to-power in man, its sanctification, its final triumph. If you have to suffer martyrdom, and if all the universe has to be destroyed in the process, still, still, still, O Christian, you shall reign as a king and set your foot on the necks of the old bosses."[17] In Lawrence's interpretation, the response to evil in Revelation represents not the establishment of divine justice, but an unholy power grab by the weak who seek to overthrow and supplant the powerbrokers, thus becoming themselves the new powerbrokers. It is a similar repulsion at Christian proclamations that they, the "weak ones," will one day be the strong and conquer their enemies that led Friedrich Nietzsche to declare Revelation "this book of hatred" and "that vilest of all written outbursts of which revenge is guilty."[18]

Violence and War

Revelation is full of violent imagery owing to its dominant metaphor of war between the armies of God and the armies of Satan. For scholars like David Barr, that metaphor itself is problematic. Violence, Barr argues, is never the solution to evil. Though he recognizes that Revelation's violent imagery stems from John's employment of the Holy War motif, Barr declares John's selection of that motif to be a rhetorical mistake as it reinforces the notion that power is the supreme value.[19] Barr similarly objects to John's shift in his symbolic depiction of Christ from that of the slaughtered Lamb to that of the divine warrior (Rev. 19:11-16).[20] Despite his concerns over Revelation's employment of violent imagery, Barr defends John by arguing that the author consistently undermines his own violent and militaristic imagery with corresponding "images of suffering and conquering testimony."[21] The perception in Revelation that God conquers evil with power is thereby deceptive as evil is really defeated by the death of the Lamb and by the suffering witness of God's people. Yet, Barr asserts, this truth "does not entirely resolve the problem" of John having employed the imagery of violence and war to begin with because the images themselves are so strong and pervasive that they tend to blind readers to John's own subversion of those images.[22]

Reflections

It is not my intention to address directly each of the criticisms of Revelation described in this chapter, though I will engage some of them to greater or lesser degrees throughout the remainder of this book. The reason for including them here is to demonstrate that Revelation's imagery is a double-edged sword that cuts both ways. On the one hand, Revelation's images of evil, violence, and warfare are provocative and powerful. They capture our attention on a visceral and emotional level and thus serve as profound vehicles for the delivery of John's message. On the other hand, the very power of those images also makes them dangerous. Their ability to engage the human imagination and provoke strong emotional response can easily lead to abuse whereby the images become distorted and twisted, forced to serve unhealthy ideologies and support ignoble agendas. However, awareness of how Revelation's imagery of evil, violence, and warfare can be easily co-opted and mis-used allows us to safeguard against the temptation to distort John's imagery in the interest of our own agendas.

Having said that, I wish to highlight several general trends revealed by these criticisms and some personal reflections as a way of placing the criticisms within an interpretive context.

First, for each of these criticisms of Revelation, the problem they identify is more one of contemporary interpretation than a problem necessarily intrinsic to John's narrative itself. On the one hand, what several of the writers above object to are irresponsible and inaccurate interpretations of Revelation, whether by apocalyptic fringe groups, those who would use Revelation as a license for bigotry, or Christians who embrace violence and imperialism as a divinely justified course of action. Such interpretations represent a distortion of John's mes-sage, not the message itself. On the other hand, some of the dissonance arises from the critic's own interpretation of Revelation. Everyone reads through the lens of his or her own particular cultural and ideological makeup and that lens to some degree determines the extent to which one finds the problems described above to, in fact, be problems. If one is a pacifist who objects on principle to the very concept of war and who rejects any possibility of a "just war," even if rendered only in literary form, then the imagery of Revelation will pose for that person a signifi-cant barrier to acceptance of John's narrative. For one who does not share those presuppositions, the "problem" of violent and militaristic imagery in Revelation is felt less acutely. Likewise, for some who find the concept of evil to be a superstitious notion that undercuts tolerance and leads to the demonization of perceived enemies, their problem with Revelation is that John has the audacity to identify *anything* as "evil." It has become fashionable in many circles to criticize Revelation in light of present-day sensibilities and concerns that were not John's. Certainly we must not ignore the social concerns of our day and engaging Revelation in light of those concerns can surface valuable insights for interpretation. We must always ask what it means to be a reader of Revelation in our own time. Yet, in any analysis of Revelation, one must be cautious of indicting John for failing to adhere to modern standards or subscribing to modern political ideologies that were not part of his world.

Second, for some interpreters the problem lies with the *imagery* John employs more than with the message he communicates through that imagery. Thus, Pippin can confess that she finds Revelation's depiction of Babylon's violent destruction to be "very cathartic," and yet she cannot get past the fact that John presents Babylon in the guise of a woman.[23] Likewise, Barr interprets Revelation as counseling non-violent resistance to Roman power and argues that John presents the victory over evil as deriving only from "keeping the word of God and the testimony of Jesus" and never through a show of force.[24] Nevertheless, Barr concludes that the violent images John employs to communicate his paradoxically non-violent message remain "morally deficient whatever interpretation we attach to them."[25]

The message cannot be easily separated from the imagery that conveys it; yet it is important to recognize that symbolism inherently facilitates multiple interpretations. In fact it may well be that the dissonance between John's imagery and his message is intentional. Essentially what Barr recognizes is that Revelation is an "incoherent text." An incoherent text is one where the surface message of the text and its subtext are at odds or, to put it another way, where a set of images paradoxically convey a message that seems contradictory to the images themselves. Film theorist Robin Wood applies the concept of an incoherent text to Vietnam War films of the 1970s.[26] These films, he argues, are full of imagery and action that appears on the surface to glorify violence, whereas the films themselves contain an underlying message of peace. Sometimes incoherence in a text is accidental, while other times deliberate. As a rhetorical tool, incoherence can be a powerful device by the way it communicates a message through subtext and by subverting the very images it uses.[27] However, an incoherent text can also be a minefield for interpretation, as the danger is always present that one might fail to recognize how a text subverts its own images. Consequently, the extent to which the imagery of Revelation offends rather than illuminates depends largely on the individual interpreter. John's imagery is the vehicle that delivers his message. For some, that vehicle travels to its destination smoothly and without incident; for others, it stalls and creates a roadblock.

Third, John clearly utilizes strong language and imagery in Revelation, including the language of demonization and war. Making sense of this language and imagery requires attention to the perspective and context of John and his audience. John's theology is contextual, not systematic. His language and imagery is designed to motivate a particular group of churches with very distinct experiences. The function of his language and imagery must be sought within that context and in response to those experiences. For those within these churches who have been victimized within Roman culture, John's harsh language and imagery gives voice to their pleas for justice. In solidarity with the martyred souls under the altar who cry out, "Sovereign Lord . . . how long will it be before you judge and avenge our blood?" (Rev. 6:10), John's language captures his audience's need for lament and the language of lament must be strong, even shocking, or it loses its cathartic and petitionary power. For others within the seven churches who have become complacent and compromised their faith, John's strong language serves as a shock to the system, waking them up from their stupor and calling them to renewed commitment.

Fourth, there is a tendency among some critics of Revelation to read the book solely as a product of John's imagination and designed to further John's personal agenda. Consequently, the concept of inspiration or divine involvement of any kind in the reception or production of Revelation is considered to be out of bounds. The key to understanding Revelation gets reduced to rhetorical strategies John uses to further his agenda. Greg Carey argues that John attacks *his* enemies, not God's enemies. John casts his own enemies in the guise of God's enemies in order to marshal outrage against them. John uses rhetoric to dehumanize and demonize his enemies in order to remove any sympathy for them among his audience and to encourage his audience to make his enemies their enemies.[28] The problem with Revelation, then, is that John silences those voices that would oppose him. Particularly posing "a fundamental problem for contemporary reflection" is that Revelation dares to make claims about truth in regard to "ultimate matters."[29] In a culture like ours that idolizes the rejection of any claim to ultimate truth and affirms the constant questioning of all authority, this is unacceptable. So Carey admonishes readers to be aware that in reading Revelation they are not encountering the truth of God but only "the truth of John."[30] At issue here is one's interpretive paradigm—whether one prioritizes the truth of John or the truth of God. Reading Revelation as the truth of John means critiquing and questioning Revelation in the light of our contemporary concerns; reading it as the truth of God means allowing Revelation to critique and question *our* concerns.

On a final note, John writes within a shared community tradition. Hauerwas correctly notes that "the question of God's justice can be posed only against the background of a community's tradition."[31] John's faith community operates with shared traditions regarding divine revelation and the nature of God and with a shared matrix of symbols and images. John does not write to convert outsiders or to influence Roman imperial policy, but to encourage, strengthen, and admonish members of his faith community. To understand Revelation, then, one must interpret its claims, narrative patterns, and symbols—whether that of a slaughtered lamb or a great whore—within the context of that faith community. As readers, we each read from a community tradition as well, be it secular or confessional, and the concerns of that community often govern the questions we ask of the text. But if we are to do justice to Revelation's message, we must first engage it within the confines of John's community and read John's narrative in line with the peculiar genre through which he chose to communicate. To that end, the next two chapters address the historical and social context of the seven churches of Revelation and the function of apocalyptic literature.

4

EVIL IN CONTEXT: THE HISTORICAL AND SOCIAL SITUATION OF REVELATION

Revelation defines evil in terms of opposition to the kingdom of God and attributes much of the suffering of its audience to that opposition. Identifying the nature of that opposition, however, is a complex task made more difficult by contemporary interpretations that divorce John's visions from their time and place and relocate them to a distant eschatological future. On the surface, Revelation might not appear to share much in common with the letters of the New Testament, but one vital feature they share is that Revelation, like the letters, is an occasional document. It is not a mystical vision of the future cut off from the flesh and blood realities of its first recipients. One of the functions of the seven letters to the seven churches in Revelation 2-3 is to ground the subsequent visions in the context of the genuine struggles and pressures experienced by these churches in western Asia Minor in the last half of the first century. Revelation serves a prophetic and pastoral function for these churches by exposing their social situation to divine revelation. The nature of that situation, though, is a matter of much debate.

Conflict or Compromise?

In the traditional view of Revelation, John wrote to respond to systematic and official persecution of Christians by the Roman Empire. Christian social isolation and religious exclusivity, their refusal to worship the image of the emperor, and their counter-imperial claims of the lordship of Christ were all taken as reasons for Roman oppression. This view had significant impact on the dating of Revelation, which was identified either with the latter years of the reign of emperor Nero (54-68 AD) or towards the end of the reign of emperor Domitian (81-96 AD), the two first-century emperors most closely associated with Christian persecution. In this view the seven churches experienced their world as a place of open opposition and imminent danger, leading John to comfort them with visions of eschatological victory while assuring them of their enemy's destruction. How else to explain the book's frequent references to the suffering of the saints (1:9; 2:9-10, 13; 6:9; 7:14), its symbolic depiction of the Roman system as demonic beasts who have declared war on the saints and are guilty of their blood (11:7; 13:1-18; 17:1-6; 18:24), and its assurances of victory for those who overcome and endure (2:7, 11, 17, 28; 3:5, 12, 21; 11:18; 13:10; 19:6-8)?

More recent reassessment of the evidence, however, has generated significant alterations to this portrait. Close analysis of first-century social and political realities revealed that the traditional theory of officially sanctioned, empire-wide persecution of Christians does not support the weight that was placed upon it. There is no record of any Roman law outlawing Christianity at that time nor any evidence that Christians were bound by law to worship the image of the emperor. The persecutions occurring during the reigns of Nero and Domitian were representative of a much more localized, temporary, and sporadic phenomenon than the traditional theory allowed. Nero's persecution of Christians was a direct response to a suspicious fire that destroyed major portions of Rome. When rumors began to spread that Nero himself was behind the fire, he sought a scapegoat to whom he could shift the blame.

Christians, already held in low regard by the populace, made an easy and convenient target. Nero's subsequent persecution of Christians was a form of punishment for supposed crimes and not for being Christian itself. In fact, once public sentiment started to turn against him due to his overly harsh treatment of Christians, Nero ended the persecution.[1] The Neronian persecution of Christians was thus short-lived and limited to Christians living in the vicinity of Rome. It was an anomaly and not representative of official Roman policy throughout the empire.

With respect to Domitian, although some Christians may also have been put to death under his reign, there is insufficient evidence for these actions being part of a systematic and widespread Roman manhunt.[2] Eusebius, the primary Christian source referring to Domitian's persecution of Christians, gives no indication of an extensive action and, in fact, says that after Domitian interviewed relatives of Jesus to learn more about Christianity, he immediately ceased the persecution.[3] Given the lack of historical evidence supporting a widespread persecution of Christians in the first century, Leonard Thompson concludes: "The solution to John's portrait of Rome in Revelation must be found within normal, not abnormal times, in established policies of the empire toward Christianity, not in eccentricities of a particular emperor."[4]

A document from the early second century AD provides insight into these "established policies of the empire" and, though written several years after Revelation, likely reflects the type of legal and political realities that governed much of Roman interaction with Christians in the first century. Pliny, the governor of the Roman province of Bithynia, wrote to the emperor Trajan around 113 AD to seek guidance regarding trials of Christians. He writes:

> I have never dealt with investigations about Christians, and therefore I don't know what is usually either punished or investigated, or to what extent. I have hesitated no small amount about whether there should be some distinction in respect to age, or whether young people, however young, should be considered

not at all different from more mature people . . . whether the
name (i.e. Christian) itself, even if there are no criminal offenses,
should be punished, or whether only the criminal offenses associated with the name should be punished. . . . Soon . . . as usually
happens, accusations became widespread and more incidences
were reported. An anonymous pamphlet was published which
contained the names of many people. I thought that those who
denied that they were or had been Christians should be dis-
missed, if they prayed to our gods, repeating the words after me,
and if they dedicated incense and wine to your image, which I
had ordered to be brought in for this purpose with the statues
of the gods, and if, moreover, they cursed Christ. It is said that
those who are truly Christians cannot be forced to do any of
these things.[5]

Several features of this document are notable. First, Pliny expresses
great uncertainty concerning investigations of Christians, including
the very basis for the investigation itself. He is unaware of any Roman
law, policy, or clear precedent establishing proper procedure for dealing with Christians, a situation virtually impossible to imagine if the
first century had been characterized by *official* imperial persecution.
Emperor Trajan's reply to Pliny's letter reinforces this conclusion when
he states that establishing any kind of general law for investigations of
Christians is impossible.[6] Second, the impetus for Roman investigations of Christians comes not from the Roman government, but from
the Christians' own neighbors. Pliny is not hunting down Christians;
he is providing legal and official inquiries in response to accusations,
some anonymous, of criminal behavior leveled against the Christian
communities. Third, refusal to worship the emperor's image is not the
reason Christians are arrested. Rather, the image functions as an acid
test for *identifying* who is and who is not a Christian since Pliny understands that genuine Christians cannot be made to worship the image
of any deity. In fact, it is notable that the emperor's image is only one

among many gods who are set up. Fourth, as Pliny reveals later in the document, some of the Christians on trial before him are put to death even though they are not proven guilty of the "criminal offenses associated with the name." Their execution, according to Pliny, is due to their stubbornness in refusing his direct orders.

It is difficult to extrapolate from this one early second-century document what the normal and established practices of the empire were with regard to Christians in the latter half of the first century; yet it is suggestive that Christians in the first century were occasionally accused of criminal behavior by their neighbors, put on trial before Roman authorities, and, in some cases, executed. We should not underestimate the impact that such sporadic clashes with Roman authority may have had on the morale and faithfulness of the affected communities. This is, however, a very different situation than widespread, officially sanctioned persecution, which appears to be lacking in the first century.

With the traditional view suffering from a lack of hard evidence, many Revelation scholars have adopted a new assessment of the social situation that represents a hundred and eighty degree turn. This new trend views Revelation as a response to the seductive power of imperial Rome rather than to its persecuting activities. Rather than a context in which John's churches faced affliction, hardship, and opposition, this new interpretation proposes that John's churches were *too comfortable* within Roman society. They were seduced by Roman promises of peace and prosperity and so made accommodations to Roman imperial culture that, in John's estimation, led to compromising their faith. If the purpose of Revelation in the traditional view is to comfort suffering churches with promises of victory, its purpose in this newer view is to call complacent churches to repentance by presenting Rome as a beast in opposition to God. If the churches will wake up from their stupor and resist the lure of Roman imperial society, *then* they will experience persecution because of their faithful opposition to Roman dominance. So Harry Maier can claim: "The problem the Apocalypse addresses is not too much persecution, but too little."[7] The shift here could not be more

severe—from John writing to comfort churches in the midst of persecution to him writing to encourage churches to become persecuted. As
evidence, those who ascribe to this view point to John's admonishment
of the churches for idolatry and sexual immorality (2:14-15, 20), the
frequent commands to "repent" (2:5, 16, 22; 3:2-3, 19), the comfortable
prosperity of Laodicea (3:17), the emphasis on Roman seduction (13:14;
17:1-3; 18:3), and the plea to come out of Babylon (18:4).

The state of the discussion on Revelation has revolved largely around
these two opposite poles: persecution or compromise. It is my con-
tention, however, that both are inadequate ways of reading Revelation
when either is made the *sole* lens through which one views the narrative.
When made that sole lens, both views suffer from a form of reduction-
ism that ignores or minimizes vital components of John's vision. The
problems with both the traditional view of Roman persecution and the
more recent embrace of cultural compromise as the underlying situation for Revelation are that neither alone successfully accounts for
the variety of evidence within the text of Revelation. Two factors can
contribute to these problems. They are an either/or mentality that often
plagues socio-historical reconstructions of New Testament documents
and an overly restrictive focus on the concept of empire.

The Either/Or Mentality

Many interpretations of Revelation operate with a false dichotomy
between persecution and compromise (either they were being persecuted or they were compromising) as though the two are mutually
exclusive experiences for a community. Maier, for instance, argues that
the churches must have been compromising because Roman persecution of the church "was relatively rare and sporadic."[8] The absence of
one, however, does not necessarily lead to the other. Real life social and
historical situations are often messy and complex, involving a smorgas-
bord of motivations, influences, and experiences. Very few churches
are uniform in the way they experience and interpret the world around
them, owing to the fact that they are made up of individuals with unique

and varied experiences. Yet our desire for neat interpretations often requires cleaning up the messy and streamlining the complex. We want to be able to say, "The situation is THIS" so that we can then say, "Therefore John writes to say THIS."

The idea that the social situation of Revelation might involve a complex intermingling of affliction *and* compromise, and thus require a multi-faceted response on John's part, works against the desire for a neatly packaged interpretation. This is why even those scholars who acknowledge the evidence for both affliction and compromise in Revelation feel compelled to select *one* as the dominant situation and thus the primary basis for interpreting the book. Usually this takes the form of paying lip service to a few who may have been suffering within John's churches, but then asserting that the "overwhelming preoccupation" of the book is to challenge the comfortable and prosperous who have compromised with Rome.[9] Of course, the argument that one type of social experience (conflict or compromise) represents the primary context for the majority of John's audience may be a valid argument to make. Unfortunately, though, in the study of Revelation such arguments have often resulted in the marginalization of the other perspective and thus essentially its elimination as a viable lens through which to read the book. An either/or choice for the situation of Revelation, however, is unnecessarily restrictive.

Another factor that sometimes encourages reduction of the social situation of Revelation to a "primary" motivation for John's writing is the agenda that drives the interpretation. Some who read Revelation primarily as a response to persecution do so because they write within a context of oppression or for an audience that experiences oppression (whether real or imagined) and thus Revelation provides the message they need to make sense of those experiences. Such focused readings have validity, but they carry with them the temptation to restrict the meaning of the book to only those types of situations, as when Boesak, who writes out of such experiences, states: "Those who do not know this suffering through oppression . . . and who do not feel in their own bodies the meaning of oppression and the freedom and joy of fighting against it shall have grave difficulty understanding this letter from Patmos."[10]

On the other hand, many who argue for cultural compromise as the primary situation for Revelation do so in service to an equally focused agenda that can lead to a restrictive interpretation of Revelation. These interpreters are often reacting to interpretations of Revelation in which prosperous and comfortable Western readers identify themselves with the oppressed Christians in John's visions and, in doing so, fail to realize how much they themselves have accommodated to the culture around them. Consequently, Revelation's message of victory over enemy forces and exaltation of the righteous translates into swapping out Roman imperialism for Christian imperialism (or, in some cases, American imperialism). The goal of some interpretations that trumpet Christian accommodation to Roman imperial culture is to promote a message of anti-imperialism and, in particular, to indict Western Christians for complicity in the Western imperialist system. Revelation becomes the antidote to capitalism and to the West's economic, military, and cultural influence in the world. Maier, for instance, acknowledges that his interpretation is "consciously political," while Richard Bauckham argues that we must read Revelation "as prosperous citizens of the first world in a system of political, military, and especially economic domination of the world, which functions both to create an ever-widening gap between rich and poor in the world and also to destroy the environment."[11] Bauckham certainly has a point. The challenge, however, is to ensure that the agenda does not determine the evidence. Unfortunately, the desire to indict comfortable and complacent twenty-first-century Christians for accommodating to Western imperial culture often generates a narrow interpretation of Revelation's social situation regarding accommodation to Roman imperial culture. This often results in minimizing or reinterpreting evidence for the oppression and affliction of John's audience in order to clarify and strengthen the critique of Western Christians.

Such agenda-driven readings of Revelation (and of course all readings are driven by some agenda) often provide helpful insights. The problem arises when the message of Revelation is reduced to fit within only that social context and to serve only that agenda. The evidence, both within the text of Revelation and from Greco-Roman society, however, is too varied and complex to be reduced to any *single* situation or purpose.

The Language of Empire

For both of the dominant perspectives on the historical and social situation of Revelation the concept of empire is the central hinge point. On one side, the focus is the empire as persecutor; on the other side, the empire as seducer. With its imagery of Babylon and its politically charged description of the beasts in Revelation 13, there is no doubt that John's conception of empire is a critical piece of the puzzle that is Revelation. The language of "empire," however, is highly charged language that requires careful articulation. When employed too narrowly, it can lead to a restriction of Revelation's message to theological reflections on military power, nationalism, and economic policies. Rather, it is better to conceive of the issues in Revelation as issues of oppositional culture. When John identifies the corporate power that stands opposed to the people of God, the terminology he chooses is "the kingdom of the world" (11:15). This phrase is much broader than any single empire or even the concept of government or nation. It identifies the counterpart to the kingdom of God, that is, the domain of the dragon. "The kingdom of the world" thereby encapsulates *all* that is under the influence of the dragon and which he employs to wage war against the kingdom of God. When we think about the social situation of Revelation in the broader context of Greco-Roman *culture*, rather than more narrowly in terms of governmental authority and policies, it provides some helpful adjustments to the concepts of both persecution and cultural compromise.

With respect to persecution, categorizing the issue in terms of an oppositional culture reveals that the term "persecution" is too narrow and specific a term for describing the social situation of Revelation, particularly when it gets identified specifically with governmental action. Affliction and opposition involve more than governmental persecution. When John states that he is their companion in "affliction" (1:9), that statement is vague enough to incorporate a variety of experiences. The environment in which these churches existed involved many social pressures and forms of opposition that do not add up to imperial persecution, but that do potentially create an oppressive situation for those who maintain faithfulness to Christ. False accusations of criminal behavior, slander from neighbors, conflicts with local synagogues, economic impoverishment, and social pressures to conform to local religious culture create an environment with many potential sources of suffering. Thompson stated that Revelation must be read in the light of normal times and normal imperial policies; yet, as the correspondence between the Roman governor Pliny and the emperor Trajan indicates, normal times and normal imperial policies were not necessarily conducive to a comfortable Christian existence. The lack of systematic and official imperial persecution does not equate to a lack of suffering or oppression.

Furthermore, any treatment of the historical and social situation of Revelation must also include the element of perception.[12] One country's patriot is another country's traitor. Likewise, the extent to which we can talk about John's audience suffering from their encounters with the Roman system has much to do with whose perspective is in play. When the United States government stormed the Branch Davidian compound in Waco, Texas in 1993, they did so with the self-perception that they were enforcing the law and keeping the peace by guarding the public against an armed fringe group. The Branch Davidians who were on the receiving end of that action, however, viewed the event very differently—they were being persecuted. Similarly, when the Romans investigated accusations against Christians in the first century, they typically did so with the assumption that they were guarding against potential unrest and protecting the populace and empire from social agitators. It is the Christian perception of those actions, however, that matters. It has become customary to downplay Christian suffering at the hands of Rome by describing events of conflict as sporadic and localized, yet even sporadic and localized outbreaks of persecution have a profound effect on the victimized communities and on all others who stand in solidarity with them.

The role of perception, for instance, helps explain the gap between ancient Christian sources that paint Domitian as a demented persecutor and official Roman documents that lack such an appraisal. It also reminds us that what Revelation captures is the Christian *experience* of their environment and not the perspective of official Roman documentation. For those in John's churches who seek to witness faithfully to the world, the problem they face is not simply imperial persecution, but the larger issue of how their environment, with all of its social pressures and entrenched animosity towards the kingdom of God, assaults their faith and weakens their resolve.

With respect to the issue of compromise, thinking in terms of an oppositional culture alerts us to the fact that the seduction identified in Revelation involves much more than accommodation to imperial power and policies. At issue in Revelation is the interaction between John's audience and their surrounding *culture*, which certainly includes aspects of economic and military practices, yet also includes a concern for how some in that audience compromise with the surrounding *religious* environment—an environment that includes Greek and foreign deities and which has roots that run much deeper than Roman policy and influence. John may be concerned with Christians who have compromised their faith in the interest of economic advancement or who have turned a blind eye to Roman military oppression in exchange for peace and security; yet he is also concerned with Christians who have compromised their faith by embracing a culture that prizes sexual liberty, that acknowledges the power of deities other than God, and that tolerates immoral behaviors (2:14-15; 20-22; 9:20-21; 21:8; 22:15). The problem of accommodation in John's churches is the problem of aligning oneself with anything that stands opposed to the kingdom of God.

Adela Collins questions whether the traditional view that John's audience was oppressed and in need of a vision that would comfort them in their misery fits the evidence in Revelation. She asks, "Were the complacent, wealthy members of the congregation in Laodicea oppressed?"[13] Yet one could just as easily turn that question around and ask, "Were the faithful yet suffering and poverty stricken members of the congregation in Smyrna compromising?" I suggest the answer to both questions is "no." What is needed, therefore, is a way of reading that gives equal weight *both* to Revelation's emphasis on the current suffering of its audience and to its stern warnings about cultural compromise.

Faith in Compromise, Faith in Conflict

The seven churches of Revelation provide seven different ways of reading the book.[14] Each church's experience is unique. Reading Revelation as a Thyatiran is a different exercise than reading it as a Philadelphian. Yet the evidence for the social situations of these churches, as gleaned from the letters and from other hints within the text of Revelation, falls broadly into two general categories. Some members of these churches experience conflict with their environment and genuine hardship in their lives, while others live lives of relative comfort and prosperity. John's apocalyptic response is thus necessarily twofold: to the first group he offers consolation, to the second a warning.[15] The seven letters contain an almost equal measure of praise and warning, devoting a total of fourteen verses to direct praise and encouragement of the faithful (2:2-3, 6, 9-10, 13, 19, 24-25; 3:4, 8-11) and seventeen verses to warnings and commands to repent (2:4-5, 14-16, 20-23; 3:1-3, 15-19). In order to flesh out these dual categories, we turn to the evidence.

Faith in Compromise

The seven letters to the seven churches in Revelation 2-3 provide the clearest window into the varied experiences of John's audience. Even a cursory glance at the letters reveals that those experiences are not uniform. Three of the seven letters demonstrate clear accommodation to the surrounding culture. The church in Laodicea is prosperous, self-reliant, and comfortable within Roman imperial culture (3:17). The letter gives no indication of any suffering or hardship in the life of this church. Later on Revelation depicts Rome as a prostitute who seduces the kings of the earth into committing adultery with her (17:2; 18:9). The purpose of their illicit union is shared complicity in the economic domination of the world (18:9-19; 13:16-17). The church in Laodicea appears to be a willing beneficiary of that economic system. Rather than suffering for their faith, this church's prosperity has left it complacent and with a faith described as "lukewarm" (3:16).

Whereas Laodicea apparently has compromised with the culture by embracing an economic system that has dulled the edges of its faith, the other instances of cultural accommodation in the letters have Christian false teachers as their catalyst. In the church at Pergamum there are "some" members who follow the teaching of "Balaam," while at Thyatira the church receives chastisement for tolerating a prophetess symbolically named Jezebel. The teachings of both Balaam and Jezebel have an identical result: they lead the faithful into committing sexual immorality and eating food sacrificed to idols (2:14, 20). The precise nature of their teaching is unknown, but it likely involves a level of comfort with Greco-Roman religious and moral culture that John does not share. The eating of food sacrificed to idols represents a participation in Greco-Roman religious life that, from John's perspective, has crossed the line into idolatry.

The references to sexual immorality are more ambiguous, as sexual immorality may function as a metaphor for religious compromise rather than as a statement of explicit sexual behavior. Biblical tradition employs the language of adultery and fornication to represent idolatrous activity and compromise with the world (Hos. 2:2-8; Jas. 4:4). Those in Thyatira who follow the teachings of Jezebel are described as committing adultery with her (Rev. 2:22), while the collusion of Rome and the kings of the earth is depicted in similar terms (17:1-2, 4-5; 18:3). Nevertheless one cannot discount the possibility that Balaam and

Jezebel's teachings lead to lax moral standards that result in improper sexual activity. Sexual immorality occurs elsewhere in Revelation in lists of moral vices (9:21; 21:8; 22:15). If sexual immorality in 2:14 and 2:20 is simply a metaphorical representation of idolatry, then its presence alongside eating meat sacrificed to idols becomes redundant. Regardless of their specific referents, however, what is clear is that some members of at least three of the seven churches, and probably more, have sacrificed faithful witness at the altar of cultural accommodation.

Other instances of possible cultural accommodation in the letters are less clear cut. In the church at Pergamum some follow the teachings of the Nicolaitans (2:15). Little is known about this group, but the general consensus is that, as with Balaam and Jezebel, their teaching involves a more liberal approach to Christian engagement with Greco-Roman culture than John counsels.[16] At Ephesus the church encountered a group described as false "apostles" (2:2), yet the content of their teaching is not given. Revelation describes the church at Sardis as unfaithful, but gives no explanation why (3:1-3).

The tendency to compromise one's faith through cultural accommodation is undoubtedly present among the churches of Revelation, though it does not account for the full experience of these churches. Only one church, Laodicea, appears uniformly accommodated to imperial culture. Although the church in Sardis is spiritually "dead" (3:1), there are "a few" who have maintained faithful witness (3:4). Although the teachings of Balaam, Jezebel, and the Nicolaitans are having a profound effect on the churches in Pergamum and Thyatira, Revelation describes those who adhere to the teaching of Balaam as only "some among you" (2:14), while the primary problem in Thyatira is not that the church has ascribed wholesale to Jezebel's influence but that they "tolerate" her (2:20). In fact, both churches in Pergamum and Thyatira are praised for their faithfulness to Christ. Pergamum remains "true to my name" (2:13), while Thyatira excels in faith beyond what they had before (2:19). The church in Ephesus actually appears resistant to cultural compromise. Whereas some in Pergamum have thrown their lot in with the Nicolaitans (2:15), the church at Ephesus receives praise for its antagonism towards that same group (2:6). If the false apostles at Ephesus spread a doctrine consistent with cultural compromise, their efforts failed (2:2). Although the Ephesian church is in need of repentance for having "abandoned the love you had at first" (2:4), the vagueness of that statement works against any clear identification of the problem. Nevertheless, many members of the seven churches do not experience Greco-Roman culture or the Roman imperial system as a particularly oppressive and adversarial enemy, but have compromised in ways that allow them to prosper and live comfortably within the Roman Empire.

Faith in Conflict

It is axiomatic in Revelation that faithful witness leads to suffering. Those members of the seven churches who have maintained faithful witness experience the world very differently than do those who have compromised their faith. When John addresses his audience as a whole at the beginning of his work, he describes himself as "your brother and participant in the affliction (*thlipsis*) and kingdom and endurance that is in Jesus" (1:9; my translation). John uses the term *thlipsis* to characterize their social situation as one that involves some form of affliction, although characterizing that affliction has proven difficult for translators as evidenced by the variety of options, such as "hardships" (NJB), "suffering" (NIV), "tribulation" (KJV), and "persecution" (NRSV). On its most basic level, *thlipsis* identifies the application of physical pressure, but that idea of pressure was adapted to represent an experience of distress, whether physical or mental. Ancient writings employ the term for the physical hardships that result from famine, war, or poverty,[17] though it can also describe the mental anguish that results from difficult circumstances.[18] Particularly within Jewish and Christian sources, *thlipsis* identifies oppression by an enemy or a form of suffering that is characteristic of the life of the believer.[19] This literature often connects *thlipsis* to the concept of endurance, highlighting that to endure *thlipsis* is a virtue.[20] Thus the term accommodates a wide spectrum of possible forms of hardship that could certainly include imperial persecution, but by no means requires it or is limited to it.

What is clear from the context of Revelation, though, is John's connection of *thlipsis* to faithful Christian witness. His initial description of their experience in Christ as one of affliction that requires endurance, along with his association of these concepts with the kingdom and with Jesus, suggests that the affliction they endure is a by-product of faithful witness. This theme of endurance runs throughout the book (2:2-3, 19; 3:10; 13:10; 14:12). In particular, praise given to churches for their past and present endurance (2:2-3, 19; 3:10) points to the continuing struggles they face, since churches that are comfortable and complacent do not require endurance.

Four of the seven letters (Ephesus, Smyrna, Pergamum, Philadelphia) describe churches that are suffering to varying degrees and for various reasons. Others like the letter to Thyatira make reference to the church's faith and endurance (2:19), but give no clear indication of the basis for that endurance. The church at Ephesus is enduring conflict because of their faithfulness ("for the sake of my name") and are not growing weary (2:2-3). The type of conflict they face is of a kind that potentially leads to weariness. That it has not yet done so is a testimony to the strength of their endurance. All indications in this letter point to their hardship deriving from internal rather than external forces. That the letter frames the church's refusal to tolerate "evildoers" (2:2b)—here identified as false apostles—with statements of the church's endurance (2:2a and 2:3) suggests that the source of their struggle is conflict with certain Christian leaders whose actions or teachings pose a threat to the stability of their faith.

The church in Smyrna has been experiencing hardship with the promise of more to come. Jesus, the First and the Last, addresses them with the statement: "I know your affliction and your poverty" (2:9). Unlike the church at Laodicea which has become complacent in its wealth, the church at Smyrna has not benefited greatly from the Roman economic system, but suffers in their impoverishment. The affliction they experience extends beyond poverty, however, to include some form of local opposition from the Jewish community at Smyrna. The letter refers to "slander" from "those who say that they are Jews and are not" (2:9). The exact nature of the "slander" is not given, though it may involve Jewish denials of any Christian claim to being the people of God. In response, the comparable Jewish claim to faithful obedience is denied ("who say that they are Jews and are not"). It is noteworthy that the church in Philadelphia experiences similar conflict with the Jewish community there. Like Smyrna, the church in Philadelphia has demonstrated faithfulness and endured despite having "little power" (3:8, 10). This church also experiences opposition from those who claim "that they are Jews and are not" (3:9).

The conflict between church and synagogue, at least at Smyrna, likely involves more than just an ideological difference of opinion over the identity of God's people. The letter to Smyrna goes on to describe Christians there being thrown into prison where they will suffer affliction that may lead to death (2:10). As this statement of imprisonment follows directly after the reference to the slander from the synagogue, it is likely that the slander includes false accusations of criminal or seditious behavior against the church that would lead to Roman involvement. The scenario described here fits well with the "normal" imperial policies regarding investigations of Christians as described in the later Pliny-Trajan correspondence where false accusations made against the Christian community by their neighbors led to imprisonments and trials of Christians, some of which resulted in death. Thus the letter to Smyrna witnesses to a situation of conflict that is combustible enough to generate imminent expectations of localized persecution. Although some of Revelation's references to the deaths of the saints are generalized or relate to a future expectation of conflict, the frequency and consistency of the theme suggests that past and present conflicts between Rome and the church are not far from the author's mind (2:10, 13; 6:9-11; 13:10, 15; 17:6; 18:24; 20:4).

The church at Pergamum has also witnessed localized persecution, as indicated by the execution of Antipas, a "faithful witness" (2:13; my translation). Although the death of Antipas was in the past, the environment that made such action possible may still be present considering that the letter links the death of Antipas to a description of the city as the place "where Satan lives" (2:13). The letter identifies Pergamum as a location where Satan's power is solidified. It is "where Satan lives" and the location of "Satan's throne." One way to interpret these statements is in reference to Roman imperial presence in Pergamum. As the first city to receive a provincial temple for the worship of a Roman emperor (Augustus, in 29 BC), Pergamum symbolized the kind of blasphemous claims and imperial worship attributed to the beast in Revelation (13:4-6, 8), which is itself connected to Satan (13:2, 4).

In summary, the evidence from the seven letters does not support the view that these churches were encountering extensive Roman persecution, but neither does it support the view that they were overly comfortable within Roman society. Rather, the evidence points to churches that represent a variety of encounters with and reactions to their environment. Some Christians are wealthy and complacent; others are poor and suffering. Some follow teachers who counsel compromise with the culture, while others resist those same teachers. Some live lives of comfort and security; others face slander, imprisonment, and death. The social and historical context of the seven churches is complex and multi-faceted. The more knowledge we gain about the realities of life in these cities, the more we can appreciate that complexity and, in particular, understand how the *same* environment can contain the seeds of both oppression and compromise. To that end, we turn to Pergamum for a specific example.

Pergamum: Conflict and Compromise

The ancient city of Pergamum offers an interesting case study for exploring the kinds of tensions that early Christians may have experienced. Archaeological excavations at Pergamum, along with other historical information, provide a snapshot of the social and religious fabric of life in a Greco-Roman city. Analyzing the religious and social life of an ancient society is a challenging task due to the vastness of the topic, so in the interest of focus and clarity, I will examine one small segment of that snapshot in order to offer a glimpse into potential Christian interaction with their environment. That small segment is the religious architecture of first-century Pergamum and the role it played in creating an environment that could be at the same time both oppressive and inviting of compromise.

Numerous studies have focused on the Roman imperial cult (emperor worship) and its influence on the book of Revelation, so I am sidestepping that issue in favor of a relatively ignored aspect of the social situation of John's audience—the pervasiveness of Greek religion. The architecture of first-century Pergamum was heavily Greek-influenced with much of the city built or rebuilt/renovated in the second century BC. The Greek gods were so integrated into the physical layout of the city that it would have been virtually impossible for any Christian living in Pergamum to navigate the city without regularly encountering them.

A Greek temple was much more than a place of worship. Temples served a variety of functions that engaged virtually all aspects of ancient life.[21] Many temples, most notably the Temple of Artemis at Ephesus, were financial institutions, in some ways the equivalent of an ancient bank. They housed great wealth, owned estates, underwrote building programs, and managed deposits, loans, and mortgages. Temples were also social hubs. Many sanctuaries contained rooms that were used for public and private meetings and banquets, as well as for educational purposes. Some prominent temples functioned as museums, displaying artwork and sculpture. The open-air portion of a sanctuary often served as a social gathering place and sometimes hosted athletic events. Greek temples were vibrant institutions that interacted with all aspects of city life—and Pergamum was no exception.

Most of the excavations at Pergamum have centered on the acropolis, the large hill which housed many of the city's administrative, social, and religious buildings. The Lower Acropolis, however, contained a marketplace (*agora*) and a prominent gymnasium, which served both educational and athletic purposes. The gymnasium, divided into three levels for different age groups, contained within its middle level an exercise ground on the western end and on the eastern end a temple for either Herakles or Hermes, an altar, religious statues, votive offerings, and small rooms used for cultic purposes.[22] Above the gymnasium stood a temple of Hera, with a temple of Demeter nearby. As the gymnasium complex illustrates, Greco-Roman society observed no separation between religion and public life. Religion was public life. The political, social, educational, and economic aspects of life were firmly immersed in the religious, and vice versa.

The Upper Acropolis of Pergamum further demonstrates this point. The main road that enters the acropolis bisects the upper *agora* (marketplace), effectively dividing this hub of commerce into two parts. The eastern side was devoted to trade, while the western side contained an altar and temple likely dedicated to Zeus.[23] Traveling from the *agora* to the renowned library of Pergamum entailed passing by the great altar, an eighteen foot high u-shaped altar often associated with Zeus and Athena and containing an extensive sculptural program that served both religious and political ends. Just prior to reaching the library, one would pass by the two-story monumental gateway that marked the entrance to the sanctuary of Athena. Athena was the patron goddess of Pergamum who was granted the epithet "protector of the city."[24] The location of her sanctuary next to the library, along with the statue of Athena that stood in the reading room, points to her role as a patron of learning.

The theater of Pergamum, which was carved out of the side of the acropolis, also represents the co-mingling of religion and public life. Gaining entrance to the theater from the marketplace required passing under the shadow of the great altar and past the temple of Zeus to come to the theater terrace, which led to the seating and staging area. Towering above the theater seats was a Temple of Athena, while below and at the end of the theater terrace was a Temple of Dionysus. The physical proximity of the theater with the Temple of Dionysus, which would have been in full view during any performance, shows the close association between this deity and the arts and public celebration.

A further feature of the physical environment of Pergamum that deserves mention is the city's prominent worship of the god Asclepius. Asclepius was a god of healing and his sanctuaries served as medical facilities. The sanctuary of Asclepius at Pergamum, remodeled during the reign of Hadrian in the early to mid-second century AD, contained a library, a theater capable of seating about three thousand, and a lecture hall, making it a center for culture and learning in addition to its medical functions.[25] Although the present remains date to the second century AD, the worship of Asclepius at the site likely extends back several centuries.[26] Another temple of Asclepius existed in the area of the Lower Acropolis.[27] The sanctuary of Asclepius at Pergamum was renowned for the medical services it provided and for the healing powers of its deity. Aelius Aristides, who came to the temple at Pergamum in the mid-second century AD to be healed, writes that "this city through the power of the god is a general source of good for all mankind."[28]

The point of this brief survey is to show that, short of leaving society for a hermetic existence, one could not live in a city like Pergamum (which is itself representative of most hellenistic cities) without constant interaction with the religious presence in the city. One could not attend the theater, participate in the athletic or educational functions of the gymnasium, visit the library, or shop in the marketplace without encountering worship, sacrificial activities, or iconography touting the power, presence, and significance of the gods. In a typical Greco-Roman city, the prominent financial, political, educational, recreational, and even medical buildings were themselves temples or closely associated with temples and deities. One simply could not participate in civic life in any form without encountering the influence of the gods.

Christians in Pergamum, who strove to maintain faithful witness to Christ and who did not enjoy the protections and accommodations afforded Judaism, would find themselves constantly at odds with a culture that did not acknowledge the sovereignty of God. The important question is not whether Christians were officially persecuted by Roman officials, but whether or not many Christians experienced hardship and suffering related to their faith, even if that suffering owes more to their perception of their surrounding environment and to the kinds of pressures that such an environment brought to bear. What does it mean to be a faithful witness in Pergamum when one is assaulted on every side with the message that this world belongs to the gods and to Rome? The pervasive involvement of deity in every aspect of life would have placed Christians in many situations requiring hard choices. Trade guilds, for instance, were a type of ancient union in which those who shared a particular profession joined together in order to facilitate their business and protect their livelihood. Typically meetings of a guild involved the offering of sacrifices and other honors to an associated deity. A Christian silversmith at Pergamum, for instance, might find himself facing the choice between maintaining a career that feeds his family yet requires an uncomfortable level of involvement in Greek religious rites or maintaining faithfulness to Christ. I once had a Korean student who informed me that, at least up until recently, many Christians in Korea faced a very similar dilemma. Certain professions involved associations that performed religious rites in honor of native deities and Christians who belonged to those professions sometimes faced a choice between compromising their faith and losing their job.

Given the various types of pressures that Christians in Pergamum may have faced, the opening line of the letter to Pergamum—"I know where you are living, where Satan's throne is"—resonates. The letter then goes on to describe Pergamum as the place "where Satan lives." As noted earlier, those statements may reference the presence and importance of the imperial cult in Pergamum. However, those statements are equally viable as references to the general religious atmosphere of Pergamum and the entrenchment of the gods in every facet of life. Considering that such a religious atmosphere was by no means unique to Pergamum, some suggest that the great altar at Pergamum is the generative force behind the language, "Satan's throne" (2:13). With its u-shaped form, the giant altar closely resembles the structure of many ancient thrones and may have served for John as the symbol of Pergamum's oppressive religious atmosphere. Regardless, the letter's emphasis on aligning Pergamum with Satan indicates that Revelation defines the Christian experience in Pergamum as one where they face great opposition, opposition made more intense *because* they "are holding fast to my name" (2:13).

If Pergamum offered Christians an environment of potential antagonism, it also offered an environment replete with temptations and opportunities for compromise. Revelation chastises some Christians in Pergamum for idolatry (2:14), essentially for becoming too engaged with the religious culture. If the argument is correct that Revelation's audience was predominately or at least heavily gentile,[29] then the pressure to accommodate to the religious culture could become acute for some due to the cultural and religious baggage they brought with them. Imagine a woman who grew up in Pergamum worshipping at the temple of Asclepius and who had successfully sought medical help there in the past. Now a Christian, her young child has become gravely ill. She has prayed to God repeatedly, but to no avail. The temptation to take her child to the sanctuary of Asclepius could become immense.

Precisely what John has in mind when he accuses some in Pergamum of idolatry is unclear. Is it some level of participation in or support of the Roman economic and military system? Is it outright worship of other deities? Or is it a more subtle crossing of lines wherein Christians engage in behavior that is not directly worship, but involves them to varying degrees in the religious life of the city, such as frequenting the theater, attending a social banquet held at a temple, seeking medical advice from the priests of Asclepius, or engaging in financial transactions at a temple? Perhaps it is justifying participation in the religious rites of a trade guild as being necessary for the economic survival of one's family. Although John's language likely symbolizes a larger idolatrous mindset, the specificity of his language is intriguing in that his example of their idolatry is that they eat food sacrificed to idols (2:14). The marketplace of the Upper Acropolis at Pergamum illustrates how easily such a situation could occur. Recall that this marketplace is divided into two by the main road, with the temple and altar of Zeus located in the western portion and the market in the eastern portion. Some of the meat sacrificed on the altar of Zeus would undoubtedly have ended up being sold in the market. Is it idolatry for a Christian to purchase meat from the marketplace knowing that it was sacrificed to Zeus? Some Christians might view that action as relatively benign, while others might view it as participation in idolatry.

I have offered many hypothetical scenarios here simply to make the point that when the worship and acknowledgment of the gods was so interwoven into every aspect of civic life, the line separating idolatry and faithfulness was not always easy to discern. Depending on how one construed Christian faithfulness, an action that appeared relatively harmless to one may seem less so to another. Those in Pergamum whose teaching leads some into idolatry are perhaps presenting a form of the Christian faith that allows for a degree of involvement in civic and social life that from John's perspective crosses the line into idolatry. Perhaps the main difference between John and his opponents is that they draw the line in a different place than he does.

The old adage about comforting the afflicted and afflicting the comfortable is an appropriate description of Revelation's general rhetorical strategy. Those who are witnessing faithfully and who are thereby encountering opposition and experiencing the harsh dissonance between the kingdom of God and their surrounding culture require a message of comfort and hope that will facilitate their continuing perseverance. Those who are compromising their faith through inappropriate accommodation to that culture need to be shocked out of their complacency and complicity. Revelation's dual situation calls for a dual response, one that is capable of speaking powerfully and persuasively to both groups. One reason why John may have chosen the apocalyptic genre as the medium of communication for his visions is because apocalyptic is uniquely suited for providing just such a response.

5

THE INDISPENSABILITY
OF APOCALYPTIC

Ernst Käsemann and Rudolf Bultmann, two of the most influential New Testament scholars of the twentieth century, were contemporaries in Germany during World War II. Their experiences with the Nazi regime, however, could not have been more different. Although not a Nazi sympathizer, Bultmann did little to draw their attention to him. Throughout the war he continued to preach and maintain his professorship in a manner that avoided conflict with the ruling power. By contrast, during Hitler's ascent to power in the 1930s, Käsemann served as a young pastor at a church in an industrial region of Germany. In his sermons he preached against the threat of Naziism, which prompted the monitoring of his sermons. As a result, he was briefly imprisoned in 1937. Upon release, Käsemann continued to preach against the Nazi party until the day they showed up at his door with an ultimatum—join the Nazi army or die. He joined and forcibly served until he was captured in 1945.

In line with their different experiences of the war, Bultmann and Käsemann had markedly different views on apocalyptic. Bultmann had very little use for apocalyptic and strongly minimized it in his interpretation of the New Testament. Käsemann, on the other hand, fiercely defended the legitimacy of apocalyptic, even going so far as to call apocalyptic "the mother of all Christian theology."[1] While visiting with Ernst Käsemann in the mid-1990s, Emory University professor Carl Holladay asked him about this difference. Why was it that Bultmann had so little interest in apocalyptic whereas Käsemann clung to it? Käsemann responded by saying that until one has experienced evil in its rawest forms, as he himself had, one could not fully appreciate the indispensability of apocalyptic for making sense of the world.[2]

Bultmann's and Käsemann's interest in apocalyptic was relative to the depth of their experience with evil. One who has experienced evil in its rawest forms, who has encountered an evil that no modern theodicy can adequately explain, discovers in apocalyptic a vision of reality that provides hope and meaning. This chapter focuses on *why* apocalyptic is indispensable for making sense of the world in the face of evil and *how* it accomplishes that. Essentially these questions of "why" and "how" are interrelated because how apocalyptic makes sense of the world is what makes it indispensable.

Apocalyptic and the Transformation of the World

John begins by identifying his work as "an apocalypse" (1:1; my translation). The Greek term *apokalupsis* means "a revelation" or "an unveiling." In calling his work an *apokalupsis*, John purports to reveal spiritual truth, to pull back the veil that separates the spiritual and physical realms so that his churches can view their world from a spiritual perspective. When John uses the term "apocalypse," he therefore does so in reference to the quality and content of his writing and not as an identification of genre. John's primary self-identification of his work's genre is "prophecy" (1:3; 22:7, 10, 18, 19), though the character of his writing puts him much more closely in line with other apocalyptically minded prophets like Ezekiel, Daniel, and Zechariah than with Hosea or Amos.

Biblical scholars, however, have imbued the terms "apocalypse" and "apocalyptic" with technical meaning designed to provide categories of reference for better understanding the book of Revelation in relation to similar writings and religious viewpoints within Judeo-Christian tradition. Often "apocalyptic" identifies a religious worldview whereas "apocalypse" defines a literary genre that is governed by and communicates that worldview. As a genre description, an apocalypse is a narrative in which supernatural beings mediate a revelation to human beings that discloses spiritual reality.[3]

The revelation of that spiritual reality provides both hope and critique, as represented by the eschatological promises and warnings to repent in the seven letters to the seven churches. This double edge to the disclosing of spiritual reality is what allows a book like Revelation to address both those whose faith is in conflict with the surrounding culture and those who have compromised their faith with the surrounding culture. John's primary concern, however, is not with the social reality of his churches, but with how their experience of that social reality (whether oppression or compromise) affects their *faith*. On the one side are those who have encountered such hardship and suffering in the world that they are in danger of losing or distorting their faith. On the other side are those who have become so comfortable with the deception that the kingdom of the world creates that they are unaware of the danger it poses to their faith. The power of apocalyptic language lies in its ability to address both groups because both groups share the same fundamental problem—a distorted view of the world. One group views the world as a place where opposition to the kingdom of God runs rampant and unchecked, thus potentially calling into question the justice and sovereignty of God; the other group experiences the world as a place where the kingdom of God and the kingdom of the world can coexist peacefully and without conflict. Both groups need an apocalypse because both groups require a new vision of the world.

In Revelation 11:15 a great voice from heaven announces: "The kingdom of the world has become the kingdom of our Lord and of his Christ." This pronouncement offers an effective analogy for what apocalyptic rhetoric itself accomplishes. Apocalyptic rhetoric is transformative language in that it transforms its audience's understanding of their reality. It shifts a person's worldview by encouraging that person to view their world differently. Through its combination of symbols and narrative, apocalyptic creates a new symbolic world contained within a new story that presents its hearers with a new interpretation of reality. This transformation is not merely an ephemeral or imaginative exercise; it effects real change. For those who accept Revelation's apocalyptic vision and who allow that new apocalyptic story to replace their old story, both they and the world they live in are transformed because they now understand that world in a new way.[4]

The dominant story communicated by Rome was that Rome and the Greek gods aligned with it rule over this world and do so benevolently. The proper response to such benevolent lordship is loyalty, obedience, and worship. John, however, presents his churches with an alternative story in which the Roman Empire is a false pretender in league with Satan and soon to come under the judgment of God, whereas God himself sits as sovereign on his throne ruling faithfully over a creation that is redeemed by a slaughtered Lamb. For those who embrace *this* story, the kingdom of the world has become the kingdom of our Lord and of his Christ because they now possess a new vision of the world, one which grants them an interpretation of the world not merely as they wish it to be, but as it is and will be.

Characteristics of Apocalyptic

How Revelation accomplishes its transformation of the world on behalf of its audience is the focus of this section. Four central characteristics of apocalyptic rhetoric illustrate its transformative function. This is not an exhaustive list of the components of apocalyptic rhetoric, but one that illustrates apocalyptic's transformative function, particularly as it relates to Revelation's approach to evil and suffering.

Transcendence
Within the apocalyptic worldview, the veil separating the material world and the spiritual world is extremely thin, allowing the spiritual world

to break into the material world at nearly every point. Visions, angels, demons, and ascents to and descents from heaven are all commonplace. In line with the meaning of "apocalypse" as "unveiling," apocalyptic pulls back the veil that separates the spiritual and the physical and, in so doing, exposes the physical world to a divine perspective. As physical beings, our natural tendency is to focus only on that which can be accessed by our five senses and then apply to that the label of "reality." In part, it is our inability to see beyond the physical that makes our suffering so unbearable because human suffering and the existence of evil become incomprehensible when viewed through such a narrow lens.

Apocalyptic writings, however, assert that the meaning of human existence and human encounters with evil cannot be deduced from our five senses nor can they be divined through the application of human reason. Such meaning "is categorically beyond the pitch of human minds and therefore must be disclosed by God."[5] By means of this disclosure, an apocalypse offers a transcendent or divine perspective on human experience.

The Jewish apocalyptic book known as 4 Ezra provides an example of the important interplay between transcendence and human experience. 4 Ezra was written around 100 AD, approximately thirty years after the destruction of the Jerusalem temple by the Romans. The story of 4 Ezra, however, is set around 556 BC, roughly thirty years after the destruction of Jerusalem and its temple by the Babylonians. The author uses that earlier destruction by the Babylonians as a literary device for addressing his own audience's suffering and disillusionment at the hands of the Romans.

In chapter three of 4 Ezra, the author questions the justice of God in the light of Israel's misfortune. In particular he wants to know how God could allow their wicked enemies to prosper while his chosen people suffer. In response to Ezra's complaint, the angel Uriel declares, "Your understanding has utterly failed regarding this world" (4:2). The angel goes on to add that Ezra's misinterpretation of his experience is because those who dwell on earth only understand earthly things (4:21). No matter how much one learns about this world, one will never understand the ways of God based upon that knowledge. One cannot comprehend the presence or purpose of human suffering from an earthly perspective alone. Understanding earthly things requires a heavenly perspective.

But as Uriel tries to inform Ezra of the heavenly mysteries, Ezra objects. He does not understand why Uriel keeps speaking about heavenly things when what he is concerned about is the earthly suffering of the Jewish people. Ezra complains:

> I did not wish to inquire about the ways above, but about those things which we daily experience: why Israel has been given over to the gentiles as a reproach; why the people whom you loved has been given to godless tribes, and the Law of our fathers has been made of no effect and the written covenants no longer exist. . . . It is about these things that I have asked (4:23-25).

With his assertion that he has no interest in "the ways above" but only in what is happening below, Ezra has missed the point that one cannot separate the two. In response to Ezra's complaint, Uriel continues to talk about heavenly things and God's plan for the end of the age. What Uriel is trying to impress upon Ezra is that when one speaks about things above, one *is* speaking about things below. Heaven and earth are inextricably linked in the apocalyptic worldview so that one does not speak about earthly things except in the context of heavenly things. An apocalypse dares to suggest that one can only understand human experience adequately when it is interpreted and critiqued in the light of God's revelation. Consequently, when one's world is exposed to transcendence, the world, for that person, becomes a different place.

Determinism

Apocalyptic writings are highly deterministic, meaning they propose that certain events are "determined" by forces outside of human control. Apocalyptic determinism has its foundation in the belief that the Creator is in control of his creation and that he has a plan for that creation. Statements in Revelation regarding "what must soon take place" (Rev. 1:1) or references to a number awaiting fulfillment (6:11) are examples of apocalyptic determinism. Although determinism and free will might seem inconsistent, the two are not mutually exclusive within the apocalyptic worldview. God does not pre-determine the choices of individual human beings or their ultimate destiny. Rather apocalyptic determinism asserts that God is active within his *creation* and will faithfully execute his plan for that creation. To that end God has determined certain events, but whether individuals choose to align themselves with God or to oppose his purposes determines their fate.

The foretelling of future events is an important aspect of apocalyptic determinism but one which is easily misconstrued. The purpose of such foretelling is not to provide a blueprint for the end of days so that alert Christians can match up historical events in a one-to-one correspondence with statements in Revelation. The purpose of such foretelling is to provide both challenge and comfort to Christians in the present by informing them of God's faithful activity. In a sense, *what* is going to happen is of less consequence than *that* it is going to happen. Determinism is about providing a glimpse into God's plan for his creation so that we can understand our experiences and make our choices in light of that plan.

One benefit of determinism is that it broadens one's view of their experiences by getting them to situate those experiences within a larger context. This is why many apocalypses spend as much time in the past as they do in the future. They recite past history in symbolic form and draw heavily from ancient traditions. The book of Revelation casts a wide temporal net in that its story extends from beginning to end, from creation to new creation. By rooting its narrative just as firmly in the past as in the future, Revelation communicates the message that God's plan for creation extends far beyond the simple events of any human life and that to understand human experiences with evil and suffering, one must interpret those experiences in the context of how God has and will deal with evil and suffering both in the past and future.

The deterministic assurance that God is in control of his creation and faithfully executing his plan addresses both those whose experience with the world is defined by conflict and those whose experience is defined by compromise. For those who suffer as a result of their faithful witness, determinism transforms despair into hope by assuring the faithful that their suffering is not in vain and that their reward is certain. For those who stand in opposition to God, whether actively or through compromise, determinism offers a strong warning, for determinism asserts that God's judgment is set and the fate of those who oppose God is assured. In light of that certainty, one must choose on which side to stand.

Symbolism

Apocalypses create a new world out of symbols. By nature symbols are polyvalent, that is, they represent a whole host of potential meanings. D. H. Lawrence writes that to read Revelation is to encounter "meanings behind meanings."[6] This is because apocalyptic language is intentionally poetic and figurative. Unfortunately, the history of interpretation of Revelation is discolored by misunderstandings regarding the purpose of apocalyptic symbolism. Many view the symbolism of Revelation as a type of code designed to obscure the message for all except the initiated. A problem with this view is that it necessitates "breaking the code" in order to understand Revelation, a process that typically involves getting rid of the poetic symbols in order to get at the prose meaning underneath. Turning poetry into prose, however, destroys its power.

Symbolism is an intentionally evocative and flexible means of communication. Whereas normal prose language can describe an experience, symbols are far more capable of *representing* that experience because symbols connect with both the heart and the mind in a way that prose language does not. An academic treatise on atonement has nowhere near the communicative power of a simple cross. Symbolic language, like poetry, is highly charged language that ignites sparks within us. Far from being an attempt at subterfuge by encrypting the message of Revelation in a symbolic code, the symbolism is the very lifeblood of Revelation. The symbols do not disguise the message; the symbols *are* the message! When Revelation presents Jesus as a slaughtered Lamb, it is not attempting to *conceal* his identity but to *reveal* something vital about his identity.

Three aspects of Revelation's symbolism are worth noting here. First, the symbols and imagery in Revelation owe their origin not only to Scripture, but also to Jewish and Greco-Roman tradition, history, and culture. Although the symbolism of Revelation can be confusing and difficult to interpret, the problem with viewing it as a code is that it implies that the symbols function to obscure the message *intentionally*. Interpreters of Revelation struggle with the meaning of the symbolism today largely because the symbols are so far removed from our time and culture. Yet the reader of Revelation should keep in mind that what is so strange and foreign to us was not nearly so strange and foreign to its original readers. Heavenly throne rooms, golden crowns, incense bowls, golden altars, and a woman standing with a globe under her feet (Rev. 12:1) all find visual representation within Jewish and Greco-Roman culture. Likewise, language about the sky rolling up like a scroll, the sun turning to darkness, war waged by an army of locusts, and a pregnant woman pursued by a red dragon all had distinct symbolic meaning to people of that time and culture. In order to appreciate the symbolism of Revelation, then, one must seek its meaning within the culture of its time.

Second, symbolic language is visual language. Reading Revelation is a visual experience that creates vibrant images in one's mind. This is even more significant considering the likelihood that most members of Revelation's original audience would have *heard* the book read to them rather than read it themselves. As visual language, the symbolism of Revelation impresses itself on one's memory and draws that person more fully into the story. In this way, Revelation's language allows a reader to experience John's visions emotionally and visually to a degree. More than just narrating John's visions, Revelation *displays* them.

Third, the inherently flexible and polyvalent quality of symbolism allows a single symbol to communicate contrasting ideas simultaneously. This is why the American flag can symbolize freedom to one person and oppression to another. The reason why one person wishes to salute the flag while another wishes to burn it is because the potential meaning of a symbol has much to do with the interpreter's own social, cultural, and ideological location. With respect to Revelation, this is why John's symbolism can communicate varying ideas simultaneously to the members of his churches. Those who are in conflict with the culture and those who compromise with the culture may hear the same symbol in different ways. To those in conflict, the symbol of the slaughtered Lamb who conquers through faithful witness might evoke in them a sense of solidarity with Christ and a renewed determination to share in his sufferings and thus share in his victory. To those, however, who have aligned themselves with the beast through compromise, the slaughtered Lamb stands as an indictment of their symbolic complicity in his slaughter. The symbolism of Babylon/Rome as a great whore (Rev. 17) might represent to those in conflict an explanation of how Rome, through its seductive lures, is able to gain allegiances that facilitate its status as economic, religious, and military powerhouse—the very status that creates potential conflict for faithful witnesses. For those who compromise, that same symbolism serves as a fitting explanation for why and how they were so easily deceived—the Roman system is an attractive and enticing consort that offers pretenses of beauty and false promises.

Dualism

Dualism organizes perception by dividing elements into two opposing categories. Most apocalyptic writings are heavily dualistic and Revelation is no exception. The root dualism that undergirds the entire narrative of Revelation is the contrast between "the kingdom of our

Lord and of his Christ" and "the kingdom of the world." The warfare theme that permeates the narrative grows out of this dualistic emphasis. The kingdom of God and the kingdom of the world are not just alternate realms but oppositional realms. They are at war and war is an inherently dualistic enterprise. It divides groups into allies and enemies and categorizes locations in terms of their territory or our territory.

Leading each respective kingdom in this battle are the "one seated on the throne" and the dragon, along with their second-in-commands: the Lamb and the beast. The armies of each respective kingdom include, on one side, the followers of the Lamb (14:4) and, on the other, the followers of the beast and "the kings of the earth" (19:19). Geography in Revelation is also dualistic and based on this contrast between the two kingdoms. On a broad level, all of the action and actors in Revelation align with one of two locations: heaven or earth. These locations should not be taken in a strict geographical sense, however, as though God has somehow abdicated authority over the earth. He remains in Revelation "the Lord of the earth" (11:4). Rather, this use of symbolic geography highlights orientation. It identifies allegiance. Thus, Revelation identifies faithful witnesses with heaven: the martyrs reside under the heavenly altar (6:9), the great multitude of the faithful stands before the heavenly throne (7:9), the 144,000 stand with the Lamb on the heavenly Mt. Zion (14:1-3). Even the two faithful witnesses of Revelation 11 who are killed on earth then ascend to heaven (11:12). In contrast, those who align themselves with the kingdom of the world are identified as "the inhabitants of the earth" (3:10; 6:10; 8:13; 11:10; 13:8, 12, 14; 17:2, 8) and "the kings of the earth" (18:3, 18; 19:19).

Other examples of dualism in Revelation are the two opposing cities that dominate the landscape of Revelation (Babylon and the new Jerusalem) and the assertion that all people find their ultimate destination by one of two bodies of water: the lake of fire (20:14-15) or the river of the water of life (22:1-4).

Revelation also operates with an ethical dualism that sets good and evil in stark contrast, though it should be observed that "good and evil" are not abstract concepts but contextually specific ones. Evil in Revelation is not some vague demonic force or cosmological principle. Evil is opposition to the kingdom of God, whether through direct action or through passive compromise. Likewise "good" is represented in Revelation by one's conformity to the pattern of faithful witness modeled by Christ. In that sense "good and evil" in Revelation are not intrinsic identity markers (as in, "this person is inherently good and that person inherently evil"), but are defined primarily by the exercise of one's choice and the formation of allegiances. The human choice between good and evil in Revelation is the choice between allegiance to the kingdom of God or allegiance to the kingdom of the world. This war allows for no neutral ground. Either one is a follower of the Lamb or a follower of the beast. No other option exists. Apocalyptic demands a radical choice.

Although dualism is a pervasive component of apocalyptic rhetoric, it is a component that is frequently rejected or criticized. The charges are that dualism deals in absolutes and easily leads to an "us versus them" mentality that contributes to prejudice, imperialism, exclusivism, and sometimes violence, a consequence that is heightened by Revelation's connection of dualism with warfare.[7] Undoubtedly history testifies to many examples, from Qumran to Waco, of how a distorted view of apocalyptic dualism has ushered in atrocities. For many the solution is to reinterpret Revelation in a way that is more palatable to contemporary sensibilities by toning down its dualism from the "harshness of moral black and white to the ambiguity of gray."[8] Toning down the dualism of Revelation, however, distorts its message.[9] To read an apocalypse as anything other than dualistic is to be reading something other than an apocalypse.

Rather than trying to neuter the dualistic language of Revelation, a more helpful approach is to inquire how dualism functions within Revelation's narrative world. Dualism is essential for Revelation's transformation of its audience and their perceptions of the world. One benefit of dualism is that it allows John to address those on opposite sides of the spectrum between conflict and compromise. For those who have suffered harshly and unjustly or who, by means of their faithfulness, have experienced firsthand the conflict between the kingdom of God and the kingdom of the world, dualism becomes a necessary aid in making sense of the world. Writing from the perspective of the social sciences, Roy Baumeister states that victims of evil tend to view their experience in absolute and dualistic categories of right and wrong, whereas the perpetrators of evil "see a large gray area."[10] For victims, maintaining the distinction between good and evil is necessary to help them categorize their experience. By transforming their world through a symbolic narrative that plays out a battle between good and evil while situating their experience within the context of that battle, Revelation provides its audience a means by which they can both make sense of their experience and gain the strength to endure it. By defining evil in terms of opposition to the kingdom of God, Revelation grants its audience a foundation for hope because such evil can be fought and overcome.

The key in Revelation is the means by which one achieves that victory, for Revelation itself guards against a corruption of its dualistic message by defining victory not in terms of violence against one's enemies but in terms of suffering witness that holds faithfully to the word of God and to the testimony of Jesus.

Just as dualism offers hope to those in conflict, it offers a stark warning to those who compromise with the kingdom of the world. Compromisers live in the gray areas because compromise only becomes a viable option when one has blurred the lines between the kingdom of God and the kingdom of the world. What dualism offers in response is clarity. Through its systematic employment of the warfare theme, Revelation symbolically transforms the world into a battlefield in which the forces of the dragon are arrayed against the forces of God. The point of this transformation of the world into a battlefield is to force a choice. There is no dual citizenship in Babylon and the new Jerusalem. Through this dualistic structure whereby one must either align oneself with the kingdom of God or with the kingdom of the world, Revelation exposes those who would compromise with Babylon as traitors. The dualism of Revelation thus provides comfort to those in conflict and an indictment for those who accommodate to the kingdom of the world. It is the antidote to the poisons of both despair and compromise.

Why Apocalyptic?

According to Käsemann, the indispensability of apocalyptic for addressing evil lies in apocalyptic's ability to grant one a new way of looking at the world. In part, apocalyptic accomplishes this through its employment of transcendence, symbolism, dualism, and determinism. The book of Revelation transforms the world by exposing the mundane events of human existence to a divinely disclosed transcendent reality, while creating for its readers a new narrative for their lives that gives them new or newly re-imagined symbols that provide commentary on and critique of their world. Revelation employs dualism to categorize their experience in the context of opposition, while enlisting determinism to encourage them to view their current experience as one small scene in a divine play that unfolds over the entire course of creation.

This explains *what* apocalyptic does, but not really *why*. The function of apocalyptic is not to provide some ethereal re-imagining of the world in order simply to change how people interpret their experience. Apocalyptic is a call to action! It is a tool wielded to accomplish the true goal: the transformation of *behavior*. One way to change how a person acts is to change how he or she thinks and feels. By transforming how his audience perceives the world, John calls upon them to act a certain way based on that new perception.[11] This is not just an intellectual exercise, for an apocalypse motivates on an emotional level as much as it convicts and informs on an intellectual one. As much as symbols cement themselves in the memory and offer flexible means of communication, their power also lies in their ability to connect with human emotion. When the rider on the white horse shows up suddenly to wage victorious battle over the opposition (Rev. 19:11-16), that image instills a feeling of hope and relief—the cavalry has arrived to save the day! The presentation of Rome as a demonic beast that wages war against the faithful and as a seductive whore who makes the inhabitants of the earth "intoxicated with the wine of her adulteries" while she herself becomes drunk on "the blood of God's people" (13:1-8; 17:1-6) functions not just to make the audience understand the abusive practices and policies of the empire but to *feel* the empire's oppressive power.

Through their symbolic transformation of the world, apocalypses like Revelation change how we think and feel in order to motivate us to action. Wayne Meeks notes that one puzzling feature of apocalyptic literature is the common inclusion of "admonitions for ordinary behavior." He writes that the images of evil in apocalyptic are set over against "the desired and promised good" and that it is the attainment of such goodness that apocalyptic promotes.[12] Rather than creating a bunker mentality as one awaits the end of days, Revelation calls upon its readers to live lives of faithful and active witness today.

How that call to witness functions varies depending on the needs of the recipients. For those whose faith is in conflict, apocalyptic offers a reality check. It asserts that their experiences of oppression, hardship, and opposition are not the whole story. It offers a vision of this world that relieves some of the tension between the claims of faith and the experiences of the world by transforming one's experiences in the light of divine revelation. So those who suffer affliction and poverty are in fact "rich" (2:9). Those with "little strength" cannot be defeated by the "hour of trial" about to afflict the earth (3:8, 10). The purpose is not simply to provide comfort and solace but to encourage these Christians to continue and perhaps even intensify their faithfulness and endurance (13:10; 14:12).

For those whose faith is in compromise, apocalyptic offers a wake-up call. It presents a transcendent vision of the world that punctures their illusions of security and prosperity. Those who think they are alive are revealed to be dead (3:1). Those who revel in their wealth and self-reliance are revealed to be "poor, blind, and naked" (3:17-18).

Revelation's transformation of the world into a battlefield in which the empire they have compromised with wages war against God serves to awaken them out of their stupor. The sharp division that Revelation establishes between the kingdom of God and the kingdom of the world makes it clear that faithful witness involves choosing sides and that in choosing God, the kingdom of the world becomes no longer an ally but an enemy. In these ways and more, the apocalyptic vision provides encouragement to those who experience the world as being against them and an indictment for those who seek a truce with a world that should be against them.

Although various apocalypses employ different conceptions of evil, they all share a view of the world that takes evil seriously. That standpoint, coupled with a transcendent perspective that situates experiences with evil and suffering in the context of God's plan for his creation, makes apocalyptic indispensable for those who encounter evil in its rawest forms as well as for those who flirt with it through the compromise of their faith. Though Revelation occupies some common ground with traditional theodicies, its goal is neither to provide a straightforward defense of God nor a comprehensive explanation of evil. It is a *revelation* of the kingdom of God and of his Christ. The goal of the book of Revelation is to encourage faithful witness by means of a story that offers an alternative interpretation of the world. In the second part of this book, we turn our attention to that story.

PART TWO
REVELATION

6

THE PATTERN OF
THE CHRIST

Experiences with evil and suffering present a challenge to faith because they call into question certain common Christian beliefs: that faithfulness will lead to blessing and prosperity, that God will place a hedge of protection around his people and keep evil at bay, and above all that a fatherly God of love and compassion would not allow his children to suffer. Most Christians live their lives with the tension between these ideas and their experiences simmering below the surface. As long as they feel mostly comfortable and secure in their own lives, they do not allow themselves to question the validity of such closely held beliefs. But when suffering becomes personal, when evil dares to intrude upon their lives, then that mildly simmering tension erupts to the surface. Revelation speaks to such situations because it offers a transformative interpretation of both the world and of faith.

The figure of Jesus Christ establishes the pattern of faithfulness in Revelation and it is this pattern that John calls upon his readers to embody. In Revelation 1:1 John identifies his work as the "revelation of Jesus Christ," an assertion that points to Jesus as a source of the messages and visions that follow, but which also hints at a deeper truth—that this book in some way *reveals* Christ. Structurally the book begins and ends with Jesus, from the opening identification of the work as the "revelation of Jesus Christ" to the closing admonition, "The grace of the Lord Jesus be with all the saints. Amen" (22:21). John's claim that the very essence of prophecy is "the testimony of Jesus" (19:10) indicates that the figure of Jesus Christ provides thematic cohesion to Revelation. Revelation's presentation of Christ, however, must not be understood apart from its presentation of God, for the function of Christ in this book is an outgrowth of the Creator's activity within his creation.

God, the Exodus, and the Cross

Chapter 1 of Revelation lays the theological and Christological foundation that undergirds the entirety of the book. Although John introduces his work as the "revelation of Jesus Christ," he quickly adds that it is a revelation "which God gave him" (1:1), thus identifying God as the ultimate source of the visions that follow. Though Revelation is written in his distinctive idiom and shaped by his hand, John's perspective is clear: this is a message from God and bearing the stamp of divine authority. In addition, John, who displays a fondness for the number three throughout Revelation, presents God by means of a threefold designation: 1) "the Alpha and the Omega"—the first and last letters of the Greek alphabet, 2) the one "who is and who was and who is to come," and 3) "the Almighty" (1:8). These titles identify a God who is powerful ("Almighty"), a God for whom temporal designations are inconsequential because he is past, present, and future, and a God who is the Creator and caretaker of all creation from its beginning to its consummation, from the alpha to the omega. Taken together these titles assert the sovereignty of God as one who not only encompasses creation from beginning to end, but who possesses the power to engage creation redemptively.

That John introduces himself in the next verse as a fellow participant in the "affliction" that his churches experience reveals an important aspect of Revelation's theological perspective. The sovereignty of

God over his creation does not result in an absence of suffering on the part of the faithful or the removal of those forms of evil that may oppose them. Rather Revelation asserts two seemingly contradictory truths without fully resolving the tension they create: 1) *suffering and encounters with evil are an intrinsic component of Christian existence* and 2) *God is sovereign*. Some find these claims impossible to reconcile. For John, however, what is most important for Christian faith is not their reconciliation, but learning how to live faithfully within the tension created by these two immutable truths. One step towards doing that is recognizing how God, in his sovereignty, has engaged evil in the past.

As stated previously, John defines "evil" in Revelation as that which stands in opposition to the kingdom of God. In Revelation 1:5-6, John evokes two formative events in the history of God's people that involve both opposition to the kingdom of God and a display of God's redemptive power: the exodus event and the cross event. John writes, "To him who loves us and freed us from our sins by his blood, and made us to be a kingdom, priests serving his God and Father." The latter part of this statement is an allusion to Exodus 19:6 in which God declares that the Israelites "shall be for me a priestly kingdom." In Exodus it is God who creates Israel as a priestly kingdom, yet in Revelation 1:5-6 that task is ascribed to Jesus. He both "freed us from our sins by his blood" and "made us to be a kingdom, priests." By conflating Christ's action on the cross with the exodus event, John encourages us to interpret one in light of the other, to see the cross as a continuation of God's redemptive activity within creation.

Both of these events are not only formative for the history of God's people, but are also formative for the narrative of Revelation. Throughout Revelation John uses the exodus and the cross to shape his audience's identity as the people of God and to provide a historical and conceptual framework for interpreting divine activity. Thematically these two events share much in common. Both involve empires (Egypt, Rome) that act oppressively towards the people of God. Both connect God's deliverance with human suffering and with violence. With the exodus account, God delivers the Israelites by means of violent plagues inflicted upon their captors. With the cross, God delivers through an act of violence perpetrated by Rome against Jesus.

Despite these connections, the exodus event and the cross event reveal different aspects of God's redemptive activity. The exodus event reveals a God who acts in *power* to redeem his people. He is the Almighty who delivers by the power of his right hand, inflicting plagues upon the Egyptians, bringing about the death of the firstborn of Egypt, and parting the waters of the sea. The cross event, however, reveals a God who delivers not through power as defined by the kingdom of the world but through *weakness* as it is perceived by the kingdom of the world. Throughout Revelation this interplay of power and perceived weakness recurs, most notably with the figure of Christ whose symbolization shifts back and forth between symbols of perceived power (lion, warrior) and of perceived weakness (a slaughtered lamb). By invoking the cross and exodus in 1:5-6 and uniting them in the figure of Christ, John lays a foundation for his transformation of the world through symbols.

With the cross he presents Christ as one who joins humanity in suffering and who thus shares in humanity's weakness; yet, by joining the cross event to the exodus he indicates that God's power to redeem comes to us through that weakness. The combination of exodus and cross is a combination of power and weakness in such a way that it unmasks the pretensions of the kingdom of the world where military might and worldly power pave the way to victory. The world becomes a very different place, however, when viewed from the perspective of the kingdom of God. Just as John can assert that Smyrna's poverty is in fact wealth (2:9), that the reputation of "life" enjoyed by the church at Sardis is really death (3:1), and that Laodicea's prosperity is really poverty (3:17), he tells us that weakness is in fact power. God's power to save and to work redemptively through the cross appears as little more than weakness in the eyes of the world. The image of a man crucified evokes defeat, weakness, and death. And yet it is that image of weakness and defeat that in Revelation provides the pattern for power and victory. In the image of the slaughtered Lamb we encounter the pattern of the Christ.

The Pattern of the Christ

Jesus is the preeminent faithful witness in the book of Revelation. As with the threefold description of God (1:8), Revelation presents a three-fold description of Jesus Christ as "the faithful witness, the firstborn of the dead, and the ruler of the kings of the earth" (1:5). This succinct description establishes a pattern for all who would claim allegiance to the kingdom of God. Christ's "faithful witness" led to his suffering and death. Yet God vindicated Christ's witness by means of his resurrection ("the firstborn of the dead") and his exaltation over "the kings of the earth." The pattern of the Christ is this movement from faithful witness to suffering/death to resurrection/vindication.

When John announces in 1:3 that blessed are all those "who keep what is written" in this book, he is announcing a call to action. That action is neither the violent overthrow of oppressors nor accommodation to Roman imperial culture as a means of preserving security and prosperity. It is the call to fulfill the pattern of the Christ. In this sense, reading Revelation exclusively as an attempt to comfort Christians in their hardships and to assure them of ultimate victory misses the point. This book calls upon Christians to engage the world as faithful witnesses (as Christ did), with the full understanding that faithful witness to God when carried out within the kingdom of the world may very well lead to their suffering and possible death (as it did with Christ), but that God will vindicate them for their faithful witness (as he did Christ).

This witness of Christ that John's readers are called to embody is an active, not passive, witness. It is not the witness of Christians sitting in church buildings and singing songs to one another, but then keeping a low profile as they move out into the world. It is the witness of those who stand up against injustice, who confront and resist evil, and who oppose that which opposes the kingdom of God. Faithful witness in Revelation is the embodiment in his followers of Christ's own witness.[1]

Therefore, Revelation's perspective is that the suffering of God's people is by no means inconsistent with the life of faithfulness; if anything, it is the inevitable outgrowth of a life of faithfulness. To participate in the witness of Christ is to participate in the sufferings of Christ. Because faithful witnesses, in imitation of their Lord, actively oppose the kingdom of the world, their suffering, like his, is thus "earned" even though not deserved.[2]

Just as participating in the witness of Christ leads to a share in his sufferings, participating in his sufferings leads to a share in his resurrection and glorification as well. Though faithful witness may lead to death, it does not go unrewarded. This participation in the glorification of Christ is not a simple reversal of fortunes so that the powerless now become the powerful and the oppressed become the new oppressors (as D. H. Lawrence objected). It is not about getting even with one's enemies. To read Revelation this way is to trade in the very same values as that of the kingdom of the world. Anyone who reads the exaltation of the faithful in Revelation as espousing a new regime in which they now get to rule over others as a form of repayment for oppression not only misreads Revelation but misreads the entirety of the New Testament. The glorification of the saints in Revelation is about taking up a place of *service* in the kingdom of God (3:12; 7:15; 22:3).[3] The reversal is akin to Jesus's statement in the Gospels regarding how the first will become last and the last become first, which should be read not as giving the downtrodden their turn at worldly power but as God's vindication of humility and faithfulness.

The first three chapters of Revelation introduce the pattern of the Christ, call upon his followers to embody that pattern, and critique their success or failure at doing so. In fact, John presents himself as one who has taken up the pattern of the Christ in his own life by virtue of his own faithful witness. He is their companion in "the affliction, kingdom, and endurance that is in Jesus" (1:9). Sharing in the affliction that faithful witness brings is sharing in the kingdom of God. John says that he was on the island of Patmos "because of the word of God and the witness of Jesus" (my translation). Traditionally this statement was taken as evidence that John was exiled to Patmos as a form of persecution by Roman imperial authority. More recently that interpretation has come under question due to a lack of historical and archaeological evidence that would identify Patmos as an official place of exile.[4] John's statement, for instance, that he is there "because of the word of God and the witness of Jesus" could as easily be a statement that he came to Patmos to preach the word of God. On the other hand, references elsewhere in Revelation to those who keep the word of God and the witness of Jesus are typically connected with suffering and opposition to the kingdom of God (6:9; 12:17; 20:4), indicating that, even if not an official exile, John's presence on Patmos may have been as a result of his faithful witness and thus one aspect of his participation in "affliction."

Regardless of the debates over the historical realities of why John was on Patmos, the theological point is that John writes as one who is himself fulfilling the pattern of the Christ. He is their companion in affliction because of his allegiance to the word of God and to the witness of Jesus. Whether or not that affliction involves exile or official persecution, although of historical interest, is immaterial to John's point. As a faithful witness, he shares in the sufferings (from whatever cause) that other faithful witnesses in the seven churches experience. When he calls upon them to embody the pattern of the Christ, he does so with the authority of one who himself embodies that pattern. Jesus set the pattern for faithful witness; John follows that pattern and calls upon his churches to do the same. The seven letters that follow in chapters two and three represent a critique of how well they are heeding that call.

Faithful Witness in Context:
Seven Letters to Seven Churches

Introducing the seven letters to the seven churches is a scene in which John sees a vision of Christ in the form of a glorified "son of man" (1:10-16). One function of this vision is to establish the divine authority of the letters that follow. The symbolism of verse sixteen highlights several important aspects of this vision. Christ, in the form of this "son of man," holds seven stars in his right hand, has a sharp, double-edged sword protruding from his mouth, and a face that shines with the full force of the sun.

Within Greco-Roman culture, rulers and other figures of influence often employed astrological and cosmological symbols as a means of communicating divine power or authority. In particular, the image of the sun's rays shooting out of a figure's head depicted the radiation of divine glory. Representations of the Greek god Helios (the sun god) appropriately utilized this imagery, as was also the case with other deities like Apollo.[5] Within Roman imperial culture this imagery communicated the glory of deified emperors or those who wished to claim divine honors for themselves. These emperors might appear (in person or in representation) wearing a radiate crown—a crown (often golden to more closely represent the sun) with projections coming out of the top that simulated the rays of the sun.[6] By representing Christ with this imagery in 1:16, Revelation offers a competing power claim to other voices of authority (whether Greek gods or Roman emperors), but also reinforces the message to these seven churches that the one speaking to them speaks with divine authority.

The seven stars in his hand work together with the sword protruding from his mouth to communicate how this figure of divine authority relates to the seven churches. The seven stars represent the angels of the seven churches (1:20). The holding of the angels of the churches in his hand evokes protection and care. This "son of man" knows these churches intimately and wants them to trust in his power and protection. Yet this same figure has a sword protruding from his mouth. This sword is an implement of war (2:16; 19:15). That this sword, however, is always associated with the mouth and in Revelation 19 is wielded by a figure identified as "The Word of God" (19:13), indicates that what this sword unleashes is not the violence of physical battle but divine judgment. Brian Blount argues that the sword represents "oppositional witness."[7] In particular it is witness *by Christ himself* against another.

The sword represents the witness of divine judgment upon those who stand in opposition to the kingdom of God. Together, these contrasting images of divine protection (the seven stars in the hand) and divine judgment (the sword) foreshadow the contrasting messages of commendation and censure that dominate the seven letters.

Although the seven letters derive from a divine authority, the glorified "son of man," the letters themselves represent the experiences of churches in real flesh and blood contexts. As such, the letters ground the subsequent visionary material of the book in the context of the struggles and challenges facing churches in the last half of the first century AD. A previous chapter already addressed the historical and social contexts of the letters; suffice it to say here that the evidence from the letters suggests a variety of experiences that can be grouped broadly into two categories: those churches encountering opposition and suffering from within their environment (from false teachers, poverty, oppression, slander, etc.) and those churches compromising with their environment (in idolatry, sexual immorality, and economic practices). Furthermore, these categories are not mutually exclusive but may overlap and intermingle within the same community. What unites all of these varied experiences and approaches to the surrounding culture, however, are John's conceptions of evil and faithful witness.

In Revelation evil is opposition to the kingdom of God, though this opposition may take a variety of forms ranging from open antagonism to subtle seduction. The identification of opposition as evil occurs prominently in the seven letters, which link opposition to the kingdom of God with the authority and activity of Satan. Even those who would ostensibly align themselves with the kingdom of God, whether Jewish or Christian, get defined in terms of evil when their teaching and activity conflict with the kingdom of God as represented by the book of Revelation. So Christian leaders in Ephesus who claim the mantle of "apostle" become exposed as "evildoers" (2:2). In both Smyrna and Philadelphia, Jewish communities whose actions include slander against the churches are each identified as "a synagogue of Satan" (2:9; 3:9). In the case of

Smyrna, the synagogue's antagonism towards the church appears to have taken the form of false accusations to the Roman authorities, accusations which may lead to imprisonment, suffering, and possibly death. Yet, it is noteworthy that John does not describe this course of action as deriving primarily from the synagogue or from Roman authorities, but from "the devil" (2:10). Similarly, the church at Pergamum had experienced the martyrdom of one of its faithful witnesses, likely at the hands of Rome. Nevertheless, Revelation connects the death of Antipas not with Rome specifically, but with Satan. It does this by framing the reference to Antipas with statements that Pergamum is the seat of "Satan's throne" and the place "where Satan lives" (2:13). Revelation similarly redefines the cultural compromise occurring at Thyatira among those who adhere to the teachings of "Jezebel" by describing those teachings as "the deep things of Satan" (2:24).

By consistently aligning opposition to the kingdom of God with Satan, John is not merely using the rhetorical strategy of demonization to marshal outrage against his own enemies and against Rome. Although the political, social, and economic realities of John's audience are very much in play, it is the *spiritual* implications behind those realities that John seeks to clarify. Roman imperial culture is not the primary enemy John identifies in Revelation. For John, the Roman Empire is only one historical manifestation of the enduring and spiritual conflict between the kingdom of God and the kingdom of the world that is under the authority of Satan. Throughout Revelation John employs imagery and symbolism drawn from several major empires that opposed God's people in one form or another (Egyptian, Babylonian, Seleucid, Roman). By this John shows that political empires come and go, but Satan remains. Opposition to the kingdom of God is always present, though it may adopt different historical forms. The real conflict in Revelation is not the church versus Rome, but God versus Satan.

The driving issue for John is how this spiritual conflict between the opposing forces of God and Satan, as currently manifested in Christian relations with their culture, affects the faith and faithfulness of the churches. John is careful, however, to maintain that the conflict between God and Satan is not some ethereal spiritual battle. The roots of that conflict grow and extend out into the social, religious, and economic realities that these seven churches face. Through the seven letters, John contends that this spiritual conflict finds purchase in their lives and communities. Ellen Charry writes: "The enemy is both within and without. In short, the cover letters undercut the clarity often associated with the cosmic struggle between God and Satan."[8] The seven letters are a reminder that evil is not simply something that is "out there" to be resisted, but something that lives among and within us. By linking Satan not only to Rome but also to the synagogue and to their fellow Christian believers, John asserts that Satan's opposition to the kingdom of God may manifest in political empires, in economic structures, in social institutions, in the synagogue, and even within the church itself. All of these entities are weapons that Satan uses to wage his war against the kingdom of God. The danger is that one can become so focused on the weapon that he or she fails to see the power that wields it. It is that power that stands behind the political, social, and economic structures that John orients his readers towards. The seven letters thus provide context for this cosmic battle by situating it in the midst of the flesh and blood struggles and temptations of these churches, while at the same time situating the experiences of these churches within the larger cosmic battle.

The seven letters further function as an analysis of the churches' faithfulness or lack of faithfulness in embodying the pattern of the Christ. The pattern of the Christ is that faithful witness to the kingdom of God leads to suffering (often generated by those in opposition), but that endurance in faith results in vindication. The alternating pattern of commendation and censure in the letters reveals the success or failure of the churches in embodying this pattern. These letters are written in the voice of the glorified "Son of Man" who appeared to John. As such, the body of each letter begins with the statement "I know" followed by information regarding the experiences of those churches. This structure identifies Jesus as one who is intimately familiar with these churches and who thereby can expose the truth about them.

Those churches or individuals who receive praise do so because they embody the pattern of the Christ. The clearest example of this pattern comes from the church at Smyrna (2:8-11). This is one of only two letters that contain no command to repent. This church has remained faithful despite experiencing affliction, poverty, and opposition from the synagogue. Nevertheless, Jesus informs them that their faithful witness will lead to even greater suffering because "the devil is about to throw some of you into prison" (2:10). As a word of encouragement for them, the latter part of verse ten lays out the pattern that they are to follow in succinct fashion: "Be faithful unto death, and I will give you the crown of life" (my translation). The phrase rendered here as "unto death" is not a gentle reminder to remain faithful for the duration of one's life until passing away peacefully in old age. It is a statement of martyrdom. He is essentially saying, "Be faithful *even to the point of death.*" In imitation of their Lord, they are called upon to maintain their faithful witness even if such witness leads to their deaths because the victory of Christ is achieved through a witness that does not falter or fade even in the most extreme circumstances. Yet, he assures them, if they share in this part of Christ's pattern, they will also share in the remainder of that pattern—Christ's glorified resurrection ("the crown of life").

Consequently, the commendation of the letters typically combines faithfulness with endurance. Those at Ephesus are "enduring patiently and bearing up for the sake of my name" (2:3). Christians at Thyatira receive praise for "faith, service, and patient endurance" and are called to "hold fast" (2:19, 25). At Philadelphia they have "kept my word of patient endurance" (3:10). Many at Pergamum are also "holding fast to my name" as they endure opposition from within and without. Antipas, called "my faithful witness," lost his life in this city "where Satan lives" (2:13). The church at Pergamum, therefore, can look to Antipas as one of their own who embodied the pattern of the Christ and therefore serves as a model for them. As the pattern of the Christ, however, is not

merely that of faithful witness that leads to suffering, but also vindication for enduring in faithful witness, each of the seven letters concludes
with an eschatological promise of reward (2:7, 11, 17, 26-28; 3:5, 12, 21).

Conversely, the censure of these letters is an indictment of the
churches for their failure to embody the pattern of the Christ, often
taking the form of compromise with and accommodation to their
surrounding culture. Some at Pergamum and Thyatira have followed
Christian teachers who promote accommodation to their surrounding culture (2:14-15, 20). Sardis is spiritually dead despite a thriving
reputation (3:1). Despite their faithful resistance to false apostles, the
Ephesian church is in danger of having its lamp stand removed (2:5)—a
symbol of their removal from the presence of Christ. The last of the
seven letters (to Laodicea) opens with an identification of Christ as "the
faithful and true witness" (3:14), a description that contrasts harshly
with the subsequent indictment of this church for its materialism and
self-reliance (2:15-17).

The seven letters indicate that living out the pattern of the Christ
often involves suffering. There is an intriguing, though not wholly consistent, relationship between faithfulness and suffering in these letters. Those churches or individuals who are among the most faithful
(Smyrna, Antipas) experience the most suffering, while those churches
that are the least faithful (Sardis, Laodicea) have no mention of past or
present suffering in their letters.[9] It is as though their level of suffering
is relative to their level of comfort within the kingdom of the world.

Three Reflections

The first three chapters of Revelation lay an important narrative foundation for the remainder of the book; they also lay a theological foundation
for understanding John's treatment of evil and suffering. Several important ideas surface in these chapters. First, these chapters indicate that
God does not define prosperity, success, and the good life in terms of
materiality but in terms of spiritual faithfulness. Faithfulness is neither
defined by material blessings nor does it necessarily lead to such. There

is no one-to-one correspondence between one's level of faithfulness and one's level of physical comfort in the world. The letters to Smyrna and to Philadelphia highly praise those churches for their faithfulness and yet each is promised a very different future experience. Those at Smyrna are told that their continued faithfulness will lead to even more suffering that may in fact result in death (2:10). Those at Philadelphia, however, are told that their continued faithfulness will lead to their being spared "from the hour of trial" that is coming (3:10). That two churches equally praised for faithfulness can expect very different outcomes in terms of suffering demonstrates that the suffering of the faithful will not always make sense when measured against a standard that equates faithfulness with comfort and prosperity. The experience of suffering in this life is not equally measured to all. Some suffer greatly while others coast through life with relative ease. What matters is not the level of suffering and hardship, but one's faithfulness in every situation.

This is why the eschatological promises that conclude each letter are so vital. Some have criticized the idea of an end-time resolution to the problem of human suffering, believing that it downplays the need to remedy injustice in the here and now. Eschatology, however, is not about taking our eyes off of the needs of this world and focusing them instead on some ultimate consolation. One who embodies the pattern of the Christ must also embody his compassion for the poor, his concern for justice, his outrage at evil, and his actions to reduce human suffering. What eschatology does, what the seven promises concluding these letters do, is challenge our assumptions that God is not faithful unless he provides blessing and comfort in *this* life. They are a reminder that God's vision encompasses much more than ours and that this material world—as important as it is—is not the totality of existence. The messages of the seven letters are strongly counter-cultural in that they dare to suggest that it is not wealth or comfort or pleasure achieved within the kingdom of the world that matters, but a life lived according to the pattern of a crucified messiah, a slaughtered Lamb, and that that pattern reinterprets all of our cultural assumptions.

Second, the seven letters transform the concept of victory. If Christ sets the pattern, then our understanding of Christian victory must conform to Christ's own victory. Christ's victory achieved on a cross was not a victory over his Roman oppressors or over his Jewish enemies, but over the power of Satan. On one level, it would have been very easy for John's audience to conclude that their struggle was against the societal forces arrayed against them. Some churches were experiencing opposition from Rome and from their Jewish neighbors, while others were materialistic, compromising in their faith, and engaging in immorality and idolatry. The former group rejected what the kingdom of the world was selling, while the latter group bought it wholesale.

John, however, makes it clear that even though their battle was being fought on the field of Roman society, their victory was not a victory over Rome but a victory over Satan. Rome, materialism, idolatry and the like were all weapons that Satan was using to wage a *spiritual* war against the people of God. To say that Christian victory in Revelation is about conquering Roman influence is like saying that knocking the gun out of an enemy soldier's hand means you have won the war. John seeks to divert his audience's attention away from the weapon itself to the one who wields it.

That each of the seven letters ends with an eschatological promise of victory places their faithful witness in the context of a spiritual battle with eternal significance. Victory in this context is not violent bloodshed or violent resistance to political power. It is faithful witness that embraces the same pattern as Christ's faithful witness—witness that endures even through suffering and death. Christian victory is not victory over one's own enemies but victory over the enemy of God. Christ conquered through active witness, suffering, and death and it is through that same active witness that his followers conquer the enemy of God (12:10-11). Such witness exposes the kingdom of the world for what it is—a pretender. Boesak writes: "When we are willing to give up our life, the power of the world is truly unmasked as powerlessness, as mere brute force, and therefore inauthentic. The church should really know this. But we don't. We are far too busy imitating the power structures of the world in the life of the church."[10] As long as the church defines victory the way the world does—in terms of power, conquest, and the defeat of one's own political, religious, or social enemies—it fails to embody the pattern of the Christ. The witness of Christ is a witness that exposes the pretensions of the kingdom of the world by demonstrating that victory comes only through faithfulness and allegiance to the kingdom of God.

Third, even though the apocalyptic dualism of Revelation generates a view of the world that divides humanity into opposing camps of enemies and allies, Revelation at the same time undercuts an "us versus them" approach by complicating the definition of "us." According to the seven letters, the issue in Revelation is not God opposing *our* enemies, but whether or not *we* stand in faithfulness or opposition to God's kingdom. The seven letters are a reminder that our willing complicity in evil always threatens or, as N. T. Wright puts it with respect to a different context, "the line between good and evil runs not between 'us' and 'them' but through every individual and every society."[11] The line between "good and evil," between ally and enemy, is permeable in Revelation and easily crossed. Those who have compromised with the enemy are commanded to "repent" and realign themselves with the kingdom of God, while those who are praised for faithfulness are also warned to endure or else they will find themselves aligned with the enemy. Twice the church at Sardis receives the admonition to be "watchful" (3:2-3). That admonition for self-critical examination stands as a warning not only to the church at Sardis but to all of the seven churches and to all Christians everywhere.

7

THE THRONE

REVELATION 4-5

When I was six years old, I was in the basement of our house as my grandmother was descending the stairs. Partway down her legs gave out and she stumbled down the few remaining steps and fell back against them. She looked up and said, "Lord, what did I do to deserve this?" What often makes suffering so unbearable is its incomprehensibility. Suffering is never harder to accept than when it appears to serve no larger purpose, to have no useful function, and to be wholly undeserved. What makes suffering and evil so difficult to incorporate within our normal range of experiences is that they often just make no *sense*. There is no comprehensive explanation, no grand plan that encompasses all human suffering and accounts for all evil. Perhaps we might explain the murder of a teenager as an act of a deranged mind corrupted by sinful impulses, but that hardly accounts for the death of a mother of two in an earthquake. We may easily write off the heart attack of an overweight fifty year old as the accumulation of a lifetime of bad choices, yet when an infant is born with a terminal illness, such reasoning falters. We can appeal to genetic anomalies, but explaining *how* such a condition arises does not satisfy the deeper urge to know *why*.

123

Much of the Christian struggle with suffering is based on two faulty assumptions. First is the assumption that suffering must make sense. Suffering is an inevitable and intrinsic part of the human experience, and one involving so many different causes and variables that no explanation can be fully satisfying in every instance. The assumption that suffering must make sense is, ironically, often a by-product of faith. If, as faith claims, God is sovereign over his creation, then suffering must have a function and purpose within the divine design. Consequently, there must be logic to suffering, a rationality that can be discerned by those who look at the world through the eyes of faith. What such a conclusion lacks is an awareness of the great divide between how suffering functions within the wisdom of God and our ability to understand it by means of human wisdom.

A second faulty assumption that underlies much Christian thinking about suffering is the persistent belief that the plan of God must be concerned first and foremost with the alleviation of *my* suffering. Without doubt, faith can sometimes be a balm to suffering, whether through the strength borne out of religious community, the comfort derived from prayer, or the hope that arises from Christian doctrine. Yet, the idea that suffering is somehow inconsistent with a life of faith and that, therefore, any divine plan for this world must involve the elimination of suffering is an egregious heresy. Faith is not a protective barrier against disease, accident, or persecution. In fact, the experience of human suffering may be exacerbated by faith rather than alleviated by it. The causes of such exacerbation may range from various forms of persecution as a result of one's Christian identification to the hardships that can arise in a life that embraces sacrifice and self-denial as a marker of its authenticity. What God offers his followers in this world is not the elimination of their suffering but the strength to endure that suffering in hope. This perspective is well-represented by the dual promise/warning Jesus made to his disciples when he informed them that, in him, they would have peace, but in this world, they would have trouble (Jn. 16:33). As human beings, we naturally focus on our own suffering and ascribe it ultimate significance. Yet,

God's divine plan is not a plan for our individual happiness, but for his entire *creation*. If we are to think deeply and theologically about human suffering, we must think about it within that larger context.

At the center of any reflection on human suffering (and evil) is the sovereignty and plan of God. Following the introductory chapters (1-3), Revelation 4-5 begins the revelation proper. It is here that the primary vision of the book begins to unfold. Not surprisingly, therefore, John begins with the sovereignty of God. For John, any discussion of the roles of suffering and evil within creation must be built off of the foundation of divine sovereignty. God *is* on his throne. Yet that is not the totality of the answer in Revelation. John is not content merely to appeal to the sovereignty of God as though that alone quells all objections. Instead, he explores the implications of that sovereignty in a way that is tailored to the specific life circumstances of his audience and, thus, leaves plenty of room for mystery within the divine providence. Revelation 4-5 sets the stage for the drama that unfolds throughout Revelation and that stage is a heavenly throne room. It is a fitting location as Revelation explores how a sovereign Lord exercises his sovereignty.

Throne Room, Part One (Revelation 4)

Revelation 4-5 constitutes a vision of the heavenly throne room of God. John's access point to this throne room comes through an open door in heaven which he passes through by becoming "in the Spirit" (4:1-2). As previously mentioned, apocalyptic language transforms one's interpretation of reality by providing a new lens through which to view the world. The open door in heaven is a transition point between heaven and earth; it represents access to a transcendent reality. By passing through this door, John gains a glimpse into the spiritual realm which then allows him to see earthly reality from a heavenly vantage point.

What John sees "in the Spirit" is a group of attendants (elders, creatures) surrounding a throne and worshipping the one seated on it. Essentially, that is it. Revelation 4 overflows with specific details and colorful descriptions that can easily distract one from the central idea, which is that everything in this chapter points towards or revolves around the throne and the one seated on it—an emphasis highlighted by the fourteen occurrences of the word "throne" in these eleven verses. John's vague description of the occupant of this throne simply as "the one who is seated on the throne" is intriguing for its obscurity. One could perhaps write it off as John's perspective "in the moment" as he enters into strange territory and is thus unsure of the identity of the one before him, except that he continues to employ this designation (5:1, 7) even *after* the elders and four living creatures clearly identify the throne's occupant as the Lord God, the Almighty (4:8, 11). What John's identification of God as "the one who is seated on the throne" does is establish an important sense of distance and mystery. It is the designation for a transcendent one who defies accurate description. This is not the informal "Daddy" God of much contemporary Christian pop theology, but the Almighty, the sovereign Lord before whom even celestial figures prostrate themselves.

At the conclusion of this chapter John witnesses the elders vacating their thrones and the living creatures casting their golden wreaths before the throne of God, while each offers up praises to God (4:9-11). The language and imagery employed in this scene is highly evocative, theologically programmatic for the remainder of Revelation, and socially connected to John's audience and their environment. Benefaction was a primary feature of the socio-economic system of the Roman Empire. In a society where the majority of resources are held by a few, benefactors become a vital component of a functioning economy. Within the Greco-Roman world, many who possessed resources, skills, or training would use them in ways that benefited the wider population. For such a system to work properly there must be motivation for individuals or groups to become or continue as benefactors. Consequently, what greased the wheels of this system was reciprocity. Those on the receiving end of the benefaction would reciprocate by bestowing public honor and gratitude on the benefactor, much like we today honor benefactors by giving them the key to the city or putting their name on a building.

Countless inscriptions and literary texts from the Greco-Roman world testify to this practice of awarding honors to benefactors, several features of which are worth noting. First, this practice was a public display of gratitude for the graciousness and help afforded by the benefactor. Second, a variety of specific "honors" could be awarded to the benefactor, including exemption from taxation and the right to occupy the best seat in the theater. One of the most common honorary awards was the granting of a golden crown, or more accurately a golden wreath (*stephanos*). The golden crown or wreath did not typically represent royalty. The standard crown of royalty was the diadem (*diadema*), a thin metal band worn around the forehead. The golden wreath primarily symbolized honor, among other concepts (victory, divine glory).[1] Third, inscriptions and literary texts that describe the awarding of golden wreaths and other honors to benefactors usually indicate that the benefactor is "worthy" of them.[2]

John's description of the actions performed by the elders and four living creatures at the end of Revelation 4 strongly evokes this practice of benefaction. While the living creatures give "honor and thanks" to the one on the throne, the elders lay golden wreaths (*stephanous*) before the throne and then declare God "worthy" to receive "honor" (4:9-11). The elders further identify the reason why God is worthy of such honor: "for you created all things" (4:11). The message of Revelation 4:9-11 is that God is the ultimate benefactor by virtue of his role as the Creator. All things in creation owe their being to the God who created and sustains them. God alone is worthy of glory and honor for he alone has created.

Yet John's audience lived in a world where the sovereignty of God and his role as the ultimate benefactor did not go unchallenged. Revelation 13 contains a vision of a beast rising out of the sea, an image that represents the Roman emperor and Roman power. On one level, this vision describes the world that John and his readers inhabit. The beast has ten horns, which are symbols of power, and wears ten diadems (*diademata*), the crown of royalty, on these horns (13:1). The beast also lays claim to power, a throne, and great authority, each of which was granted to it by the dragon, or Satan (13:2). Furthermore, the beast receives the worship of the whole world—a clear reference to the imperial cult, the worship of the Roman emperor (13:4, 8). In short, the world as experienced by John's readers is a place where Rome is sovereign, where Rome lays claim to all power, authority, and divine glory. In the world as envisioned in Revelation 13, the Roman emperor is the one who sits on the throne and exercises sovereignty over the earth. It is also worth noting that Roman society hailed the emperor as its supreme benefactor. As sovereign ruler of the world, the emperor was the source of all good things that came to his citizens.

Both God and Rome lay claim to a throne, to power, to authority, and to the right of worship. The stage is certainly set for a turf war. One of the driving theological questions in the book of Revelation is this: Who rules in this world? Is this world under the authority of God or under the authority of the dragon and his beasts? Given that both God and the dragon/beast assert their right to rule over this world, it is not surprising that one of the dominant structural metaphors in the book of Revelation is war.

In light of this, one way to read Revelation 4 is as a counter-claim to Roman imperial power.[3] When the twenty-four elders vacate their heavenly thrones and cast their golden wreaths at the feet of God, it is a statement that *only* God is worthy to sit on a throne, that *only* God is worthy to receive divine honor, because *only* God is the creator of all things. Transcendence exposes truth. As John, "in the Spirit," enters the heavenly throne room, he experiences an apocalypse—that is, an unveiling. The curtain separating the spiritual and physical realms is pulled back and John sees the Creator on his throne ruling faithfully over his creation, an image that exposes the posturing of the dragon and beast as mere pretension. With this image John undercuts the desire for accommodation to Roman authority by highlighting the inadequacy of Roman claims to sovereignty when viewed from the shadow cast by "the Lord God, the Almighty" reigning from his heavenly throne, while at the same time offering comfort to the suffering faithful that, despite the presumption of appearances to the contrary, God is in control.

John's vision of the sovereignty of the Creator over his creation holds certain implications for how one understands evil and suffering. If God is indeed sovereign over *all* creation, then one must assert that even evil and suffering fall under his reign.[4] One cannot simply appeal to limitations of God's power to resolve the issue, as though he were incapable of remedying evil and suffering, because John asserts that the one on the throne is "the Almighty" (4:8). This implies that God has created a world in which evil is always a possibility due to the free will of humanity and in which suffering is a necessary and intrinsic component of life.

However, for many of us, the problem is that God does not deal with evil in the way we would prefer, which usually involves the immediate and total eradication of evil and its attendant suffering—or at least the eradication of evil and suffering from *our* lives. Or, we compartmentalize and question why God could not have at least created a world in which children did not get cancer or hurricanes did not exist. If we are honest, we confess that there are no simple answers to those kinds of questions. Explaining why God did *not* create the world differently is an exercise in pointless conjecture that does nothing to change the fact that the world is as it is.

John makes no attempt to justify or even to explain the existence of evil and suffering as entities within creation; rather, his focus is on how one maintains faithfulness within the world as it is. Revelation 4 suggests that if one acknowledges God as Creator, then one must also acknowledge that he is sovereign over that creation. What John's vision in Revelation 4 assures his readers is that their trust in the sovereignty of God is trust in a divine benefactor whose rule over creation is beneficent and not oppressive.

Furthermore, whereas many Christians end their reflections on evil and suffering with the assertion that God is on his throne, for John that is the *beginning* point. Asserting that one merely turn everything over to God and trust in his control may sound like a noble position of faith, but it offers little comfort to the victim, little guidance to the confused, and little solace to those in pain. John understands that an acknowledgment of the sovereignty of God is the place where the response of faith *begins* and everything else must grow out of that foundational claim; yet, if such an acknowledgment alone were sufficient, John could have ended his book with chapter four. Instead John explores the implications and significance of this claim of divine sovereignty throughout the remaining eighteen chapters. This is because, for John, God's sovereignty is not a passive declaration. The Creator is active within his creation and the remainder of the book of Revelation unveils how the God who is past, present, and future has, is, and will exercise that sovereignty.

Throne Room, Part Two (Revelation 5)

In Revelation 5 the narrative focus shifts from theology to Christology, from God to Christ. Everything in Revelation 4 revolves around God's throne, with no mention whatsoever of Christ. That all changes in chapter five as Christ becomes a central player in the drama. This is not to suggest that God somehow recedes from the main stage. The events of Revelation 5 occur within God's throne room, he holds the all-important scroll in his hand (5:1), and he receives the worship of all creation at the conclusion of the chapter (5:13). Chapter five does not represent a shift away from God to Christ, but a declaration of how Christ fits within God's sovereign plan for his creation.

With Revelation 4 providing a bird's eye view of the heavenly throne and the one seated on it, Revelation 5 zeroes in on one specific aspect of that scene—a scroll held in the right hand of the one on the throne. This scroll contains writing on it and within it and is sealed with seven seals (5:1). Identification of the content of the scroll is a matter of much scholarly debate, as Revelation offers no clear description of its content even after the scroll has been opened. The best suggestion for the content of the sealed scroll is that it contains a revelation of God's plan for his creation, a revelation that is not only about the future, but also the past and present.[5] In other words, it contains the content of the visions that follow.

That the image of a sealed scroll was a common prophetic motif may offer some help. Ezekiel 2:9-10 depicts a scene similar to that of Revelation 5: "I looked, and a hand was stretched out to me, and a written scroll was in it. He spread it before me; it had writing on the front and on the back, and written on it were words of lamentation and mourning and woe." Ezekiel's scroll contains words of judgment on the house of Israel, which suggests that the scroll of Revelation 5 may likewise contain the judgments that unfold in the book of Revelation, either in whole or in part.[6] Although judgment is certainly a component of the scroll's content, other stark differences between Ezekiel's and John's scrolls—Ezekiel's is not sealed with seven seals and John's is not spread out before him—caution against a specific identification of the two. As with Ezekiel's scroll, however, John's scroll functions as a message for his audience and their situation.

The sealing of a scroll or other document would typically occur by pouring wax on the document until it began to harden and then using a "seal"—a stamping or rolling device—to make an engraving on the wax. The seal thus served as a symbol of the document's author and protected its content from unauthorized eyes. Only those with the proper authority were to break the seals. So, with the introduction of this seal in the hand of God, a mighty angel proclaims, "Who is worthy to open the scroll and break its seals?" A search commences throughout all creation for one with the proper authority, but none is found and John begins to weep (5:2-4). John weeps because the failure to open this scroll means that the plan of God will go unfulfilled. As Boesak states: "If the scroll is not opened, the 'why' behind the suffering of God's people will not be heard or answered."[7] One might wonder why God himself could not open the scroll, but God is the author of the scroll. It is intended for someone else. It is intended for the one who will bring about the fulfillment of God's plan.

John's grief turns out to be premature as an elder suddenly announces that the one for whom the scroll was intended has been found. He is "the Lion of the tribe of Judah, the Root of David" (5:5). These descriptions identify this figure as one of undeniable power. The Lion of Judah is a king who will rule his people with might (Gen. 49:9-10), while the Root of David is an image derived from Isaiah 11 that identifies one who possesses the spirit of strength (Is. 11:2) and who will strike the earth "with the rod of his mouth" and slay the wicked with nothing but his breath (11:4). The impression generated by Revelation 5:5 is that this figure possesses the authority to open the scroll because of his great *power*. The elder, in fact, anoints him in this regard by ascribing his worthiness to open the scroll to the fact that he "has conquered."

The idea that deliverance comes only through a display of power is a consistent human deception that has proven difficult to shake, whether by those ancient Jews who envisioned a Messiah who would marshal an army to lead them in revolt against the occupying Romans or by Americans who constantly build stronger tanks, bigger guns, and ever more devastating bombs because we are certain that only military power can ensure security and peace. We take great pride in strength as we desire faster automobiles, more powerful operating systems for our computers, and fitter bodies. Christianity is certainly not immune from this desire for power. When Christians fall ill or encounter obstacles in their lives, what kind of deliverer do they seek? They seek a God of power who will destroy the cause of suffering in their lives, who will overwhelm their enemies with force, or miraculously heal whatever ails.

For John's audience, power was an issue because Rome possessed it all. Those who sought compromise with Rome did so to align themselves with the primary powerbroker in that world, the only tangible source of security and economic prosperity. In contrast, those who resisted the lure of Roman power received affliction and poverty. They, like those at Philadelphia, had "little power" (3:8). The image of a Lion of Judah come to fulfill the plan of God was thus a highly provocative image for both groups because it tapped into the human desire for power and reinforced the hope for a mighty deliverer who would rectify the imbalance and provide the security and victory they craved. The announcement of the Lion of Judah is a triumphant exclamation point for the expectations of John's audience. Yet, for John and his audience, that exclamation point quickly turns into a question mark as the Lion of Judah undergoes a startling transformation.

John never actually sees a lion. In verse five he *hears* the elder describe the Lion of the tribe of Judah as the one worthy to open the scroll, but when he turns to look at the one the elder is describing, John *sees* "a Lamb standing as if it had been slaughtered" (5:6). John hears about a lion, but sees a slaughtered Lamb. Several times throughout Revelation, John employs this same rhetorical device whereby he first hears something only to have that auditory experience redefined by what he then sees (1:10-12; 7:4, 9; 9:16-17). Through this redefinition, John learns that the Lion he had been led to expect is actually a Lamb, and a slaughtered one at that. The expectation of power gets redefined in terms of weakness. It is an image that would no doubt resonate with those in John's audience who had "little power," who thus see in the slaughtered Lamb one who stands in solidarity with them in their suffering. Yet the slaughtered Lamb as symbol communicates much more than just solidarity in suffering. This Lamb is the Christ of Revelation 1:5, "the faithful witness" who "freed us from our sins by his blood." He has been slaughtered because of his witness.

This image of a slaughtered Lamb has generated much scholarly debate. Some see in it a representation of sacrifice, "the gentle lamb led to the slaughter" (Jer. 11:19; Is. 53:7).[8] For others the Lamb is not a powerless sacrificial lamb, but the militant ram found in some Jewish apocalyptic texts.[9] Blount forges something of a middle ground. Though he takes the slaughtered Lamb to be a symbol of power, it is not the militant power of the apocalyptic ram, but the power of active, nonviolent resistance. He rejects the idea of the slaughtered Lamb as sacrifice because he equates sacrifice with passive victimization and unearned suffering rather than with the earned, though not deserved, suffering of active witness.[10] Writing within the context of the black church, Blount's reaction against sacrificial language owes much to his recognition that, historically, the idealization of sacrificial suffering has often served as a "deceptive and evil ruse" designed to hold back the flood of active witness.[11] Although I agree with Blount's identification of the slaughtered Lamb as representative of oppositional, nonviolent witness, I believe that his outright rejection of any sacrificial connotation here results from an overly narrow definition of sacrifice as victimization. Sacrifice as a voluntary choice, such as in choosing the path that leads to a cross, is a form of earned suffering. To stand up and actively witness, knowing full well that such witness will lead to opposition and suffering, *is* a sacrificial act.

The image of the slaughtered Lamb deliberately embodies elements of each of these perspectives because John is intentionally playing with expectations regarding power and weakness.[12] That the Lamb is "slaughtered" naturally evokes the image of sacrifice, yet this same Lamb is later going to lead an army (Rev. 14:1-5). Rome is power and so the obvious temptation for John's audience is to seek power, whether by accommodating to Roman authority and culture, by looking to physical forms of resistance against Rome, or by beseeching God to lay waste to their enemies. The announcement of the Lion of the tribe of Judah thereby sounds like good news. But the solution John offers is not the Lion but the Lamb. Following its initial appearance in 5:5, the Lion disappears completely from the narrative. That title does not occur again in Revelation. The Lamb, however, is referenced twenty-eight more times. It is the Lamb who provides the model for John's audience. John is not suggesting, however, that Christian victory comes through weakness rather than through power. What he is doing with the transformation of the Lion into a Lamb is transforming his readers' conception of power. The Lamb is the *embodiment* of the Lion, not its replacement. John hears the introduction of the Lion, but when he turns what he sees is the Lamb. In other words, just as the Lion is the Lamb, the Lamb is the Lion.

Although the image of a slaughtered lamb evokes weakness, this Lamb possesses seven horns and seven eyes (5:6). The number seven in apocalyptic numerology represents completeness. As the horn symbolizes power and eyes symbolize knowledge, the seven horns and seven eyes of this Lamb identify the Lamb as the possessor of all power and all wisdom. Or, as Blount states it, "The slaughtered Lamb is *how* the Lion manifests himself in the world."[13] This apocalyptic merging of Lion and Lamb communicates that Christ's victory and Christ's power manifest in forms that appear weak to the world. If one looks at the cross without 2000 years of religious interpretation, one sees only weakness. On the cross is a man broken, bleeding, dying. There is no power there. It is an execution. Yet, for those who view the cross through the eyes of faith, there is nothing there but power.

The subsequent disappearance of the Lion from the narrative is because the slaughtered Lamb is the image John wants to hold before us since it is the image that best captures the pattern of the Christ. It is an image testifying that Christian victory is not found in worldly power structures or in economic security. Christian victory is found in embodying the pattern of the Christ. God's plan for his creation involves a slaughtered Lamb. And all who would follow this Lamb must achieve victory not through violent resistance or force, not through compromise with the enemy, but through faithful witness, knowing that such witness has the appearance of weakness within the kingdom of the world.

Revelation 5 reveals that a fundamental component of God's plan for his creation is the cross of Christ and that Christian victory can only be defined in light of it. As the Lamb takes the scroll from the right hand of God, the elders and living creatures offer up bowls of incense which contain "the prayers of the saints" (5:8). The elders and creatures immediately follow this by singing a "new song," which suggests that the prayers of the saints are prayers for deliverance. The singing of a "new song" is a recurring motif in the Old Testament where it identifies a song that praises God for deliverance and victory (Ps. 33:3;

40:3; 96:1; 98:1; 144:9; 149:1; Is. 42:10). The "new song" that the elders and creatures sing declares Christ worthy to take the scroll because "you were slaughtered and by your blood you ransomed for God saints from every tribe and language and people and nation" (5:9). The subsequent assertion that by this act Christ has made them "a kingdom and priests" (5:10) again echoes Exodus 19:6. The combination of the cross of Christ with this Exodus reference both here in 5:9-10 and earlier in 1:5-6 provides another form of redefinition. John defines the cross as a new exodus. Whereas the exodus event was God's supreme act of deliverance on behalf of his people and an act by which he made them into a nation, here John defines the cross event as the supreme act of deliverance by which God provides saints from all nations and peoples with a similarly common identity.

This heavenly announcement of the Lamb's worthiness occurs as an explosion of praise building to a powerful crescendo. It begins with the new song of the elders and four living creatures (5:9-10) and then expands as countless angels join in with "full voice" (5:11-12). Then, just as it seems the energy has reached its peak, all creation breaks forth with the acclamation of "blessing and honor and glory and might forever and ever!" (5:13). With the crescendo at its climax, the praise concludes with a bang as the four living creatures shout "Amen!" and the elders fall to the ground in worship (5:14).

Along with this intensification of worship that closes out chapter five, Revelation 4-5 displays an interesting progression in the object of worship. In chapter four God alone receives the worship of the heavenly hosts (4:9-11). Then, the first two songs in Revelation 5 direct their praise to the Lamb only (5:9-12). Finally, when all creation joins together in praise, they sing, "To the one seated on the throne and to the Lamb" (5:13). This uniting of God and the Lamb in the final declaration of praise highlights the centrality of the Lamb within the divine plan. The worship in these chapters begins at the center, around the throne, and then radiates outward encompassing all creation, only to return to the center at the end. Thus the entire scene of Revelation 4-5 ends where it began—at the throne of God. As sovereign over all creation, God's sovereignty finds its clearest and most powerful expression in the figure of a slaughtered Lamb.

As Revelation 5 makes clear, any attempt to understand Revelation's perspective on evil and suffering must take account of the cross of Christ since it forms the essence of God's plan for his creation. The cross represents the pattern of the Christ—the pattern of faithful witness, suffering, and victory. At the end of chapter five, all creation breaks out in praise of the slaughtered Lamb because the cross provides victory not only for those who have been bought with his blood but for all creation. Those who would follow the Lamb are to take up his pattern of faithful witness with the assurance that the sovereign Lord who rules faithfully over his creation will also rule faithfully over their lives.

Yet, as the pattern of the Christ reveals, faithfulness is not a shield against suffering. Christ's expression of faithfulness was that of joining humanity in suffering. Evil in the form of opposition is the primary threat in Revelation, whether the evil of oppression or the evil of accommodation for accommodation is its own form of opposition to God. The exodus and cross, both of which John aligns in Revelation 5 and which serve as frequently recurring themes throughout the book, offer a glimpse into how God deals with evil. In both cases God redeems his people *through* suffering more than *from* suffering. Likewise, in both the cross and the exodus, God does not do away with evil as such, but saves his people from evil by working in and through the very situations created by evil actions.

With the image of the slaughtered Lamb, Revelation subverts worldly notions of power and victory. It asserts that the power of God manifests most profoundly not in machines of war, or in economic prosperity, or in physical security, but in the suffering witness of the cross and in those who take up that pattern. If evil is the problem, Revelation 5 suggests that suffering is actually a part of its resolution. Victory comes through faithful witness and the suffering that often attends it. The irony, though, is that whereas the faithful suffering of

Christ and his followers helps provide the resolution, that suffering must also itself be resolved. The need for such resolution rises to the forefront in Revelation 6-7.

8

THE SEVEN SEALS

REVELATION 6:1-8:1

Revelation 5 introduced a scroll sealed with seven seals and then identified the slaughtered Lamb as the only one possessing the authority to break those seals. Revelation 6:1-8:1 records that activity. As the Lamb opens each of the seven seals, a brief scene unfolds, the interpretation of which is widely debated. Are these prophetic signs preceding the end of the world that can be matched to contemporary events? Are they historical judgments on the Roman Empire or eschatological judgments on all enemies of God? This debate over the external referents for the seals, though important, runs the risk of diverting attention away from the *theology* of the seals. This is vital because what the opened seals actually reveal is less about *what* is going to happen than about *who* is acting. In other words, the seals unpack the implications of Revelation 4-5 which asserts that God is on his throne and ruling over his creation. The opening of the seals highlights certain aspects of that creation and how the one on the throne exercises his sovereignty over it. In doing so, Revelation 6-7 contains elements of theodicy, yet does not function as a systematic explanation of all aspects of God's involvement with his creation. What the seals do is explore how the justice of God manifests with respect to certain expressions of evil and suffering.

The Four Horsemen: Seals 1-4 (6:1-8)

Of the seven seals, the first four mark a clearly defined unit (6:1-8). In addition to containing similar themes, they share an identical literary pattern: the Lamb opens the seal, one of the four living creatures calls out "Come!" and a colored horse with a rider appears. These riders bring with them conquest, war, famine, and death, and their appearance concludes with the statement that a fourth of the earth dies by sword, famine, pestilence, and wild animals (6:8). The literary and thematic cohesion of these first four seals argues for interpreting them as a unit. Furthermore, although John narrates the opening of the seals sequentially, nothing indicates that the events they record occur in a chronological fashion. What is of primary concern here is *thematic* order, not chronological order. John is giving order to a message, not to an historical timetable.

The first four seals describe great suffering afflicting the earth, yet they contain nothing specific to indicate that the source of this suffering is human evil or opposition to God. They may very well be so, but the lack of any indication to that effect suggests that the message of these first four seals is not primarily about *human* action. Through the narrative structure, John makes it clear that the events of the first four seals fall under the purview of divine authority. They have their origin, ultimately, in the heavenly throne room of Revelation 4-5. The scroll that contains these seals comes from the right hand of God, the Lamb is the one who opens the seals, and the command to the riders to go out into the world comes from the four living creatures that surround God's throne. John does, however, carefully avoid having God directly command or decree the unfolding of these events through his use of the passive voice. The first rider "was given" a crown, the second rider "was permitted" to induce slaughter, while Death and Hades "were given authority" to kill (6:2, 4, 8). Bauckham proposes that this may be an example of the "divine passive," which he describes as "the Jewish reverential habit of protecting the transcendence of God by not stating his agency in the world directly but only as the implied agent of verbs in the passive."[1] Regardless, the narrative connection of these seals to the divine throne is unmistakable.

What does this say about God's relation to these events? A natural assumption would be that the events of the first four seals are divine judgments upon those who stand in opposition to God. The prophetic theme of God sending "four kinds of destroyers" in judgment provides some justification for this (Jer. 15:2). Similarly, Ezekiel invokes the same four types of judgment described in Revelation 6:8 when he states, "For thus says the Lord God: How much more when I send upon Jerusalem my four deadly acts of judgment, sword, famine, wild animals, and pestilence, to cut off humans and animals from it!" (Ezek.14:21). In Leviticus God also sends sword, famine, wild animals, and pestilence as forms of punishment against his people, yet does so with the explicit intention that these judgments will lead to repentance and reconciliation (26:18-26, 33-36). If judgments, then the first four seals of Revelation represent the sovereignty of God in the use of suffering as a means of both punishment and reconciliation.

Despite the similarity to such Old Testament prophetic judgments, there is reason to be cautious in assigning these acts the label of "judgment." First, the seals contain no specific language of judgment or wrath, unlike with the fifth and sixth seals (Rev. 6:10, 16-17). In fact, the point of the fifth seal is that it is not yet the time for judgment (6:11). Second, the first four seals identify no specific recipient of these actions. With no mention of "the inhabitants of the earth," the "followers of the beast," or any other specific group being on the receiving end, the first four seals leave the impression that conquest, war, famine, and death are indiscriminate events affecting both the faithful and the unfaithful. Third, even if the four seals represent judgment, it is clearly not final, end-time judgment owing to the limited scope of the seals. Revelation 6:8 indicates that the four acts of sword, famine, pestilence, and wild animals affect only one-fourth of the earth. Fourth, the book of Zechariah provides a possible alternative interpretation for the seals. Like Revelation, Zechariah introduces four colored horses (red, black, white, and gray). Although they sometimes bear riders (Zech. 1:8), at other times they pull chariots (6:1-3). The colored horses of Zechariah do not ride out to inflict judgment on the earth; rather, they go out "to patrol the earth" (1:9-11; 6:5-7). They represent God's knowing presence throughout the earth and his involvement in the affairs of this world.

One important difference between the horses of Revelation 6 and those of Zechariah is that the horses of Revelation execute destructive actions on the earth, indicating that what may be at play here is a merging of prophetic traditions. In one sense, the seals provide a general description of the world as it is. Conquest, war, famine, and death are common occurrences in this world. They represent a fundamental component of human experience. The connection to Zechariah where the horses patrol the earth as representative of God's knowledge of and involvement with the world suggests that God is not removed from these human experiences but active within them to accomplish his plan for creation. As the prophetic tradition of the four kinds of destroyers attest, one aspect of that plan may include God's employment of conquest, war, famine, and death as agents of judgment.

This connection between the first four seals and the throne room of God is not a declaration that God is the deliberate source of all war, famine, and death on the earth, though it is certainly suggestive that God may utilize such for his own ends (see Rev. 18:8). Elsewhere Revelation assigns the origin of much warfare, violence, and destruction to the dragon and its pawn, the beast (11:7-8; 12:17; 13:7-8; 17:6; 18:24). The theological point of Revelation 6:1-8 is not causality but control. If God is indeed on his throne and sovereign over his creation as Revelation 4-5 assures, then he is sovereign over conquest, war, famine, and death and can employ even these in service to his divine plan. Revelation does not allow for any limitation of God's sovereignty in his dealings with evil and suffering. According to Revelation's perspective, the reason why

God does not do away with suffering and opposition is not because he *cannot*. John's vision of the Almighty ruling from his throne governs all of Revelation. Although John is not specific on exactly why God allows suffering and opposition to seemingly hold sway in this world, he suggests that God does so because it serves his larger purpose for creation. Despite ambiguity regarding the specific referents for the first four seals, the larger theological message of these seals asserts that the existence of suffering and violence in the world by no means nullifies the sovereignty of God over his creation.

Souls in Asylum: The Fifth Seal (6:9-11)

The fifth seal deviates from the previous four both in its literary structure and in its thematic focus. Unlike the generalized nature of the first four seals, the fifth seal narrows in on a particular group and its experiences. As the Lamb opens the seal, "the souls of those who had been slaughtered for the word of God and for the testimony they had given" cry out from beneath the altar (6:9-10). These are the souls of faithful witnesses whose faithful witness has led to their slaughter at the hands of "the inhabitants of the earth" (6:10), a phrase that functions as a symbolic marker of the opposition. Just as God and those faithful to him are aligned with heaven in Revelation, the opposition belongs to the earth, to the kingdom of the world. Revelation's use of "earth" and "kingdom of the world" are not about geographical location, for God is sovereign over all creation, but they are about *orientation*. The "inhabitants of the earth" have given their allegiance to a kingdom that stands opposed to the kingdom of heaven.

John's reference to these souls as "slaughtered" aligns their witness with that of the Lamb.[2] Faithful witness to God challenges the power structures and values of the kingdom of the world and so those belonging to that kingdom slaughtered them, just as they had with Christ. The souls under the altar have fulfilled the pattern of the Christ that links faithful witness with suffering, yet the ultimate fulfillment of that pattern includes vindication of the suffering witness. Thus the cry that rises up from beneath the altar is a plea for justice and vengeance against the inhabitants of the earth (6:10). Some critics of Revelation might see in this plea for vengeance little more than personal vindictiveness so that the cry of the souls under the altar becomes the cry of people who cloak their own desires for revenge in the language of justice. Powerless to exact revenge upon their perceived enemies themselves, they look to God to do it for them. This perspective on the fifth seal is really more of a response to Revelation's troubled history of interpretation than it is to the text itself, for within that history are many who have used Revelation's language of justice and vengeance to justify their own violent actions or their own selfish desires for revenge.

Yet within the social and narrative world of Revelation, there is another way to interpret this language—as a faithful expression of genuine unjust suffering. The souls under the altar are those whose faithful witness against the deceptions of the kingdom of the world have earned them a share in the sufferings of Christ. The words "how long?" that mark their plea are the words of lament. In the Psalms these words express concern that justice or deliverance is lacking and that the world is not as it ought to be (Ps. 6:2-3; 13:1-2; 35:17; 74:10-11; 80:4-7). "How long" is the question asked by all who look at the world and see the absence of justice, who see violence and oppression holding sway. In 1983 the Irish rock group U2 recorded an album titled "War." Two songs on that album, "Sunday Bloody Sunday" and "40," deliberately take up the language of the psalms and pose the question, "How long?" How long must we witness injustice and violence in the world? How long must we see bodies lying in the street and families torn apart by war? These songs expose the frustration arising from the hopes and prayers for peace in this world when balanced against the reality of war.

The question of "how long?" was asked thousands of years before the composition of Revelation's fifth seal and has been asked for a couple thousand years since. It is the plea of all those who stood before the smoke of the crematoriums at Auschwitz, of those who stood before the rubble of the Twin Towers on 9/11, of those who witnessed genocidal actions in Rwanda. The cry for justice and vengeance is the cry of all who have experienced atrocities both great and small throughout the world. When the souls under the altar cry out to God, "how long will it be before you judge and avenge our blood," they stand in solidarity with all those, both ancient and modern, who have suffered unjustly. Their plea is an acknowledgment that true justice sometimes requires vengeance, not the petty revenge borne out of resentment or selfish desires or hurt feelings, but the divine vengeance that acts to bring order out of chaos and to set right what has gone horribly wrong. In their plea the souls under the altar address God as "Sovereign Lord" (6:10), a thematic link back to the throne room of Revelation 4-5. With that address, the souls cry out that the one who sits on the throne, whose sovereignty over creation is manifest in the first four seals, bring that sovereignty to bear on their situation.

The use of the word "slaughtered" in conjunction with an altar certainly evokes an association with sacrifice. However, I would argue that sacrifice is not the primary theme at issue here. For one thing, the altar in question is most likely not the altar of burnt offering, but the golden altar of incense that is associated with prayer and not with animal sacrifices (see Rev. 8:3-4). Likewise the primary issue in this scene is not the sacrifice of the martyrs (although their *faithfulness* to the point of death may represent a sort of offering to God), but their prayers for justice and vengeance. Another interpretive context for Revelation 6:9-10 provides insight into the symbolism of an altar and the souls who cry out from it for justice and vengeance. It is the practice of Greek altar asylum.[3] The ancient Greeks had developed a system whereby those who were victims of violence, oppression, or injustice could find help and safety. These "supplicants" could gain asylum by coming into physical contact with an altar. Greek literature abounds with examples of this practice and Greek vases often depict supplicants seeking asylum by sitting on or grasping an altar.

In particular, the practice of altar asylum revolved around three themes. The first was *protection*. A supplicant seeking asylum at an altar comes under the protection of the deity to whom that altar belongs. As long as the person maintains contact with the altar, he or she must not be harmed. Refugees in war, those fleeing political enemies, the falsely accused, and slaves suffering under the hand of harsh masters all sought asylum at altars. On one occasion even the Jewish high priest, Onias III, fled to a Greek temple seeking asylum from his enemies (2 Macc. 4:33-34). Greek writers typically praised the protection afforded by an altar. Apuleius calls an altar a "source of help."[4] Plutarch states: "For a slave there is an altar to which he can flee."[5] Aeschylus says that for those who seek protection in times of war, "there is an altar, a shelter against harm," while elsewhere he adds, "Stronger than a castle is an altar—tis a shield invulnerable."[6] One of the most arresting visual representations of the protection granted by altar asylum occurs on a series of Greek vases depicting Menelaus, armed with a sword, in pursuit of Helen of Troy. The scene shows Helen reaching out to grasp the altar and at the moment she does so, Menelaus drops his sword.[7] Once Helen comes under the protection of the altar, she is untouchable.

A second theme pertaining to altar asylum is *justice*. Seeking asylum at an altar was a plea for justice on the part of the oppressed, a plea that often initiated legal proceedings with the priests of the sanctuary acting as advocates for the accused. The belief behind this was that the gods procure justice on behalf of their supplicants. The altar was the last refuge for the falsely accused and the oppressed, a place for the innocent to find justice in an unjust world. In reality, however, abuses of altar asylum were rampant as many guilty parties took advantage of the system as a way to avoid paying for their crimes. Such abuses were a distinct violation of the intent of altar asylum, which was designed to correct injustice, not facilitate it. One character in a Greek novel by Achilles Tatius protests abuses of altar asylum at the Temple of Artemis in Ephesus by declaring that Artemis only aids the innocent. "She alone has the right to rescue those who seek sanctuary with her, but only provided the court has not passed its sentence. The goddess has never released a prisoner from his shackles nor freed a condemned man from the death penalty. Her altars are for the *unfortunate*, not the wicked."[8]

The third theme pertaining to altar asylum is *wrath*. Justice involves not only protecting the innocent but punishing the guilty—those who either oppress the suppliants or who violate the sanctity of the deity's asylum. Often in times of war or civil unrest, those seeking asylum were slaughtered while grasping the altar. The more pious instigators would drag the individuals away from the altar first and then kill them, thinking perhaps that adherence to the "letter of the law" would absolve them of violating its spirit. The truly creative types circumvented the protection of the altar by tricking suppliants into leaving the altar or barricading them in and waiting until they died of exposure or starvation. The operative belief, though, was that such violations of the altar's protection would bring divine retribution. The deity would exact vengeance on those who dared violate his or her sanctuary. Pausanias records many examples of this retribution, such as when he writes, "The disaster that befell Helice is but one of the many proofs that the wrath of the God of Suppliants is inexorable."[9]

The fifth seal of Revelation presents the slaughtered souls of the saints in the guise of suppliants in physical proximity to an altar while crying out for justice and wrath. Whether intentionally designed as such by John or not, the scene is highly evocative of Greek altar asylum and likely would have been understood as such by many in western Asia Minor whose primary experiences with altars were not with that of the Jerusalem Temple, but with the altars of the Greco-Roman societies they inhabited. [10] That these souls maintain physical connection to the altar says that they have come under God's protection. No longer will they be harmed, for the one on the throne will guard them. They have found asylum, but asylum is not merely about protection. It is about righting what is wrong. From the altar they therefore cry out for justice and for the wrath of God to bring divine retribution on those who have violated God's faithful. They express no doubt that the God who is "holy and true" will grant them the justice they seek. Their question is not "Will you?" but "How long?"

Ironically, God's immediate reply to the saints' plea for vengeance is that it is not the wicked who will suffer initially but the righteous! He answers their question of "How long?" with "a little longer" (6:11). Before God will act to avenge their blood, they are told, they must wait "until the number would be complete both of their fellow servants and of their brothers and sisters, who were soon to be killed as they themselves had been killed" (6:11). This statement indicates that one reason why God does not simply do away with the suffering of his people or, at the very least, stamp out any opposition that would threaten the faithful is because the suffering of the saints serves a larger purpose within God's design. It is important to note that the suffering of these saints is not the suffering of a devastating illness or a tragic accident. This is the suffering borne from faithful witness. It is the suffering of the slaughtered Lamb. Just as God did not stop the suffering of his son, he also allows the suffering of these saints and, in fact, decrees that even more must join them. This is because, within the divine plan, the suffering that results from faithful witness is a primary means by which God challenges the kingdom of the world with a different kind of power and a different conception of victory.

The fifth seal is an example of apocalyptic determinism, which asserts divine control over events that are unfolding or will unfold. The Jewish apocalyptic book of 4 Ezra, roughly contemporary with Revelation, contains a scene of apocalyptic determinism that bears a strikingly similar narrative pattern to the fifth seal of Revelation.

> "Did not the souls of the righteous in their chambers ask about these matters, saying 'How long are we to remain here? And when will come the harvest of our reward?' And Jeremiel the archangel answered them and said, "When the number of those like yourselves is completed; for he has weighed the age in the balance, and measured the times by measure, and numbered

the times by number, and he will not move or arouse them until that measure is fulfilled" (4 Ezra 4:35-37).[11]

Apocalyptic determinism provides assurance that God is actively engaged with his creation and faithfully executing his plan. God is not the cause of martyrdom, but even it falls under his purview and is subject to his sovereignty. When taken with the first four seals, the fifth seal forms an argument from the greater to the lesser. If God is sovereign over conquest, war, famine, and death (in essence sovereign over the suffering in this world), then God is sovereign over martyrdom and over the suffering of his saints as well.

Wrath and Reward: The Sixth Seal (6:12-7:17)

The sixth seal of Revelation encompasses Revelation 6:12 through the end of chapter seven, with the breaking of the seventh seal then occurring in 8:1. Although some take Revelation 7 to be an interlude or digression from the sixth seal, it is best understood as an extension of the scene and an integral part of its message. The initial scene of the sixth seal (Rev. 6:12-17) serves as a response to the question posed in the fifth seal. The souls under the altar asked, "How long?" They were then told to wait a while longer as God's divine plan was still unfolding. Yet the justice of God demands that he respond to the suffering of his faithful witnesses and the sixth seal reveals that he will in fact do so. The focus is neither on *when* he will act nor on the exact details of *how* he will act, but *that* he will act. In response to the fifth seal's question of "How long?" the sixth seal assures that the day of wrath will come (6:16-17).

When the Lamb opens the sixth seal, the entire creation is shaken to its core. There is a great earthquake, the sun turns black and the moon blood red, stars fall from the sky while the sky itself rolls up like a scroll, and mountains and islands are uprooted (6:12-14). Often these phenomena are interpreted as end-time destruction of the earth and the final judgment of the wicked. While possible, especially considering that a scene of eschatological reward follows (7:9-17), forcing an end-time scenario on this description as the only viable option fails to take account of the prophetic context of this language and confuses the literal with the symbolic. These events, whether referencing an eschatological occurrence or not, do not comprise a literal description of events nor are they a prophetic timetable that readers can match to their daily newspaper. Whether there are earthquakes in China or a comet streaking across the night sky is irrelevant. The sixth seal offers a symbolic assurance that the day of wrath will come as a manifestation of God's presence. The symbolism of Revelation captures the *meaning* of events, not their literal description.

The kind of cosmic disruption language in Revelation 6:12-14 is standard prophetic language used to describe events that in reality look nothing like their symbolic or poetic description. The Old Testament prophetic books often communicate God's judgment and activities through poetic and figurative language. Isaiah 34:4-5 recounts God's historical judgment on the nation of Edom with these words: "All the host of heaven shall rot away, and the skies roll up like a scroll. All their host shall wither like a leaf withering on a vine, or fruit withering on a fig tree. When my sword has drunk its fill in the heavens, lo, it will descend upon Edom, upon the people I have doomed to judgment." When God's judgment actually came upon Edom, the stars of heaven neither rotted away nor did the sky literally roll up like a scroll.

The language of cosmic disruption is the language of a *theophany* (the appearance of God). When a person steps into a still puddle of water, suddenly everything within that puddle is thrown into chaos. The result is massive disruption and upheaval within that system because an outside force has entered it. When the prophets wanted to depict God acting powerfully within history, they used the language of stars falling from the sky, the moon turning to blood, earthquakes, and the sky rolling up like a scroll because God had entered into history and was bringing his will to bear. The symbolic disruption of all creation highlights the power of God's appearance.

New Testament writers employ these prophetic texts in similar fashion. Luke applies Isaiah 40's assertion that every valley will be lifted up and every mountain made low to the activity of John the Baptist. The symbolic upheaval and reversal of nature accompanies the appearance of God in the person of Jesus as announced by John (Lk. 3:5). On the day of Pentecost, Peter quotes Joel 2 to the effect that the sun is becoming dark and the moon turning to blood and then assures his audience that this prophetic text is being fulfilled *right now* in their midst (Acts 2:16). Peter can attest that the sun is turning to darkness and the moon to blood because with the events of Pentecost God is accomplishing his will and thus disrupting creation by his powerful presence.

The point of the cosmic disruption language in the sixth seal is simply that God will act on behalf of his people in a powerful way. God will make an appearance in order to avenge the blood of the saints. The importance of the fifth and sixth seals, when taken together, lies in what they reveal about God. Though his justice may at times seem slow in coming, God will not abandon his faithful. The one who is "holy and true" will manifest that holiness in wrath. And not God alone, for what is coming is "the great day of *their* wrath"—that of the one seated on the throne and "the wrath of the Lamb" (6:16-17). Identifying with the slaughtered souls by virtue of being slaughtered himself, the Lamb seeks justice on their behalf. Justice, however, involves more than wrath against those who kill God's faithful witnesses. These witnesses embody the pattern of the Christ. Their faithful witness has led to their suffering and death, yet that pattern is not complete without vindication. Consequently, the question posed at the end of Revelation 6 ("who is able to stand" in the day of wrath?) does not go unanswered.

Revelation 7 is a continuation of the sixth seal. In essence, it provides the answer to the question, "the great day of their wrath has come, and who is able to stand?" The chapter contains two separate, yet interconnected scenes. The first (7:1-8) is a vision of four angels holding back the destructive power of the four winds of the earth until "the servants of our God" can be marked with a seal on their foreheads. The seals on the forehead are identity markers. They identify those who belong to God and therefore fall under his protection. The number of those sealed is 144,000, a number made up of twelve thousand from each of the twelve tribes of Israel. The second scene (7:9-17) depicts a vision of an innumerable, multi-national crowd of people standing before the throne of God and singing praises to him.

There are substantive reasons for viewing these two groups as distinct and separate entities. One is a specific number (144,000); the other an innumerable multitude. One has a specific ethnic identity (tribes of Israel); the other comprises "all tribes and peoples and languages" (7:9). One depicts the faithful on earth prior to the outpouring of divine wrath; the other depicts the faithful in heaven after the outpouring of divine wrath. Nevertheless, sufficient justification also exists for interpreting these two as the same group viewed from different perspectives. The argument that 144,000 is a specific number and therefore necessarily distinct from the innumerable multitude is mitigated by the fact that the number twelve functions as a symbol of completeness. The enumeration of 144,000, as a multiple of twelve, may thus represent symbolically the totality of God's people, rendered as Israel in 7:1-8 and then in its multi-national capacity in 7:9-17.

We have also seen how elsewhere in Revelation John employs the rhetorical device of hearing versus seeing as a way of equating two separate symbolic descriptions and allowing them to interpret each other. In chapter five, John hears about a Lion but when he looks, he actually sees a Lamb. Likewise, John only *hears* the number of those who are sealed from the twelve tribes of Israel (7:4). When he actually looks (7:9), what he sees is an innumerable and multi-national crowd. These two visions in chapter seven may thereby be another example of John's transformation of symbols. Just as the Lion is in actuality a Lamb, and vice versa, so also the 144,000 of Israel is actually an innumerable and multi-national crowd and vice versa. This may be John's way of describing the totality of God's people as comprising both Jew and Gentile. According to this view, the contrast between the scenes is one of perspective. Revelation

7:1-8 depicts the sealed on earth prior to the wrath of God promised in 6:17, while 7:9-17 depicts the sealed in heaven following that wrath.

Regardless of the specific identification of these two groups relative to each other, the larger message of Revelation 7 remains the same: God's faithful witnesses belong to him, are under his protection, and will receive vindication. Revelation 7 asserts that those who are able to stand in the great day of God's wrath are those who have shown themselves faithful through their embodiment of the pattern of the Christ. In 7:14 an elder offers a specific identification of the great multitude before the throne by stating, "These are they who have come out of the great ordeal." That they have "come out" of the great ordeal indicates that God's deliverance of these faithful was not a deliverance *from* suffering but a deliverance *through* suffering. That they have washed their robes "in the blood of the Lamb" (7:14) connects them specifically to the death of Christ and may be an indication that, like the martyred souls under the altar, they have borne their witness to the point of death.

At any rate, Revelation 7:9-17 presents a vision of the glorification and vindication of those who have embodied Christ's pattern of faithful witness. Chapter seven offers no hint of the type of self-aggrandizing glorification that many critics of Revelation decry whereby Christians trumpet their rise to power and their exaltation over their former oppressors. In this vision, their reward for faithfulness is cast in terms of service and shelter. Their fortunes are reversed but it is not the reversal of impoverishment to power, but the reversal from suffering to shelter. No longer do they hunger, or thirst, or grieve, or wilt under scorching heat; instead the Lamb shepherds them and they serve God day and night in his temple (7:15-17).

Concluding Reflections

The seven seals of Revelation 6:1-8:1 are an exploration of the sovereignty of God that Revelation 4-5 asserts. They reveal that suffering is a normal part of human experience. For as long as humans have lived in community, there has been conquest, war, famine, and death. The first four seals demonstrate that the existence of these in no way nulli-fies divine sovereignty or God's active involvement with his creation. If the scroll that came from the right hand of God represents God's plan for his creation, then the breaking of the seals must be understood in connection with that plan. Regardless of the specific cause or origin of the sufferings depicted in the seals, the seals indicate that even the suffering in this world ultimately falls under God's reign and bows to his authority.

Certainly some of that suffering derives from opposition to the king-dom of God, as represented by the "inhabitants of the earth" who are held responsible for the deaths of the souls under the altar. Suffering is a particular component of *Christian* existence (6:9-11; 7:13-14) because faithful witness brings one into conflict with the kingdom of the world. Yet if the suffering of God's faithful occurs at the hands of evil (in the form of opposition from the inhabitants of the earth), the suffering of God's faithful also incorporates God's response to evil. In his divine sovereignty, the martyrdom of the faithful must continue for a time (6:11). Similarly, the faithful multitude are not spared from suffering but brought "out of" it (7:14). Just as the witness of Christ on the cross forms the essence of God's response to evil, so too does the suffering witness of the saints.

In one sense, the seven seals encompass the larger narrative claim of Revelation in condensed form. The righteous are those who, rather than accommodate to and compromise with the kingdom of the world, witness faithfully to it. Because the kingdom of the world stands at odds with the kingdom of God, those who take up the mantle of faith-ful witness will suffer for it. Yet God is on his throne and his justice is assured. His wrath will come upon those who oppose his kingdom and the faithful who share in the sufferings of the slaughtered Lamb will also share in his glory.

9

THE SEVEN TRUMPETS

Wrath and mercy are concepts that have experienced a long and troubled history within Christian thought and practice. While recognizing that the Bible asserts both as fundamental components of the divine nature, Christians have struggled with how the two stand in relationship to each other or whether they are capable of cohabiting at all. Wrath and mercy appear to be such contradictory categories that many Christian movements have—in practice if not in theory—opted for one over the other as their primary, and often exclusive, understanding of God. On one extreme are those who view God as a judicial figure, holding all accountable to a rigid standard and meting out punishment for the slightest infraction. As servants of a wrathful God, they preach fire and brimstone sermons and offer dire warnings of hell as they attempt to motivate others by means of the same fear that motivates them. They tread lightly before this God for fear that they too might slip up and fall under his divine wrath. Such exclusive belief in a God of wrath creates followers who are often legalistic, judgmental, and insecure due to recognition of their own inability to measure up to the standard. On the other extreme are those who view God as a kindly Father, full of compassion and love for all people. They proclaim grace to all and announce a God who accepts them as they are with no judgment. The language of sin and repentance is downplayed and marginalized within these communities. That deficiency often leads to a form of spiritual malnourishment that produces moral laxity, complacency, and a lack of accountability.

What both of these extremes fail to account for is that mercy and wrath are not contradictory but complementary aspects of God's nature. In particular each provides a vital corrective function for distortions of the other. The message of grace and love counteracts the legalism, judgmentalism, and insecurity that characterize communities that have attached themselves to a God of wrath, while the message of judgment counteracts the moral laxity, complacency, and lack of accountability that threaten those who have embraced a God of love. Maintaining the uneasy tension between wrath and mercy is a healthy expression of Christian faith. Wrath and mercy function together as an integrated expression of divine justice. While divine wrath is the more prominent theme in Revelation owing to the specifics of John's rhetorical focus, Revelation occasionally hits notes of divine mercy that help to clarify the function of God's wrath in Revelation. One place where this interaction between wrath and mercy plays out is in the seven trumpets that comprise Revelation 8-11.

Rising Prayer, Descending Wrath

The seven seals conclude with the announcement of the great day of God's wrath (6:16-17) and with a vision of those faithful who are able to stand in that day (7:1-17). The breaking of the seventh seal (8:1) then inaugurates a transitional scene between the seals and the trumpets. John sees seven angels holding seven trumpets (8:2). The angels, however, do not blow their trumpets immediately. Instead, John presents a scene in which an angel offers on the golden altar before God's throne incense that is mingled with the prayers of the saints. The symbolism of this scene initially points upward as the incense and prayers ascend to God from the altar. A reversal of this upward motion occurs, however, when the angel then takes burning coals from the altar and hurls them downward upon the earth, provoking thunder, lightning, and an earthquake.

The similarities between this scene and that of the fifth seal are instructive. In both instances the prayers of the saints rise up to God from the altar, implying that both sets of prayers share the same focus—justice and vengeance against the inhabitants of the earth. The response to the prayers in 8:4, however, is much more direct and immediate than with the fifth seal. The same censer used to offer up the prayers of the saints is then used to cast fire down on the earth. With this imagery, Revelation 8:2-5 presents a symbolic description of answered prayer: the prayers rise up and fire comes down. The fire cast down upon the earth is the fiery judgment of God poured out on those who oppose his kingdom and his faithful witnesses and the seven trumpets that follow depict in more detail this outpouring of judgment, as evidenced by references to fire in five of the first six trumpets (8:7, 8, 10; 9:2, 17-18).

The heavenly altar scene sets up the blowing of the seven trumpets by introducing them as the divine response to the prayers of the saints for justice. Trumpets were typically employed in cultic contexts or in times of war to announce something. In this case, they announce God coming in judgment. As with the first four seals, the first four trumpets function together as a unit. These trumpets share a relatively generalized description which identifies no specific human recipients as the objects of these actions. In fact, with the first four trumpets, the emphasis is less on humanity than it is on creation itself. The judgments of the first four trumpets encompass the earth (9:7), the seas (9:8-9), the inland waters (9:10-11), and the celestial sphere (sun, moon, stars—9:12). In short, these trumpets depict *all* of creation under God's sovereign control. Though it is not God's creation itself that is the object of his judgment, all of creation is affected by these actions. The first four trumpets do not represent final, end-of-time, judgment by virtue of their limitation to one-third of creation. That these judgments are limited in scope and under the authority of the sovereign Lord of all creation is an important part of the message of the trumpets. God's wrath comes in response to the prayers of the saints, but it is not wrath wantonly poured out and indiscriminate in the destruction it brings. It is wrath with a purpose—a purpose that is an expression of God's sovereign plan for his creation.

A Plague of Locusts (The Fifth Trumpet)

Prior to the blowing of the fifth trumpet, an eagle (often used as a messenger for divine beings) announces, "Woe, woe, woe to the inhabitants of the earth, at the blasts of the other trumpets that the three angels are about to blow!" (8:13). This announcement provides the structure for the following trumpets by revealing that each of the final three trumpets corresponds to one of the three "woes." Consequently, once the fifth trumpet concludes, the text states, "The first woe has passed. There are still two woes to come" (9:12). The eagle's announcement also highlights a specific recipient for the actions of the remaining trumpets: "the inhabitants of the earth." Since the souls under the altar had cried out for God to avenge their blood against "the inhabitants of the earth" (6:10), it would appear that the final three trumpets depict the divine response to those prayers. Yet, are the judgments that unfold merely vengeance? The fifth trumpet offers a clue.

Movement from heaven to earth permeates the narrative of the first five trumpets, indicating the heavenly origin of these judgments. Coals from the heavenly altar are cast down from heaven to earth (8:5), fire and hail rain down upon the land (8:7), a great star falls upon the rivers of the earth (8:10), and now, as the fifth trumpet sounds, an angel in the form of a star descends upon the earth (9:1). Revelation's description of this angel as having "fallen from heaven to earth" does not indicate a "fallen angel" in the sense of one cast out of heaven for disobedience. The falling of the star from heaven is not a judgment but a means of transportation. The angel has come down to do God's will.

This angel unleashes a plague of locusts upon the land, but rather than bringing widespread destruction, the locusts are directed only against "those people who do not have the seal of God on their foreheads"

(9:4). As previously noted, the seal of God is a mark of identification that protects the faithful from divine judgment. The locusts attack the unsealed (i.e. the inhabitants of the earth) and torture them for five months (9:5, 10). Once again the limitation of judgment occurs. Not only is the time frame limited to five months, but no one among those tormented dies from this judgment (9:6). The limitation of the activity of the trumpets to one-third (first four trumpets) and five months (fifth trumpet) suggests that the function of judgment here is not solely punishment or vengeance, but that another factor is also at play.

John's description of this locust plague is strongly reminiscent of the prophet Joel's description of an army of locusts invading the land to bring judgment on the disobedient (Joel 1-2). In both accounts the locusts are associated with fire (Rev. 9:2; Joel 2:3, 5), they appear like horses in battle (Rev. 9:7; Joel 2: 4), have teeth like that of a lion (Rev. 9:8; Joel 1:6), and their activity leads to the darkening of the sun (Rev. 9:2; Joel 2:10). Although one must be cautious of reading too much of the Joel text into Revelation 9 due to some significant differences—such as the fact that the locusts in Joel lay waste to the land whereas those in Revelation 9 are forbidden to do so (9:4)—the overt similarities between the two locust plagues raise the question of whether the judgment by locust plague might serve the same function as the judgment by locust plague in Joel 1-2. In Joel the plague of locusts functions to generate repentance (Joel 1:13-16; 2:12-14). Is John, through this association with Joel, indicating that the judgments of the trumpets have at least the partial goal of calling people to repentance and that the limitations of these judgments function to allow for such an opportunity? An answer to that question requires an examination of the theme of repentance in the sixth trumpet.

The Sixth Trumpet, Scene One (9:13-21)

Vital to understanding the function of the sixth trumpet is the recognition that this trumpet comprises *all* of the material from 9:13 through 11:13. As with the sixth seal, which unfolded across three scenes (6:12-17; 7:1-8; 7:9-17), the sixth trumpet also unfolds across three scenes (9:13-21; 10:1-11; 11:1-13). That 10:1-11:13 should be considered part of the sixth trumpet is clear from the statement in 11:14 that, "The second woe has passed. The third woe is coming very soon." The eagle in 8:13 declares that the three woes correspond to the remaining three trumpets. Consequently, immediately after the fifth trumpet there comes the announcement that the first woe has passed. The similar announcement that the second woe has passed comes only after 11:13, indicating that the entire section from 9:13 through 11:13 must be interpreted as the sixth trumpet. This recognition is important because a reference to repentance occurs in the first and third scenes of the sixth trumpet and interpreting them in reference to each other allows the distinctive emphasis of this trumpet to become clear.

With the blowing of the sixth trumpet, four angels are sent out to kill one-third of humankind by plagues of fire, smoke, and sulfur (9:13-15, 18). The limitation of this trumpet to one-third directs our focus to the survivors more than to the victims. Throughout the sixth trumpet (9:13-11:13), it is the actions of the survivors of judgment that receive attention. John, therefore, follows the description of these plagues with the statement: "The rest of humankind, who were not killed by these plagues, did not repent of the works of their hands" (9:20-21). The judgments of the trumpets fail to generate repentance by the inhabitants of the earth.

One way to read this failure of repentance is in line with the exodus tradition where the plagues inflicted on Egypt fail to generate repentance by Pharaoh, as represented by the recurring theme that Pharaoh's heart was hardened (Ex. 7:13, 22; 8:15). Similarities between some of the Egyptian plagues and some plagues of the trumpets strengthen this connection. In the exodus tradition, statements regarding Pharaoh's hardness of heart lead into the declaration that this occurred "as the Lord had said" (Ex. 7:13, 22; 8:15), implying that Pharaoh's resistance was part of God's divine plan and thus repentance was never the point. According to this view, repentance was never the goal of the trumpets and so the statement that the survivors fail to repent merely highlights their recalcitrance.[1]

There are, however, some important deviations from the exodus tradition, as well as other factors at play, that caution against interpreting the failure of repentance in Revelation 9:20-21 so closely with that tradition. First, the trumpets lack any kind of statement that the failure to repent is in line with God's plan or will, such as the "as the Lord had said" statements in the exodus tradition. Second, in Exodus the focus is on *Pharaoh's* failure to repent. The primary symbolic counterpart to Pharaoh in Revelation is the beast, yet here it is not the beast who fails to repent but humankind. Third, the connection between the exodus tradition and the plagues of Revelation is much stronger with the seven bowls that come later, whose plagues more closely resemble those of the exodus. The bowls do contain two statements regarding the failure of those afflicted to repent (16:9, 11), highlighting the recalcitrance of those who are opposing God and thus the justice of God's actions in judgment. Yet, their refusal to repent only makes sense if repentance was a viable option that they have rejected. Fourth, the seven trumpets not only invoke the exodus tradition but also the Joel tradition whereby the judgment of God by locust plague was designed to generate repentance. Fifth, that the sixth trumpet later indicates repentance on the part of some (11:13) indicates both that repentance is a lively option here and that the theme of repentance is of more concern to John here than simply as a marker of recalcitrance.

In line with the Joel tradition employed in the fifth trumpet, I argue that the judgments of the sixth trumpet at least partially function to generate repentance. One reason for the limitation of these judgments is to provide for that opportunity. That judgment (as in Joel) *can* function as a catalyst for repentance (whether or not that option is taken), demonstrates that judgment should not be defined solely in terms of wrath but can also be a manifestation of mercy.

The judgments of the trumpets involve the infliction of suffering upon humanity, which inevitably leads to the question: Can an action that causes suffering to another ever be an act of mercy? The answer to that question depends heavily on one's view of suffering. If we define suffering as the experience of pain, then we would have to answer "yes." Through acts of discipline, parents regularly inflict suffering on their children—whether slapping the hand of a child reaching out for a hot stove or taking eagerly desired privileges away from a disobedient teenager—and we recognize those actions as manifestations of love and care. Physicians often inflict suffering on their patients (shots, surgeries, chemotherapy, etc.) as a means of facilitating healing. Yet, when the discussion turns to God, many become uncomfortable with the thought of God utilizing suffering as a manifestation of love or mercy. If one views suffering, for instance, as an inherent form of evil or only as an agent of destruction, then such sensitivity makes sense.[2]

Viewing suffering from an apocalyptic perspective, however, means drawing a sharp contrast between the physical and the spiritual and allowing spiritual reality to redefine human experience. In the Jewish apocalyptic work of 4 Ezra, the angel Uriel instructs Ezra that "those who dwell upon earth can understand only what is on earth" (4 Ezra 4:21). The apocalyptic tradition claims that suffering interpreted solely from an earthly perspective is necessarily limited and insufficient. Exposing suffering to a heavenly perspective grants it a new evaluation. By this, apocalyptic does not suggest that all suffering suddenly makes sense or has a definable purpose. Rather, it suggests that viewing suffering from above (from a heavenly perspective) rather than from below (from an earthly perspective) allows one to interpret suffering in the light of God's larger purpose for his creation and, in doing so, indicates that suffering can potentially play a positive role in human lives.

Luke Timothy Johnson writes: "The reason why Christians can give some kinds of suffering a positive evaluation, and why even negative experiences of suffering can be transformed . . . by the perspective of faith" is because "God raises the dead to new life." Jesus endured the suffering of the cross, Johnson argues, because he did not equate *life* with the survival or health of his physical body.[3] With the resurrection,

God shows himself able to take the most deplorable acts of suffering and evil and turn them into a means of new creation. Jesus is the slaughtered Lamb of Revelation, but through that identification he also serves as "the firstborn of the dead" (1:5) and he who holds "the keys of Death and of Hades" (1:18). The resurrection defines the Christian perspective of both evil and suffering.[4] The awareness that God can transform death into life, destruction into creation, and opposition into victory is a necessary perspective for those who are called to be faithful witnesses "even to the point of death" (2:10).

Suffering, in the form of judgment, can function positively as a wake-up call. One aspect of Revelation's social situation is the ever-present temptation to compromise with Roman society and so dull the edges of one's faith. Compromise is often subtle and gradual; ones who have compromised often do not realize the extent or seriousness of their actions. John writes to expose those actions by revealing Roman hegemony as a demonic beast in league with Satan (Rev. 12-13)—and thus as an enemy of God—and to warn his communities against compromise with the enemy. The judgments of the seven trumpets do exactly that. These judgments serve both as a warning of what awaits all who compromise with the opponents of God and as an opportunity to reject compromise and return to God. A judgment is coming in Revelation that is not limited as are the trumpets. In light of that forthcoming judgment, the trumpets serve as a vital wake-up call. The opportunity to repent and turn to God remains, at least partially explaining why the martyred souls' cry of "How long?" is answered by "Not yet" (6:10-11). Yes, the opponents of God (the inhabitants of the earth) reject this opportunity, but John is not writing to the opponents of God but to members of his communities who find themselves with one foot in the enemy's camp. The trumpets serve to wake them up from their self-delusion and call them back to faithfulness.

For the Hebrew prophets, wrath and mercy were inextricable components of judgment. They placed promises of restoration and hope side by side with oracles of doom. By heeding the prophet's call to repent, some experienced the announcement of judgment as a form of mercy. The author of Revelation presents himself as a prophet calling the people of God to repentance while promising the wrath of God upon those who oppose his kingdom. In this way the suffering that attends prophetic judgment can serve as an expression of both divine wrath and mercy.

I should caution here that I am drawing general assertions from Revelation and from the prophetic tradition regarding *potential* roles of suffering within God's creation. Human suffering is a multi-faceted experience that involves many different causes, functions, and evaluations, both positive and negative. It is not the place of any person to define the specific suffering of another. Too often Christians try to comfort others with generic pronouncements about how God is using their suffering for good or how God has a specific purpose for the trouble that afflicts them. It is the height of arrogance for a person who is not suffering to tell one who is that their suffering is because God is either punishing them or trying to get them to repent. That God, in his sovereignty, *may* use suffering in a particular way does not mean that he is doing so in a particular situation or that we possess the ability to identify such functions for others.

Yet, if one function of apocalyptic is exposing human experience to transcendence so that people learn to view their physical experiences from a spiritual perspective, then they may *themselves* discern a greater meaning for their suffering. Human suffering can, at times, be a catalyst for redemption and renewal. Many years ago I met a man named Joe who, growing up, had been the quintessential All-American kid—tall, handsome, athletic, and intelligent. Joe had been raised in a Christian family by loving parents, yet during high school he rebelled against everything that Christianity stood for and against the values his parents had instilled in him. He determined that the sole purpose of life was to have a good time and threw himself wholeheartedly into that pursuit. Drugs, alcohol, women—nothing was off-limits. Joe's relentless pursuit of pleasure resulted in expulsion from several schools and eventually from his own home. School leaders, his minister, and his parents all tried to talk to him, but Joe refused to listen. One night, just a couple of months before Joe's nineteenth birthday, he got in an argument at a party with his ex-girlfriend. She threatened to kill herself if he didn't come back to her. This was a cycle they had been through several times before, so this time Joe was fed up. He went over to her house later and she met him on the front lawn with a gun. To make matters worse, both of them were drunk. As they drunkenly struggled over the gun, she grabbed it and it went off. The blast hit Joe in the neck, severing his spinal cord.

That was over twenty-seven years ago and Joe has spent every day since then paralyzed from the neck down. Many people in that situation would be very bitter. They might blame God in anger or decry the lack of justice since the police bungled the investigation and the woman was never charged. Others might take the experience as clear evidence that a loving and merciful God could not exist. But not Joe. Joe once told me that this experience, with all its tragedy and hardship, was paradoxically one of the best things that ever happened to him because it provided him with a much-needed wake-up call. Joe sobered up and cleaned up. He reunited with his parents and rededicated his life to God. Now some might argue that this is an awfully high price to pay for reconciliation, and perhaps it is; but given the choice between the person Joe was before this tragedy and the person he became after, Joe recognized the value attached to that price because he came to understand that life is about more than the body.

Theologians can quibble endlessly over whether or not God had any involvement in Joe's suffering and how best to characterize it. For Joe, however, things are much simpler. He sees the hand of God at work in his sufferings. In a talk that Joe once gave at a high school, he summed up his experience this way: "My problem was that I wouldn't sit still long enough to listen to anyone. So God put me in a chair that I couldn't get out of." Joe views his suffering, not as the product of a vengeful and angry God who wants to punish him for how he lived, but as the product of a merciful God who took his body to save his soul.

Revelation indicates that the presence of suffering in the world is neither a sign of God's absence from the world nor his lack of control over it. God sits on the throne and even suffering falls under his dominion. The symbolism of the seals and the trumpets, which have their origin in the throne room of God, shows that suffering can serve many functions within God's creation: from an expression of divine wrath in the service of justice to an expression of divine mercy in the service of reconciliation and redemption.

Of course, Revelation 9:20-21 states that the judgments of the trumpets fail to generate repentance. This assertion is important because the remainder of the sixth trumpet (10:1-11:13) explores the implications of this failure noted at the end of scene one, just as the remainder of the sixth seal (7:1-17) explored the answer to the question posed at the end of its first scene (6:17). In particular, the final two scenes of the sixth trumpet address the responsibility of God's faithful witnesses. Reading Revelation simply as a book about what God is doing and will do for the faithful and to the unfaithful misses a vital part of its message because the focus falls solely on God's activity. When Revelation is read that way, readers can too easily become passive observers who wait to see what God will do. Revelation, however, is a call for the faithful to be *active* in their witness and the remainder of the trumpets reinforces that call.

The Sixth Trumpet, Scene Two (10:1-11)

In Revelation 10 the theme of failed repentance that concluded chapter nine gives way to the theme of prophetic witness. John sees another angel coming down from heaven and proclaiming, "There will be no more delay, but in the days when the seventh angel is to blow his trumpet, the mystery of God will be fulfilled, as he announced to his servants the prophets" (10:6-7). The time for delay is drawing to a close. The limitations of the seals and the trumpets will soon come to an end for there is a final judgment coming in Revelation. In particular, this movement towards a more complete judgment is tied up with the seventh trumpet where "the mystery of God" will be revealed. This angel also holds in his hand a "little scroll" that he gives to John along with an admonition to eat it (10:9-10).

Revelation 10 functions as John's prophetic call. He receives his commission as a prophet in a manner that deliberately evokes the prior commissions of the prophets Daniel (Dan. 10:5-6; 12:4-7) and Ezekiel (Ezek. 2:8-3:3). The first half of chapter ten, where the angel descends and announces "the mystery of God," follows the Daniel tradition more closely, while the second half of the chapter bears stronger resemblance to the call of Ezekiel. Both John and Ezekiel are offered a scroll to eat and they do so as a symbolic means of internalizing the message. The scroll contains the content of the prophecy that John is to proclaim. The message of Ezekiel's scroll involved words of "lament and mourning and woe" (Ezek. 2:10) and though the content of John's scroll is not so clearly defined, the fact that it turns his stomach bitter likely indicates a similar message of judgment. The scroll's initial sweet taste in his mouth, however, may suggest that John's message also incorporates an element of hope.[5] Upon eating the scroll, John receives his specific prophetic commission: "You must prophesy again about many peoples and nations and languages and kings" (10:11).[6] Revelation 10 thus sets the stage for the story of the two witnesses in 11:1-13 by introducing it with this narrative of a prophetic call.

The Sixth Trumpet, Scene Three (11:1-13)

Both structurally and theologically, chapter eleven stands at the center of the book of Revelation. From the very beginning of Revelation John has called upon his churches to take up the role of faithful witness in imitation of the faithful witness of Christ. Such witness certainly includes challenging the religious, political, and economic influence of the Roman Empire, but it is much more than that. John's choice of Babylon (the sixth century BC empire that oppressed the people of God) as a symbolic identifier of Rome indicates that his concern lies more with the manifestation of evil in the guise of institutionalized power than it does with Rome exclusively. Rome just happens to be the current incarnation of this recurring phenomenon. It is not the Roman Empire itself that is the threat, but the Roman Empire as one component of "the kingdom of the world"—a kingdom that opposes and obstructs the will of God. Consequently, opposition to the kingdom of God in Revelation involves not just participation in the imperial cult but also participation in the wider religious environment of the Greco-Roman world, not just accommodation to the military and economic policies of the empire, but also compromise of one's moral and ethical principles through accommodation to the values of the kingdom of the world.

Revelation 11 addresses such a context by clarifying both the nature of the opposition and the responsibility of the church in the face of such opposition. The chapter begins on earth with a brief scene at a temple that is modeled on the Jerusalem Temple, particularly with reference to the outer court of the gentiles (11:1-2). Worshippers gather inside the temple, while the nations trample on the outer court.

Revelation 11:1-2 contrasts what is inside with what is outside and what is measured with what is unmeasured. Inside are the temple, the altar, and the worshippers; outside are the outer court of the gentiles and the holy city. This depiction relies upon the physical layout of the Jerusalem Temple where the temple building, altar, and inner courts were accessible only to Israelites, while the outer court was accessible to gentiles. Furthermore, John measures the temple, altar, and worshippers, while being expressly forbidden to measure the outer court. One function of measuring by a prophet is to mark out a particular territory for divine protection (Zech. 2:1-5). Consequently, this scene depicts the faithful worshippers protected by God even as the nations trample the unmeasured outer court and the holy city for forty-two months (11:2). These contrasts set the stage for the scenes that follow.

Chapter 11 provides the most extensive description of the opposition so far in Revelation. Those who threaten God's temple and the worshippers gathered there are "the nations" (11:2), also called "the inhabitants of the earth" (11:10). They are associated symbolically with Sodom and Egypt, representing respectively immorality and oppression of God's people (11:8). They seek to harm God's two witnesses (11:5) and align themselves with the beast who has declared war on the witnesses of God (11:7). Perhaps most instructive is the statement that the nations will exercise their threatening actions for forty-two months (11:2). Forty-two months, or three and a half years, is a time-frame derived from Daniel's "a time, two times, and half a time" (with a "time" equal to one year—Dan. 7:25). The forty-two months in Daniel represent the duration of time that the Seleucid King Antiochus Epiphanes waged war upon the Jewish people and their religion in the second century B.C, events commonly called the Maccabean Revolt. Antiochus came to represent for the Jews a stereotypical opponent of God and the embodiment of evil (much like Hitler functions in contemporary times). From the time of Antiochus through the first century AD, "apocalyptically minded Jews were incorporating their human opponents into the framework of the scenario of the end as special manifestations of the power of evil."[7] The actions of Antiochus were part of a larger mythic pattern of evil that repeats itself throughout history, finding ever new yet familiar expressions in willing associates who embody the distinct characteristics of these figures of opposition, namely "blasphemy against God and persecution of God's faithful."[8]

In Revelation 13:5, the beast (a symbolic representation of Roman hegemony) exercises his authority for forty-two months, the identical time-frame during which the nations trample the holy city. By identifying the time frame during which the beast blasphemes God and wages war against God's faithful (11:7; 13:5-7) with the time frame of Antiochus's similar actions in Daniel, John makes it clear that Roman authority is merely one manifestation of this mythic pattern of evil in which the kingdom of the world takes a stand against the kingdom of God.

Revelation 11 thus begins with a symbolic depiction of God's people under attack by the agents of evil even as the people of God find shelter under God's protection. The forty-two months represent this period of opposition. It is not a literal description of elapsed time, but a symbolic description of any period of time when God's people find themselves threatened by the kingdom of the world. In Revelation, this would encompass both persecution already experienced by some members of John's churches and the potential conflict his churches would face if they take up the pattern of the Christ. The theological message of Revelation 11:1-13, however, focuses less on the specific experiences of John's audience than on the present responsibility of the church in the world. For that, we turn to the story of the two witnesses.

Some interpreters identify the two prophetic witnesses in Revelation 11:3-13 with specific individuals from Jewish (Moses and Elijah) or early Christian (Peter and Paul) history. Revelation itself undercuts such specific identifications by describing the two witnesses as an amalgam of prophetic stereotypes and traditions. They wear the standard prophetic garb of sackcloth and are identified as "the two olive trees and the two lampstands" from the book of Zechariah (Rev. 11:3-4; Zech. 4:1-14). They have authority to shut up the sky in the tradition of Elijah (Rev. 11:6; 1 Kings 17:1) and to strike the earth with plagues that resemble the actions of Moses (Rev. 11:6; Ex. 7:20). Furthermore, the fire that pours forth from their mouth is reminiscent of the prophet Jeremiah (Rev. 11:5; Jer. 5:14). That there are two witnesses, rather than being a literal description of historical figures, likely derives from Deuteronomy 19:15 where the testimony of two witnesses lends credibility to the message. Given the patchwork description of these witnesses, it makes the most sense to treat them as a symbolic representation of the prophetic witness of the community of God.[9]

The two witnesses engage in their prophetic activity for 1260 days, a time period equivalent to the forty-two months during which the nations trample and the beast exercises his authority. In other words, the period of witness is equal to the period of opposition. This is because the two have a mutually dependent relationship. Faithful witness to the kingdom of God creates opposition from the kingdom of the world, while at the same time the proper Christian response to opposition is faithful witness. As long as there is faithful witness, there will be opposition; as long as there is opposition, there must be faithful witness. As a symbolic representation of the community of God's faithful, the two witnesses demonstrate that the responsibility of the church is to witness faithfully in the face of opposition and in accordance with the pattern of the Christ.

The prophetic activity of the two witnesses remarkably resembles the prophetic activity of Christ. They witness faithfully and as a result of their witness are killed by the beast (Rome) in the city "where also their Lord was crucified" (Rev. 11:7-8). After three and a half days they are resurrected (11:11) and then ascend up to heaven (11:12). These two witnesses fully embody the pattern of the Christ: faithful witness—suffering/death—resurrection/vindication. The two witnesses represent the call to all of God's people to take up Christ's pattern in the world. When Christians witness faithfully, they will face opposition as Jesus did, yet God will be with them as he was with Jesus. Their faithful witness may lead to suffering and even death as with Jesus, yet also like Jesus, their faithful witness will result in vindication.

It is vital that the church embodies the pattern of the Christ in the world because through this pattern God challenges the kingdom of the world. John states that the inhabitants of the earth were tormented by the prophetic activity of the two witnesses (11:10). Their torment stemmed from how the faithful witness of God's people challenged the kingdom of the world with a different kind of power and a different conception of victory. The responsibility of the church in a world beset by suffering, evil, and opposition to the will of God is not violent resistance, nor triumphalistic desires for revenge, nor defeatist surrender due to an inability to reconcile injustice and evil with belief in a benevolent and all-powerful God. The responsibility of the church in a world beset by evil, suffering and opposition to the will of God is to witness as Christ witnessed because that is where God is active. That is where the benevolence, the power, and the goodness of God find its most profound expression. It is through the cross and the subsequent embodiment of that pattern in the lives of those who have been called to take up their own cross that God challenges the power structures and values of the world.

In Revelation 11 the postscript to this harsh treatment of God's witnesses is the judgment of God. A great earthquake strikes the city where God's witnesses were martyred, killing seven thousand people. The focus, though, is on the survivors of the earthquake who, upon witnessing the resurrection and ascension of the witnesses and experiencing the judgment of God, give "glory to the God of heaven," a statement suggesting repentance/conversion.[10] Recall that the first scene of the sixth trumpet concluded with a statement regarding the lack of repentance by the inhabitants of the earth (9:20-21). The last scene of the sixth trumpet concludes with repentance by those who opposed God's witnesses (11:13). This movement from no repentance to repentance is crucial for understanding the function of the sixth trumpet.

What accounts for the difference between judgment *without* repentance (9:13-21) and judgment *with* repentance (11:13)? Sandwiched between these two is John's call to prophetic witness (10:1-11) and the prophetic witness of the community of God as represented by the two witnesses (11:1-12). Within the narrative flow of the sixth trumpet, judgment alone fails to generate repentance, but judgment coupled with the faithful witness of God's people does. Judgment in Revelation is not merely a punitive exercise, but is designed to function in consort with the witness of God's people. When the church models its witness on the witness of Christ, that witness impacts the kingdom of the world beyond what judgment alone can accomplish.

The first six trumpets reveal that divine wrath and judgment cannot be easily separated from divine mercy. Yes, God may bring judgment as an expression of his wrath, yet he also uses judgment as a catalyst for repentance. This is not an either/or scenario, for the same judgment that grows out of the wrath of God may also spark the repentance/conversion that manifests the mercy and love of God. What the trumpets demonstrate is that suffering as an outgrowth of divine wrath and suffering as an outgrowth of divine mercy both fall under the sovereignty of God and function to accomplish his plan for creation.

The Mystery of God (the Seventh Trumpet)

In Revelation 10 an angel announces that "the mystery of God" will be fulfilled with the blowing of the seventh trumpet (10:7). When the seventh trumpet blows, the revelation of that mystery comes as celebration breaks out in heaven and the host of heaven declares: "The kingdom of the world has become the kingdom of our Lord and of his Messiah" (11:15). The division between these two kingdoms governs the entirety of Revelation. John's pervasive warfare language describes the opposition and animosity between them. Yet with the blowing of the seventh trumpet, that opposition is overcome through a merging of the two kingdoms. This is not a willing surrender of power but a submission by the kingdom of the world due to the activity of God and of his people. God acts in sovereignty and in faithfulness to his creation by bringing the recalcitrant kingdom of the world under his authority, yet he does not do this simply through the force of will. As Revelation 10:1-11:13 indicates, God works through the prophetic witness of his community. It is the faithful, prophetic witness of those who embody the pattern of the Christ that results in the kingdom of the world becoming the kingdom of the Lord and of his Christ.

The first six trumpets also reveal that the prophetic witness of God's people, as with the Hebrew prophets, often works in consort with the wrath of God. Consequently, the twenty-four elders proclaim that the time for judgment and wrath has now come (11:16-18). If *now* is the time for judgment and wrath to begin, what has been occurring previously in Revelation? Certainly some of what has transpired to this point would qualify as judgment and wrath. What the seventh trumpet envisions is an eschatological scenario, one that will be unpacked further in the final chapters of Revelation. The previous acts of judgment and wrath were limited in part because they were temporary or circumscribed actions. The seventh trumpet, however, declares a time when the kingdom of the world has become the kingdom of God, when God's judgment and wrath are not limited, and when God's servants receive vindication.

There is a note of finality and completion here that is lacking in previous descriptions. John provides in Revelation 11:16-18 a skeleton description of God's actions that will receive flesh in chapters 14-22.

The focus in chapter eleven is on the God who will balance the scales and establish justice by reconciling the two kingdoms and bringing order out of chaos. These verses end with the assertion that God's wrath will result in "destroying those who destroy the earth" (11:18). Bauckham notes that this is an example of *lex talionis* ("measure for measure"), or as we might say, "The punishment fits the crime." Identifying the destroyers of the earth as "the powers of evil who are ruining God's creation with their violence, oppression, and idolatrous religion," Bauckham acknowledges that God's judgment of such opposition is not the cruel whim of a vengeful and spiteful deity, but the establishment of *justice*.[11]

Revelation 11 concludes where it begins—at the temple, only this time it is the heavenly temple with the Ark of the Covenant fully visible within (11:19). The accompanying lightning, thunder, hail, and earthquake mark this as a *theophany*—an appearance of God. Though God himself receives no description, the appearance of the ark within the temple represents his presence. With this imagery, 11:19 reiterates the point of verses 16-18—that God has come to set things right—while firmly situating that establishment of justice in the context of covenant. By judging the dead, destroying those who destroy the earth, and rewarding his servants, God shows himself faithful to his covenant.

Of course, at the time of John's writing, the Ark of the Covenant no longer existed within the Jerusalem Temple, having either been destroyed centuries earlier or lost to history. The physical loss of the ark, though, in no way minimized its importance as an enduring symbol for the Jewish people. During the second-century AD revolt against Rome, the Jewish rebels minted coins that depicted the Jerusalem Temple with the Ark of the Covenant visible within.[12] This imagery represented the hope of the Jewish nation for victory and restoration, a hope based in their dependence on God's covenant faithfulness.

In Revelation 11, the appearance of the ark also gains particular import from the movement from earth to heaven represented in the chapter. The events of this chapter begin on earth and conclude in heaven. The two witnesses conduct their ministry on earth (11:3-10) only to then ascend "up to heaven" (11:12). The kingdom of the world, represented by the beast that comes up out of the earth (11:7), exercises its opposition on earth as the nations trample on the holy city (11:2) and then kills the two witnesses while the inhabitants of the earth gloat over them (11:7-10). Yet, at the conclusion of the chapter we learn "in heaven" that the kingdom of the world has become the kingdom of God (11:15). Most striking is the contrast of the temples. Revelation 11 begins at the temple on earth, a temple that is threatened by the marauding nations and that contained no ark. It ends at the temple "in heaven," a temple that is untouched, secure from all threats, and within which the Ark of the Covenant blazes in glory.

Through this movement John communicates the contrast between earthly reality and heavenly reality. On earth God's people, if they are faithful, are threatened, at war, forever in opposition to the world in which they live. Despite their faithfulness and at times because of it they suffer and sometimes die, while those who oppose them seemingly prosper. For many Christians, this perceived inequity might call the justice and faithfulness of God into question. The movement from earth to heaven in this chapter, however, makes the point that spiritual reality must govern one's perspective of earthly reality, not the other way around. This is the transformative language of apocalyptic. It asserts that one's earthly experiences must be viewed in the light of God's heavenly reality. The heavenly appearance of the ark makes the point that no matter what transpires on earth, God's covenant remains in effect and he will faithfully execute it.

The apocalyptic perspective of the seventh trumpet is that God's sovereignty is secure, that the kingdom of the world will never ultimately triumph over the kingdom of God, and that God will act in justice to set everything right. It is this perspective that instills in the community of faith an assurance that faithful witness according to the pattern of the Christ will, by the covenant faithfulness of God, receive vindication and be an instrument through which God will faithfully exercise his sovereignty over creation.

10

THE CHRISTIAN STORY RECAST

Before narrating the judgment promised at the conclusion of the seventh trumpet, John tells a story. It is a story that provides a distinct interpretation of Christian experience through a symbolic re-telling of the Christian story in mythological form. Revelation 12 in particular is a pastiche of mythological traditions—Jewish, Greek, Roman, ancient Near Eastern—that gives the chapter a truly cosmopolitan flavor. As the seven churches of Asia contained both Jewish and gentile converts to Christianity, John draws from stories and traditions familiar to each group and weaves them together to produce a masterful recasting of the Christian story that both identifies why Christians suffer for their faithful witness and clarifies the nature of the enemy.

The Cast of Characters

John's story in Revelation 12 revolves around three characters—a pregnant woman, the child she bears, and a great red dragon bent on their destruction. John introduces the woman with cosmic language. She is clothed with the sun, has a crown of twelve stars on her head, and the moon under her feet (12:1). Although one interpretive tradition

identifies the woman narrowly as Mary, she is more properly understood as the larger messianic community of Israel. She has a corporate,
not individual, identity.[1] The woman of Revelation 12 is the community
of Israel as it prepares to give birth to the Messiah. Her connection to
the sun, moon, and stars may hearken back to Genesis and Joseph's
dream in which the sun, moon, and stars represent his father, mother,
and brothers (Gen. 37:9-10), with the crown of twelve stars representing the twelve tribes.[2] The depiction of Israel as a pregnant woman
goes back at least to the time of Isaiah, although there it functions as a
description of Israel's distress before the Lord (Is. 26:17-18).

The moon under the woman's feet also carries with it another
meaning by virtue of its placement. In Roman iconography, the globe
played a prominent role as an image of imperial power and victory.
The globe would appear next to or under the feet of a Roman emperor,
the goddess Roma, or the goddess Nike (Victory) as a visual depiction
of Roman authority and victory over the earth.[3] The early second-century Fountain of Trajan at Ephesus contained a statue of the emperor
Trajan with a globe at his feet.[4] The emperor Domitian produced a
gold coin with a picture of his deceased son sitting on a globe as seven
stars circled his head as an assertion of his son's deification.[5] Certain
Roman coins bore images of either the goddess Roma or the goddess
Nike standing on a globe.[6] John's image of the pregnant woman standing on a globe (the moon) takes this standard form of Roman imperial
propaganda and co-opts it. This woman, and particularly the child she
will bear, represents a competing claim to power and victory. Her child
is the Messiah "who is to rule all the nations with a rod of iron" (Rev.
12:5; Ps. 2:9), a statement that at first blush appears to match Roman
assertions of power. Yet, as he did with the Lion/Lamb imagery, John
inverts this language by attributing the power, kingdom, authority, and
victory of the Messiah not to impressive displays of physical might but
to "the blood of the Lamb" and to the faithful witness of his followers
"who did not cling to life even in the face of death" (12:10-11).

The third major character in this drama is the red dragon (12:3-4). The dragon was a common symbol in ancient Near Eastern and Greek mythology, representing chaos, disorder, and opposition to the divine. In some tales, the dragon appears red in color.[7] The dragon goes by many names in ancient mythology (Python, Typhon, Leviathan), though Revelation identifies the dragon as "that ancient serpent, who is called the Devil and Satan, the deceiver of the whole world" (12:9). This dragon has ten horns (a symbol of power) and wears seven diadems on its seven heads. The diadem represents royal authority and that there are seven indicates a claim to complete and total authority. Revelation asserts, however, that the dragon is "the deceiver of the whole world." One aspect of that deception is the Dragon's claim to wield authority and power over this world.

The Story of Revelation 12

In Revelation 12 John offers a tantalizing interpretation of the Christian story recast in symbolic form. Although a variety of traditions influence the symbolism in this story, I highlight four distinct traditions—two Greek and two Jewish—that shape the structure and meaning of the chapter.

The Combat Myth

After introducing the primary characters in the story, Revelation 12 narrates the dragon's intent to devour the pregnant woman's child once it is born. Instead, however, the child is taken away to God while the woman flees into the wilderness where she finds protection. The dragon then wages battle against the forces of heaven until he is defeated (12:1-9). The form of this story bears strong similarities to a mythological tradition that was widespread throughout the ancient Mediterranean world and that is commonly known as the Combat Myth. The Combat Myth, which appears in a variety of incarnations, has at its center "a struggle between two divine beings and their allies for universal kingship."[8]

Essentially it is a battle between the spiritual forces of chaos and those of order. Typically one of the participants in this battle is a dragon.

Numerous variations of the Combat Myth are found in the ancient Near Eastern and Greek world, though the two versions that show the closest similarity to Revelation 12 are the Egyptian Isis/Seth-Typhon myth and the Greek Leto/Python myth. In the former story the dragon Seth-Typhon pursues the goddess Isis in order to kill her child Horus. In the Greek version, the dragon Python pursues the pregnant woman Leto in order to kill her child Apollo. Revelation 12 likely represents a mingling of these two traditions, though I will use the Leto/Python myth here as a means of illustrating the narrative patterns at work. The general similarities between the story in Revelation and the Leto/Python myth can be charted as follows:

Leto/Python Myth	Revelation 12:1-11
1) A woman (Leto) is pregnant with a child (Apollo)	1) A woman is pregnant with a child (Jesus)
2) A red dragon (Python) pursues the woman in order to kill her child	2) A red dragon (Satan) pursues the woman in order to kill her child
3) Zeus rescues the woman and Poseidon protects her	3) God rescues the woman and protects her
4) The child (Apollo) defeats the dragon	4) The child defeats the dragon (Rev. 12:11)

In some versions of the myth, the defeat of the dragon occurs with the aid of a champion (a role fulfilled by Michael in Revelation 12:7-9), though Revelation makes it clear that the dragon's defeat here ultimately derives from the cross of Christ (12:11).

Why John would tell his story in such mythological form is a question that will receive more extensive attention after I have surveyed the various traditions operating in Revelation 12. For now, I only note that John employs traditions like the Combat Myth as a way of defining the Christian story within the context of warfare, but particularly a certain kind of warfare—not the warfare engaged in by military forces, but the warfare between spiritual entities. Nevertheless, though the Combat Myth is a story about spiritual warfare, it also has political implications since Roman emperors would employ versions of the Combat Myth to identify the emperor with the victorious agents of order. John, then, may in fact be deliberately subverting such political associations by instead identifying the dragon—and by extension its cohort the beast, which represents the Roman imperial system (Revelation 13)—with the defeated agents of chaos rather than with the victorious agents of order.[9]

The Gigantomachy

Once the woman and her child find protection (Rev. 12:5-6), a war breaks out "in heaven" between Michael and his angels and the dragon and his angels. Michael's forces are victorious and the dragon is thrown down to the earth (12:7-9). The concept of a war in heaven between opposing forces was prevalent in the Greco-Roman world and sometimes served as a component of the Combat Myth. One common version of the "war in heaven" is known as the Gigantomachy (Battle of the Giants). This story relates a heavenly battle between the gods (Athena, Apollo, etc.), as the forces of goodness and order, and the Giants (sometimes called Titans) as the representatives of evil and chaos.[10] The Giants were creatures who were human from the waist up, but with serpents for legs. The Gigantomachy was a common theme on vases and in the sculpture on some sacred architecture. At Pergamum, for instance, the eighteen-foot-high Great Altar contained an extensive sculptural program made up of scenes from the Gigantomachy.

The following chart highlights general parallels between the Gigantomachy and Revelation 12:7-9:

Gigantomachy	Revelation 12:7-9
1) The gods fight a war in heaven against hybrid human-dragons (Giants)	1) Michael and his angels fight a war in heaven against the dragon and his angels
2) The gods are victorious	2) Michael and his angels are victorious
3) The Giants are cast out of heaven	3) The dragon and his angels are cast out of heaven

Just as the Gigantomachy highlights the defeat of the forces of chaos, Revelation 12:7-9 adopts a similar pattern to describe the defeat of Satan. It is essential to note that the focus in Revelation 12:7-9 is not on the primordial origin of Satan, but on his spiritual defeat. John is not describing the casting out of rebellious angels from heaven at the dawn of creation.[11] Within the narrative flow of Revelation 12, the casting of Satan out of heaven occurs *after* the birth of the child (the Messiah) and is depicted as a direct result of the dragon's failure to devour the child. The casting down of Satan from heaven is a representation of spiritual defeat that occurs as result of this child.[12]

Accompanying the announcement of the dragon's fall from heaven is a hymn declaring that the dragon's fall has inaugurated "the salvation and the power and the kingdom of our God and the authority of his Messiah" and that his defeat derives in part from "the blood of the Lamb" (12:10-11). What the war in heaven and the subsequent casting down of the dragon symbolically depict is the defeat of Satan by the cross. The deceptive power of Satan is unmasked as mere illusion by the faithful witness to the point of death of God's Messiah. Yet the hymn asserts that the dragon owes his defeat not only to the cross, but also to all those who have taken up the pattern of the Christ. They defeated him "by the word of their testimony, for they did not cling to life even in the face of death" (12:11). Revelation 12 depicts not the primordial defeat of Satan, but the *perpetual* defeat of Satan begun with the cross of Christ and continuing in the lives of those who take up their cross after him. It testifies that the kingdom of God is present, victory is present, power is present, and the dragon is defeated *whenever* God's people witness faithfully according to the pattern of the Christ.

The hymn concludes with a contrast between the rejoicing that occurs in heaven over the dragon's defeat and the announcement of "woe to the earth" because the dragon has gone down to it (12:12). This contrast between rejoicing and woe is a contrast between heavenly reality and earthly experience. The victory has been decided in heaven, but that victory has not yet become fully manifest on earth. The dragon has been and is continually defeated by the blood of the Lamb and the faithful witness of the saints, but he has not ceased fighting. In describing the activity of the dragon on earth, therefore, John turns to another ancient story to provide symbolic structure and meaning—the exodus.

The Exodus

Revelation 12:13-16 describes the dragon's activities upon being thrown down to earth. He once again pursues the woman and she once again receives protection. But in this portion of the narrative, John models his description on Pharaoh's pursuit of Israel in the exodus event. Here the dragon takes on a new symbolic identity as Pharaoh. Ezekiel offers a precedent for this association, as he twice describes "Pharaoh king of Egypt" as a dragon thrashing in the seas (Ezek. 29:3-5; 32:1-4). Furthermore, John's statement that the woman in Revelation 12 "was given the two wings of the great eagle, so that she could fly . . . into the wilderness" recalls Exodus 19:2-3 where God states that he bore Israel to safety in the wilderness "on eagles' wings." This clear allusion to the exodus narrative, combined with the prophetic tradition of symbolically identifying Pharaoh as a dragon, lends credence to the idea that John relates this portion of the Christian story by recasting it in the form of the exodus.

The story John tells in Revelation 12:13-16 is not a one-to-one correspondence with the exodus account, but it does possess symbolic coherence with that narrative. The following chart highlights the overarching parallels between John's story and the exodus:

The Exodus Narrative	Revelation 12:13-16
1) Pharaoh pursues after the Israelites	1) The dragon pursues after the woman
2) God carries the Israelites "on eagles' wings" to the wilderness where they are protected (Ex. 19:2-4)	2) The woman is given eagles' wings to fly to the wilderness where she is protected
3) Pharaoh sends an army to overtake the Israelites	3) The dragon sends a river to overtake the woman
4) The sea opens and swallows the army	4) The earth opens and swallows the river

By using the exodus account to provide symbolic and narrative structure for Revelation 12:13-16, John retains the themes of opposition and combat while connecting his audience's interactions with Rome to this earlier manifestation of opposition to the kingdom of God. In doing so he reminds them that the emperor stands in a long line of tyrants who do not have the interests of the kingdom of God at heart, but just as God proved faithful to the Israelites in Egypt, he will do the same for them. Before examining these larger implications of John's story in Revelation 12, however, one final Jewish tradition requires attention.

Genesis Three

Of all the traditions active within Revelation 12, Genesis 3 is arguably the most important because it both sets up the conclusion and grants a sense of cohesion to the story as a whole. Like Revelation 12, Genesis 3 is a story about a woman and a serpent/dragon. John's identification of the dragon as "that ancient serpent . . . the deceiver" (Rev. 12:9) evokes the serpent's deception of Eve into eating from the forbidden tree, an act that prompts a series of curses. These resulting curses aimed at the woman and the serpent are what John adapts for his narrative. God tells the woman in Genesis 3 that "in pain you shall bring forth children" (Gen. 3:16), a curse that Revelation 12 echoes when describing the woman who is clothed with the sun as "crying out in birth pangs" (Rev. 12:2). Most important is the curse placed upon the serpent. God declares to the serpent that he "will put enmity between you and the woman" (Gen. 3:15). Revelation 12 is a narrative expression of this enmity as the serpent/dragon seeks to destroy the woman both before (12:1-6) and after giving birth (12:13-17). But the enmity does not exist only between the serpent/dragon and the woman, for the Genesis account asserts that the enmity shall also extend to the woman's offspring (Gen. 3:16). This aspect of the curse sets up the conclusion of John's story as the serpent/dragon, filled with rage at the woman but unable to get at her, "went off to make war against the rest of her offspring" (Rev. 12:17; NIV). The following chart highlights these similarities between Revelation twelve and the Genesis three account:

Genesis Three	Revelation Twelve
1) A serpent deceives Eve	1) A serpent deceives the whole world (v.9)
2) The woman will give birth in pain	2) The woman cries out in the pains of birth
3) There is to be enmity between the serpent and the woman	3) The serpent seeks to kill the woman
4) There is to be enmity between the serpent and the woman's offspring	4) The serpent goes off to make war on the woman's offspring

The woman's first child was the Messiah (12:5) who defeated the serpent/dragon by his blood (12:11). Stinging from this defeat, the serpent/dragon renews his attack against the *rest* of the woman's offspring, identified as "those who keep the commandments of God and hold the testimony of Jesus" (12:17). The rest of the woman's offspring are thus God's faithful witnesses—those who embody the pattern of the Christ.

The themes of opposition and war infuse Revelation 12 from beginning to end. Each of the four traditions that structure John's story (the Combat Myth, Gigantomachy, Exodus, Genesis 3) all have opposition and conflict at their center. Having examined these individual pieces, we now turn to an exploration of how they function together to create the theological message of Revelation 12.

The Theological Message of Revelation 12

At first glance, Revelation 12 is a strange and fantastical story several steps removed from reality. But the more that one lives within the story, the more one recognizes its familiarity. The tale that John weaves is a symbolic re-telling of the Christian story. The story moves from the pregnant woman to the woman's child to the initial defeat of the dragon to the dragon's declaration of war on the woman's offspring. Another way to describe this movement is from Israel (the woman) to the Messiah (the child) to the cross (the dragon's defeat) to the period of Christian existence (the dragon's war on the offspring). Israel gives birth to the Messiah who defeats Satan by means of the cross. Satan then declares war on "those who hold to the testimony of Jesus." This is the story of Revelation 12 and it is a familiar one. It is the story of Israel, the Messiah, the cross, and the church. In particular, Revelation 12:13-17 describes the period of Christian existence, the period in which the dragon has gone down to the earth. These verses are critical for understanding Revelation because they represent the time period in which John's readers live and they describe the experience of John's audience. Another way to put it is that Revelation 12 *"ends at the place where the book of Revelation begins."*[13] Through this symbolic re-telling of the Christian story, John offers an apocalyptic perspective on his audience's Christian experience.

Why do the faithful suffer injustice and opposition? John declares it is because they are at war. Satan has declared war on those who hold to the testimony of Jesus. Revelation thus redefines the world as a battlefield and Christian existence as warfare. One reason why the world does not look as it should is because there is a war going on—and Christians are caught in the middle of it. This war is not a physical battle, but a spiritual one; not a battle fought with force of arms, but one fought with a different kind of power (faithful witness) and one that results in a different kind of victory that cannot be measured by spoils, land, or subjects.

Although it is a spiritual war, it is one waged within the very concrete structures of the social, religious, and political realities within which we live. One function of Revelation 12 is to clarify the relationship between this spiritual war and the various social, religious, and political forms in which it manifests. The four traditions that John employs (Combat Myth, Gigantomachy, Exodus, Genesis 3) help to accomplish this. John's use of both Greek and Jewish traditions likely has to do, in part, with the makeup of his audience. It is difficult to identify the cultural and ethnic makeup of the seven churches with any certainty, but circumstantial evidence leads to the conclusion that they likely incorporated both Jewish and Gentile Christians. By drawing upon both Jewish and non-Jewish traditions, John recasts the Christian story in a new form that communicates to both groups and unites their respective stories into one. As both Jew and Gentile unite in Christ, so too do their stories and traditions. All four traditions represent ancient (in some cases extending back to creation), universal stories that define opposition on a cosmic scale. Through the use of these traditions, John redefines the Christian experience of suffering and opposition as something that is not new, but ancient, and as part of the eternal battle between good and evil.

For those in John's audience who are suffering as result of their faithful witness, Revelation 12 gives meaning to their experience. It assures them that they do not suffer because of their failings but because of their *faithfulness* and that they stand in solidarity with all of God's faithful witnesses who have gone before. By redefining their experience as one of warfare, John provides them the motivation to fight by means of continued faithful witness, or, to use John's words, "Here is a call for the endurance and faith of the saints" (13:10). For others who have been lulled into complacency through prosperity, the hope of security, or their own distorted perceptions of the world, this chapter offers an important wake-up call opening their eyes to their participation in a war that perhaps they did not even realize was going on. In fact, one vital function of Revelation 12 is to bring clarity on the true nature of the enemy. That John's description of Roman authority in the guise of the two beasts (Revelation thirteen) follows directly after Revelation twelve is significant. The beast does not have a strong presence in Revelation prior to chapter twelve, being mentioned only once (11:7), but immediately following Revelation twelve it becomes a major player in the drama. Revelation twelve sets the stage for the appearance of the beasts and is thus essential for a proper understanding of their role and the empire they represent.

Revelation 12 introduces the true power behind the throne. It identifies who the *real* enemy is—and it is not Rome. Their true opponent, according to Revelation 12, is not a first-century political empire, but

Satan. John expands their theological horizons by informing them that their primary struggle is not a social, political, or physical conflict with Rome (though it certainly manifests in that way), but a spiritual conflict with Satan. This forces them to expand the limits of their thinking and to contextualize their present circumstances in the light of what the God "who was and is and is to come" has been doing, is doing, and will do within his creation.

In any war, it is important to know who the enemy is and Revelation 12 clarifies that. But what then of Rome? If Revelation 12 identifies the real enemy, Revelation 13 identifies one way that that enemy manifests in the social reality of the seven churches.

The Two Beasts (Revelation 13)

Revelation 13:2 announces that the beast receives his power, throne, and authority from the dragon. By linking Roman authority (the beast) with Satan (the dragon), John is redefining the Roman Empire as one present manifestation of an eternal *spiritual* conflict and thus getting his audience to understand their interactions with Rome in the context of a much larger, ongoing war. If the dragon is the enemy who has declared war on God's faithful witnesses (chapter twelve), then the beast is the weapon used to wage that war (chapter thirteen).

Commentators almost unanimously identify the two beasts of Revelation 13 as a representation of Roman imperial power and authority. John's description of the first beast, which rises out of the sea (13:1-8), derives partially from Daniel 7. Daniel sees a vision of four beasts—a lion, a bear, a leopard, and a fourth beast with ten horns (Dan. 7:2-7)—and then learns that the four beasts represent four kings (Dan. 7:17). John's beast combines all four of Daniel's beasts into one (Rev. 13:1-2), thus creating a characterization of the Roman Empire as the culmination of institutionalized evil whose roots of imperial authority run deep. The Roman Empire is just one manifestation of a weapon Satan uses to oppose the kingdom of God, just as he used Egypt, Babylon, and the Seleucids (Antiochus IV) before them.

If "Babylon" is the empire in Revelation, the beasts are its human faces. The beast from the sea (13:1-10) is a symbolic representation of Roman imperial authority as embodied in the emperor. According to the ancient practice of gematria whereby a person's name was converted into a numerical equivalent, the number of the beast (six hundred and sixty-six) is "the number of a person" (13:18). In particular the characteristics of this beast highlight its opposition to the kingdom of God. The ten diadems that it wears on its horns and its throne are a declaration of royal authority and power (13:1-2). That "the inhabitants of the earth" worship this beast is a reference to the imperial cult, the worship of the Roman emperor (13:4, 8). The beast wears blasphemous names on its heads (a reference either to divine claims by certain emperors or to the practice of addressing emperors with titles such as "Lord," "Savior," or "son of a god") and speaks blasphemies against God and all who dwell in heaven (13:1, 5-6). By the authority of the dragon, the beast wages war against the saints (13:7).

If the beast from the sea represents Roman imperial authority as embodied in the emperor, the beast from the land (13:11-17) represents a subordinate functionary who enacts and enforces the policies of the first beast. It exercises its authority on behalf of the first beast by promoting the imperial cult (13:12-15) and enforcing the economic policies of the empire (13:16-17). This description points to those who wield some form of authority in the Roman provinces. Common identifications for the beast from the land include a provincial high priest, a provincial governor,[14] or the larger network of people and institutions in Asia Minor that supported the imperial cults.[15]

Despite the power that these beasts wield, John makes it clear that they function *only* under the authority of the dragon. The dragon "gave" the beast his power, throne, and authority (13:2, 4). Furthermore, throughout Revelation 13 John uses the passive voice to describe the subordinate nature of both beasts. The beast from the sea "was given" its blasphemous words to speak (13:5), "was given" its authority to exercise over the earth (13:5, 7), and "was given" permission to make war on the saints (13:7). Likewise, the beast from the land "was given" the signs that it used to deceive the inhabitants of the earth (13:14, 15). The dragon is the real power behind the throne.

The combination of the beasts and Babylon represent the institutionalization of evil as a weapon the dragon uses to oppose the kingdom of God. Bauckham writes: "Revelation exposes the Roman Empire as a system of violent oppression, founded on conquest, maintained by military brutality. It is a system both of political tyranny (the beast from the sea) and of economic exploitation (Babylon)."[16] It is not necessarily the case, though, that this institutionalized opposition to the kingdom of God manifests primarily as physical persecution, although it is no doubt occasionally present. The issue here is more one of dueling interests and ideologies. One need not posit exceptional circumstances of persecution to account for Revelation's perception of Rome. The normal policies of the empire were a sufficient warning signal that the state and the church were on a collision course. As Boesak writes, "conflict between the interests of the state and the demands of the Word of God was both necessary and unavoidable."[17] Faithful and active witness to the kingdom of God will eventually run one afoul of the kingdom of the world. So John counsels that this requires "endurance and faith" on the part of the saints (13:10). John further links endurance and faith with the specter of captivity and death (13:10), indicating that the endurance required is endurance *through* suffering and opposition. Faithful witness, rather than protecting one from suffering, may in fact be the catalyst for it.[18]

Revelation 12 and 13 provide an apocalyptic perspective on the social realities of John's audience. Unless John's churches learn to view their economic, political, and social experiences within Roman imperial society in *spiritual* terms, they will continue to live under a deception. The apocalyptic reality that John calls his audience to see is that Satan is the real opponent who has declared war against them. Satan's current weapon of choice, however, is the beast and it has a human number (13:18). In other words, they are embroiled in a heavenly battle, but one that takes earthly form.[19] Revelation identifies their experiences as part of the *eternal* conflict between good and evil and informs them that the social, economic, and political choices they make have *spiritual* consequences.

Is this transcendent perspective in Revelation 12-13 a matter of John describing reality as it is in order to explain to the oppressed why they are suffering or is it John demonizing Roman imperial society in order to awaken compromisers from their stupor? The answer is probably a bit of both. The dragon's war does not always manifest itself in overt expressions of opposition. It is a war that is also waged through effecting compromise and complacency (Laodicea). An effective battle plan involves not only overt displays of force, but also subtle maneuvers designed to bait the enemy into a trap. Revelation 12-13 engages those on the receiving end of both strategies. On the one hand, for those who have crossed the line in their compromise with Roman imperial society, Revelation 12-13 exposes who exactly they have gotten into bed with—a demonic beast who seduces them with its deceptions and who takes its orders from another. On the other hand, for those faithful witnesses who experience Roman imperial authority as oppressive and antagonistic, Revelation 12-13 grants them an expanded perspective that allows them to see Rome for what it is—a weapon wielded by their real enemy—and to recognize that they already possess the necessary armaments to defeat that real enemy—faithful witness according to the pattern of the Christ.

"IT IS DONE!"

REVELATION 14-20

Conflict between faith and experience can lead to a distorted understanding of God. This is true whether that conflict arises from the difficulty of reconciling faith in the sovereignty and goodness of God with the chaos and suffering of this world or whether it arises from an inability to perceive how one's alliances with the surrounding culture stand in tension with the faithfulness that God requires. The former situation can lead one to question the justice and benevolence of God, while the latter perceives God to be tolerant with, if not complicit in, one's alliances because one fails to recognize those alliances as unholy. For this multifaceted context, Revelation offers a narrative vision of divine action that offers both comfort to the oppressed and a warning to those who compromise with the kingdom of the world. The two themes of justice and wrath that dominate Revelation 14-20 form the basis of that comfort and warning.

The throne room scene of Revelation 4 asserted the sovereignty of God over his creation, effectively removing the option of appealing to any deficiency in God's power to explain evil and suffering. With that option removed, the primary question becomes whether or not God's use of his sovereignty relative to evil and suffering is *just*. Justice is a balancing of the scales, a restoration of order in the midst of chaos. It implies the reception of deserved consequences for one's actions. Revelation 14-20 operates with the assumption that the world is not as it ought to be. Chaos reigns and God's faithful witnesses suffer while their oppressors and those who compromise with them prosper. Justice is required.

Revelation 14-20 is a series of visions that portray God restoring order to creation as a manifestation of his justice. These visions of God's unfolding plan include an eschatological component with their depiction of the ultimate and final defeat of evil. Yet, it would be a mistake to read these visions as a blueprint for the end of days. The purpose of these chapters is not to provide a literal detailing of events preceding or accompanying the return of Christ, but to provide an assurance of the justice of God. When or how these events occur is of much less importance than the assertion that God will act to provide justice.

The eschatological component to these visions is vital, not for computing end-time scenarios or for correlating contemporary newsworthy events with the text of Revelation, but for how it re-frames *present* Christian experience and broadens our understanding of God's activity. Depicting God establishing justice in the future provides comfort to the oppressed by assuring them that order will be restored and their faithfulness rewarded and provides a warning to compromisers by revealing the ultimate fate awaiting the empire that has seduced them. Furthermore, eschatology is central to any discussion of the justice of God. If we are to think at all about how God in his sovereignty engages evil and suffering, then we must not do so strictly in light of what God has done and is doing. We must also think about what God *will* do. God is "the one who was, is, and *is to come*." To evaluate God's involvement with his creation only in terms of our past and present experiences with evil and suffering is insufficient because the story is not over. Revelation 14-20 reminds us that God is actively at work within his creation and that his plan for this creation is a comprehensive one comprising past, present, and future so that any discussion of divine justice that ignores the eschatological is necessarily incomplete.

Two dominant themes infuse the visions of Revelation 14-20: 1) the opposition will receive the consequences of their actions, and 2) God is just in assuring this. However, these themes appear in a section of material that complicates these seemingly straightforward assertions. Many of the objections that scholars raise regarding Revelation's treatment of evil and suffering derive from chapters 14-20, including the pervasive use of warfare imagery (e.g. 16:14; 17:14; 19:11-16, 19-20), the specter of coercion in God's dealings with humanity (14:9-11; 16:8-11), the perception of a misogynistic orientation (17:1-6), and the triumphalistic rejoicing over the demise of one's enemies (19:1-3).

I make no pretense of offering an interpretation of Revelation that provides a satisfactory resolution to these issues for all. As argued earlier, these and other objections grow out of a variety of theological, ideological, and political concerns to the extent that a one-size-fits-all explanation is not possible. What I attempt here is rather an interpretation of Revelation that takes seriously its character as a book written within an ancient community of faith to ancient communities of faith and that, by virtue of its inclusion in Scripture, continues to engage communities of faith today. Nevertheless, before proceeding it may be helpful to address some of the underlying issues involved with these common objections as a way of establishing the context for my approach to Revelation 14-20.

Metaphor and Judgment

A metaphor is a means by which we gain perspective on one thing by comparing it with another. We understand our reality by means of the symbols and language we use to describe it so that metaphor becomes one way of categorizing human experience. Metaphors and symbols provide access to truth about human experience; they provide us with a conceptual framework for understanding how things really are.[1] When John describes Christian experience as warfare, he employs a metaphor and it must be evaluated *as a metaphor*. John's warfare imagery is not an attempt to advocate militant Christianity or to justify violence. Treating it as such misunderstands the nature of metaphor. Through this metaphor, John is categorizing Christian experience in terms of *spiritual* opposition and conflict. The metaphor of warfare provides both an explanation for why Christians suffer and a way of conceptualizing God's response to opposition. In Revelation's use of this metaphor, it becomes clear that this is God's battle and he will wage it in faithfulness and with justice. As a metaphor for the spiritual nature of Christian existence, the warfare language suggests that Christians must fight but that they do so not with blades of steel. Whereas the dragon fights with the weapons of imperial domination, economic control, and religious and cultural seduction, God, in return, employs his own weapons: the faithfulness of Christ on the cross and the faithful witness of those who take up that pattern.

Another metaphor John employs that has generated much discussion and even disdain is his description of the Roman Empire as "the great whore" (17:1), a phrase that has left him vulnerable to the charge of misogyny. The issue of how to appropriate this metaphor for our much more sensitive culture today is an important debate to have, but the charge that John is misogynistic is problematic. One cannot move easily from a metaphor to the social mindset behind it. Equating John's use of this metaphor with his general viewpoint on women is further complicated by the fact that John also employs much more positive female imagery (the woman clothed with the sun, the bride of Christ) as well as negative male images (the dragon, beast, false prophet).[2] As one cannot assume that John's use of negative male stereotypes indicates his disrespect for men, one should be equally cautious of turning his use of negative female stereotypes into a charge of misogyny.

A metaphor reveals truth through comparison, but it often does so in a limited and focused way. John's use of the whore metaphor is designed to reveal something about the Roman Empire, not about women. He is exposing the seductive power of Rome and so defines

Rome using what would have been the most provocative and effective image of seduction in that culture, one that was certainly not of John's invention since his description of Babylon as a whore has its roots in Jeremiah's description of Babylon as a female who seduces the nations into intoxication (Jer. 51:7). The metaphor must be interpreted in light of its function within the whole narrative rather than treated in isolated fashion as a window into the author's prejudices.[3]

Furthermore, the judgment language in Revelation should be understood as an extension of John's warfare metaphor. John links the two when describing the rider on the white horse as one who "judges and makes war" (19:11). Fundamental to Revelation is the awareness that this is a defensive war that started on the other side.[4] God is not coercing obedience; he is combating opposition. His judgment in Revelation 14-20 is a response to those who have aligned themselves with the dragon and the beast, set themselves up in opposition to God by means of this alliance, and rejected all opportunities for repentance. Essential to Revelation's presentation of judgment, therefore, is the recognition that there are things worthy of being judged.

Critics who read Revelation as merely the product of a human mind would argue that we cannot trust John's identifications of evil and of those worthy of judgment because those evaluations are simply John's. If viewed from such a secular perspective, these cautions make sense. But John writes within and to communities of faith. Reading Revelation within a community of faith means reading it as Scripture. It means reading Revelation as *revelation*. This requires an acceptance of certain fundamental assumptions about the text .

First is the assumption that God is the arbiter of what is right, good, and holy. Against the temptation to set ourselves up as the arbiters of what is right and then hold God accountable to that standard, readers of Scripture acknowledge that we must allow the text to hold us accountable. We all bring our contemporary questions and issues to the text, but reading Revelation as Scripture means letting it challenge our beliefs and ideologies, not cater to them. In other words, Revelation should challenge both the pacifist who indicts the book for its militaristic imagery and the militant who finds in it a sympathetic co-conspirator.

Second is the assumption that suffering serves a vital purpose in our world. Within the narrative world of Revelation, suffering fulfills varied functions and receives varied evaluations. Though it holds the unjust suffering of the righteous to be an evil, it also presents suffering as an expression of divine justice. This suggests that in Revelation the moral evaluation of suffering is determined not by the experience of pain itself, but by the act that generates it.

Third is the assumption that God is sovereign and his judgments are just. It cannot be stressed too strongly that in Revelation judgment belongs to God alone. The faithful are never counseled to seek vengeance for themselves or to make determinations regarding who is a worthy candidate for judgment. Only God and his Christ act in judgment. The followers of the Lamb are called only to continued faithful witness and endurance. Human beings possess neither the ability nor the authority to declare who is worthy of divine judgment, let alone to execute it. But neither dare we criticize God for that determination. Revelation begins and ends with God on the throne. That is both the starting point and the ending point, the alpha and the omega. The image of the divine throne asserts that God rules faithfully over his creation and he will likewise judge it faithfully. To those who would object that the violent depictions of judgment in Revelation are theologically or morally deficient because they depict an angry God, Miroslav Volf counters that any God who is *not* angry at evil in the world "would be an accomplice in injustice, deception, and violence."[5]

Justice and Judgment

The kingdom of the world opposes God's kingdom and all that it represents and John characterizes this opposition as a declaration of war. The forces arrayed against each other in this war include a city, an animal figure, and those who bear that figure's mark. On the one side are the city of Babylon, the beast, and those with the mark of the beast on their foreheads. On the other side are Zion (14:1), the Lamb, and those with the mark of the Lamb on their foreheads. With these opposing sides clearly defined, Revelation 14-20 presents visions of God systematically dealing with each one of these opposing forces.

Although the dragon remains the real enemy directing this war against the kingdom of God and the beast continues to play a prominent role in that war, the central focus in 14-20 shifts slightly to Babylon. The ancient Babylonian Empire was a regime characterized by arrogance, wealth, and oppression of the Jewish people. Around 586 BC the Babylonians destroyed Jerusalem and its temple and it is possible that John employs Babylon as a symbol for Rome because Rome was likewise responsible for the destruction of Jerusalem and its temple in 70 AD. However, John never makes such a connection explicit and it requires a post-70 dating of Revelation which, though likely, is not assured. Regardless, their shared arrogance, economic oppression, and antagonism towards the people of God are a sufficient basis for a symbolic equating of Rome and Babylon. In Revelation 14-18, Babylon becomes the dominant representation of the kingdom of the world. One reason for identifying Rome with Babylon is that historical Babylon previously received the judgment of God and thereby foreshadows the ultimate fate awaiting Rome as well.

The constant assurance throughout Revelation 14-20 is that these judgments represent divine justice. These are not the capricious whims of a cruel deity, but the proper balancing of the scales. Justice in Revelation is God reconciling the two kingdoms and restoring order out of chaos. As Bauckham states, "An interpretation of Revelation that is faithful to its own priorities must surely give this affirmation of divine justice hermeneutical priority."[6] In addition to the recurring refrain that God's judgments are just (15:3; 16:5, 7; 19:2), two features highlight Revelation's depiction of divine justice in these chapters. First, God's judgment is on behalf of genuine victims. In two instances, John links these judgments back to the prayers of the souls under the altar who "had been slaughtered for the word of God and for the testimony they had given" (6:9). When the third angel pours out his bowl of divine wrath, "the angel of the waters" declares that this wrath is in response to the shedding of the blood of saints and prophets (16:5-6). The altar itself then speaks and says, "Yes, O Lord God, the Almighty, your judgments are true and just!" (16:7). That this announcement of divine justice comes from the altar suggests that the slaughtered souls' pleas for vengeance are being answered. The time for waiting is over and the great day of God's wrath has come. This view receives further confirmation from Revelation 19:2 where God's "true and just" judgments are described in terms of God having "avenged . . . the blood of his servants," language which evokes the souls' prayer for God to "avenge our blood" (6:10).

The second feature is that God's judgments represent the deserved consequences of actions and choices. Those aligned with the kingdom of the world have brought the wrath of God down upon themselves as a consequence of their own opposition. Revelation 16:6 lays out the principle well. After the rivers and springs of water are turned into blood, an angel announces that "because they shed the blood of saints and prophets, you have given them blood to drink." The punishment not only fits the crime, but is in direct correlation to it. Likewise, Revelation 18:6-7 depicts the judgment of Babylon as the appropriate consequence of her behavior: "Render to her as she herself has rendered." Because Babylon glorified herself in luxury, she is to be given "a like measure of torment and grief." The cup of judgment she drinks, according to a voice from heaven, is one that she herself mixed. What makes the judgments of Revelation 14-20 just is that they are merely reaping what they have first sown. They declared war so war is what they get.

Dealing with the Opposition (14:1-19:10)

Revelation 14 begins with a general announcement of judgment to come. Three angels make three public declarations that increase in specificity and severity. The first announces that the hour of judgment has now come (14:7). The second declares that Babylon the Great has fallen, thereby foreshadowing as already accomplished fact the judgment to be described later (14:8). The third angel restricts its focus to those who bear the mark of the beast. They have willingly aligned themselves with evil and will therefore drink God's wrath undiluted (14:9-11). Framing these announcements of wrath upon Babylon and the followers of the beast (14:8-11) are the admonitions to "Fear God and give him glory" (14:7) and to maintain endurance and faithfulness (14:12). By means of this structure John offers a choice to his audience. They can choose between allegiance to the kingdom of the world or allegiance to the kingdom of God. The need to choose has reached a critical mass in the narrative because the time has now come for the harvest and for the treading of "the great wine press of the wrath of God" (14:14-20).

It is important to keep in mind the rhetorical focus of Revelation 14 that sets the stage for the judgments to follow. That focus is not the forced conversion of those who stand adamantly opposed to the kingdom of God, but rather on those who claim the name of Christ and yet have so accommodated to the kingdom of the world that they do not realize the extent to which their allegiance to God has been compromised. These chapters are about waking them up to the dire consequences they face if they fail to clarify their allegiance to God. The later plea to come out of Babylon so as to not share in her sins (18:4) highlights the central rhetorical focus of Revelation 14-20. These chapters assert that neutrality is not an option in this war. All must declare their allegiance and prepare for the consequences of that choice.

Revelation's third series of seven, the seven bowls of wrath, envisions God's judgment upon the kingdom of the beast and those who bear his mark (16:2, 10). Chapter fifteen sets the stage for the outpouring of the bowls by introducing the actors and equipment employed in the series, but also by clarifying the thematic context of the bowls. Revelation 15 presents the bowls of wrath as a symbolic representation of the exodus event. The identification of the seven bowls as "plagues" (Rev. 15:1; Ex. 7:14-12:30), the interconnection of sea and fire (Rev. 15:2;

Ex. 14:23-24), the singing of "the song of Moses" (Rev. 15:3; Ex. 15:1-18), and the appearance of "the tabernacle of witness" (Rev. 15:5; Ex. 25:8-9) all give this vision the flavor of the exodus. Furthermore, several of the plagues unleashed by the bowls recall those of the exodus: sores (Rev. 16:2, 11; Ex. 9:8-12), frogs (Rev. 16:13; Ex. 8:1-15), darkness (Rev. 16:10; Ex. 10:21-29), and water turning to blood (Rev. 16:4; Ex. 7:14-24).

Once again, the association of Rome with both Babylon and Egypt in these chapters reveals that these judgments result from the perpetual conflict between the kingdom of God and the kingdom of the world as manifest in oppressive imperial power. Revelation 15 represents a deliberate attempt to link its audience's present experience with the past. It encourages *remembrance*. Just as God previously acted in faithfulness by bringing justice to bear on Egypt and Babylon, he will do the same with Rome. Just as God previously acted in faithfulness to deliver his people from slavery (Egypt) and from exile (Babylon), he will deliver them as well.

After crossing the sea, the Israelites in Egypt sang the Song of Moses to praise God for his actions on their behalf (Exodus 15). In Revelation 15, those who are victorious over the beast due to their faithful witness sing "the song of Moses . . . and the song of the Lamb" (15:3). The inclusion of the Lamb here once again links present and past, cross and exodus, and affirms that God's actions on behalf of his people are part of a pattern of faithfulness and justice. The content of the song itself highlights this by praising God for his deeds of power, justice, and holiness (15:3-4). The statements that those on the receiving end of these plagues refused to repent of their deeds and instead cursed God (16:9, 11) expose their commitment to opposition, thereby lending support to the proclamation from the altar that God's "judgments are true and just" (16:7).

The description of the sixth bowl does not contain a greatly extended scene as with the seals and trumpets, but instead depicts the armies of the kingdom of the world gathering for battle against God (16:12-16). Demonic spirits assemble the kings of the earth at a place called, in Hebrew, Armageddon (16:16), a reference to the Israelite city of Megiddo.[7] In Israelite history, Megiddo was a strategic location that was the site of many ancient battles (Judg. 5:19; 1 Kings 23:29; 2 Chron. 35:20-22). John is employing symbolic geography by using Megiddo's history of military conflict to represent the final showdown between these opposing forces. Yet, Revelation 16:16 depicts only the gathering for battle, with the conflict itself being held off until chapter nineteen.

With the seven seals and the seven trumpets, there was an emphasis on the limitation or even temporary nature of those actions. The seven bowls contain no such limitation. There is a sense of finality to the bowls that was lacking in the seals and trumpets. Thus, the seventh bowl brings the series to a close with the declaration, "It is done!" (16:17). Justice has been accomplished as John announces the fall of Babylon and of "the cities of the nations" (16:19). By announcing the fall of Babylon as accomplished fact, the seventh bowl provides an overview of God's judgment on Babylon that will be worked out in more detail in the following chapters.

From Revelation 17:1-19:10, John envisions the judgment of Babylon unfolding in three parts: a description of Babylon as the "great whore" who sits atop the beast (17:1-18), an oracle of doom pronounced over Babylon and modeled on Jeremiah 50-51 (18:1-24), and a heavenly celebration over the accomplishment of God's judgment (19:1-10). The symbolization of Babylon as a whore reveals the seductive power of the Roman Empire and its ability to deceive people into an unholy alliance. John also describes this deceptive quality as "sorcery" (18:23). Rome has essentially put people under its spell, including members of John's own faith communities who have been deceived into believing they are upstanding citizens of the kingdom of God while forming bonds of allegiance with the kingdom of the world. John's declaration of judgment on Babylon puts them on notice regarding the fate they too will share if they continue playing this game of dual allegiance. The plea from heaven to "Come out of her, my people, so that you do not take part in her sins" (18:4) is a plea to reject accommodation and compromise and to give one's sole allegiance to the kingdom of God.

John's depiction of Babylon/Rome as a seductive whore also functions as an explanation for the extent of the opposition against the kingdom of God. By employing her seductive powers, she has gained numerous allies. John describes the actions of "the great whore" as "fornication" (17:2, 4). Many scholars identify the "fornication" referenced here as a symbol for idolatry. Certainly in the Hebrew prophets the language of sexual immorality could function as a representation of idolatrous relationships and John himself links fornication and idolatry earlier in the book (Rev. 2:14, 20). The primary focus in Revelation 17-18, however, is less on idolatry than it is on the illicit nature of the relationship between the great whore and those with whom she engages in this behavior. The fornication that John describes here is specifically between the great whore and "the kings of the earth" (17:2; 18:3, 9). The kings of the earth are the leaders of the subject kingdoms and client-states that make up the Roman Empire. Babylon has employed its seductive lures to join its power with that of the kings of the earth in one immoral union, thus strengthening its opposition to God. In fact, it is these very kings who align with the beast to wage war against the kingdom of God (16:14; 19:19).

In addition to Babylon's fornication with the kings of the earth, three other charges form the basis of Babylon's judgment: economic exploitation (18:3, 7, 11-13, 15-19), pride/self-glorification (18:7), and violent oppression of God's people (17:6; 18:24). Revelation 18's concluding assertion that Babylon is responsible for "the blood of prophets and of saints, and of all who have been slaughtered on earth" (18:24) indicates that this is judgment not simply on Rome but on Rome as one historical manifestation of the kingdom of the world that repeatedly expresses its opposition to God. Rome is just the current incarnation of the perpetual battle between good and evil.

Although Revelation 18 clearly highlights the reasons for judgment on Babylon/Rome, the precise historical nature of that judgment is unclear, owing in part to its poetic description. Yet, the statement in Revelation 17:16 to the effect that ten kings (represented as "horns"), along with the beast, will "hate the whore" and "devour her flesh" may provide one clue. This representation points to the self-destructive nature of evil and may indicate that God's judgment on Babylon involves, at least in part, internal corruption and civil war. Most striking, however, is the subsequent statement that these kings give their kingdoms over to the beast at God's subtle direction, indicating that God is working through these kings and through the beast itself to execute his judgment. God "put it into their hearts" to give their kingdoms to the beast and in doing so they "carry out his purpose . . . until the words of God will be fulfilled" (17:17). This is God's sovereignty at work, which sometimes expresses itself in paradoxical form. Just as God works through suffering in order to redeem us from suffering, he works through the opposition to bring judgment upon the opposition.

Following the judgment on Babylon, celebration breaks out in heaven (19:1-3), a celebration first mandated in 18:20 with the command, "Rejoice over her, O heaven, you saints and apostles and prophets! For God has given judgment for you against her." Revelation here presents rejoicing over the downfall of Babylon as a proper response, a feature of the text that has generated much criticism. Is it appropriate to rejoice over the devastation of others? If taken as a prescription for proper Christian behavior, does not such celebratory rhetoric lead to triumphalism and the justification of violence? Does it not feed into the unfortunate human tendency to identify ourselves, whether justified or not, as the righteous victims combating evil and thus provide justification for vengeful attitudes towards and violent treatment of those we deem our oppressors?

In an attempt to orient the discussion to a modern context, Greg Carey asks the question, "What does it mean to defend these songs in Revelation, if one also experienced horror that people could rejoice over the events of September 11?"[8] Many Americans expressed anger, shock, and dismay at scenes of Muslims around the world celebrating the destruction of the Twin Towers and the thousands of lives that perished with them. While I was writing this very chapter, the news broke that Osama bin Laden, the terrorist deemed responsible for the attack on the Twin Towers, was killed by American forces in Pakistan. In an interesting parallel to the days following 9/11, news programs aired scenes of crowds and individuals around the world celebrating this man's death. It was obvious from the sheer joy exuded by some and their expressed desires for more violence that some had crossed the line into an inappropriate triumphalism, especially so when such thirst for vengeance came from Christians whose words seemed incongruous with the admonition of their own master to "Love your enemies" (Mt. 5:44) and who modeled such a response himself by praying on the cross for his own persecutors (Lk. 23:33-34).

Yet the reality of inappropriate rejoicing does not negate the possibility of appropriate rejoicing. Regarding the death of Osama bin Laden, President Obama declared to the families of 9/11 victims, "Justice has been done." For these individuals who had their lives shattered on that day, their rejoicing was not one of celebratory glee so much as rejoicing borne out of a recognition that a measure of order had been restored to their lives, that their lost loved ones had received the justice denied them, and that a man who callously murdered thousands of innocent men, women, and children received the consequences of his actions.

When interpreting the celebratory language of Revelation 18-19, it is important not to confuse the message of Revelation with its misuse. The interpretation of this language requires examination of both its narrative context and rhetorical function. Within the narrative context, three features stand out as vital for framing the issue. First, all of the rejoicing described in Revelation 18-19 occurs *in heaven*, not on earth. The celebration in 19:1-3 is that of "a great multitude in heaven," while the command in 18:20 is for "heaven" to rejoice, which is then defined as saints, apostles, and prophets.

Recognition of this symbolic location is important for the second feature, which is that Revelation presents this as the rejoicing of genuine victims. These are those who have been slaughtered for their faithful witness now rejoicing in heaven that God "has avenged on her the blood of his servants" (19:2). Those who are not victims must tread cautiously when calling into question the justice that true victims seek and their response when that justice is acquired. It is the height of arrogance to tell Auschwitz survivors that it is inappropriate for them to rejoice at the fall of Nazism or to tell a rape victim not to rejoice when her attacker is sentenced. Their rejoicing is not triumphalistic glee, but the relief shared by all who suffer unjustly when order is restored, when the scales are balanced, and evil receives its due.

The third feature of the narrative context of Revelation 18-19 is the recognition that rejoicing is the appropriate response because it is a response to divine justice. It is the Creator God who enacts this judgment and therefore "his judgments are true and just" (19:2). This rejoicing occurs "in heaven" because this is about the accomplishment of *divine*, not human, justice. Wayne Meeks argues that "the apocalyptic rhetoric that puts ultimate judgment exclusively in the court of God exercises a healthy restraint on our moral fervor" by restraining "our own rush to judgment."[9]

Like much of its language, Revelation's judgment language functions in a dual manner. On the one hand, it provides comfort to those who suffer for their faithful witness within Roman imperial society. Judgment language assures them that God will not forget their faithfulness and endurance, but will likewise show himself faithful to them. On the other hand, for those believers who adopt an accommodationist stance with the idolatrous, immoral, economically oppressive aspects of Roman imperial society, John draws a clear line in the sand between the kingdom of God and the kingdom of the world and admonishes them to choose a side on which to stand.[10] In regard to such accommodationists, Bauckham writes that God's judgment on Babylon "will seem excessive to those taken in by the propaganda of the beasts because they themselves profit from Babylon's prosperity. Such people cannot see the violent and foul underside of their own history until their eyes are opened by such prophetic vision as Revelation provides."[11] The judgment on Babylon in chapters eighteen and nineteen provides that eye-opening prophetic vision. It establishes a clear division between the fate of Babylon and all who allow themselves to be seduced by its charms and the fate of those who embrace the pattern of the Christ and reject the compromise of their faith even to the point of death. Justice will be done and that justice will not be kind to those who cast their lot with Babylon.

The frequent contrasts in Revelation between heaven and earth, along with the association of the righteous with heaven and the identification of their opponents as "inhabitants of the earth," underscore the opposition between the kingdom of God and the kingdom of the world. Revelation 18 emphasizes Babylon's influence on earth. Those who weep and wail over her demise are "the kings of the earth" (18:3, 9) and "the merchants of the earth" (18:3, 11), also called "the magnates of the earth" (18:23). In addition, Babylon is declared culpable for all the righteous slaughtered "on earth" (18:24). Thus the rejoicing of those *in heaven* at the accomplishment of God's judgment contrasts sharply with those who have been seduced *on earth* and reinforces the clarion call for God's people to come out of Babylon (18:4).

The Final Conflict (19:11-20:15)

Having accomplished the judgment of Babylon, the focus shifts to the remaining opponents: the beasts (and those aligned with them) and the dragon. The justice of God demands a full accounting. Inaugurating this final conflict is Christ in the form of a rider on a white horse leading the armies of heaven into battle (19:11-16) while the beast and the kings of the earth gather for their final stand against him. The slaughtered Lamb has transformed into an eschatological warrior king. As warrior, he "judges and makes war" in righteousness (19:11). By connecting judgment with defensive war (as this war began with the opposition), John asserts that God's judgment is not a capricious attack on the unsuspecting and innocent but a just response to those who have chosen opposition. Some attempt to downplay the violent imagery of this scene by declaring that there is in fact no battle depicted.[12] The armies gather for battle and then victory is announced with no intervening conflict described. Yet a battle is described, though in minimalist fashion. The kings of the earth and the armies of the beast are "killed by the sword of the rider on the horse" (19:21) and the beast and false prophet are captured (19:20).

Though the image of Christ as warrior occurs earlier in Revelation (2:16), this appearance of the warrior on the horse stands in stark contrast to the dominant image of Christ employed throughout Revelation. How does one reconcile this depiction of violent conquest by the warrior Christ with the image of the slaughtered Lamb?

Reading this depiction of the warrior king in light of the larger narrative of Revelation reveals that the warrior and the Lamb are not as incongruous as they may appear. Throughout Revelation John juxtaposes language and imagery of conquest with that of faithful witness. The sword with which the rider strikes down the nations comes out of his mouth (19:15), while in the letter to Pergamum Christ threatens to make war against them "with the sword of my mouth" (2:16). The connection of sword and mouth suggests that the means by which Christ makes war and executes judgment is through witness, an association strengthened by the designation of the rider as "The Word of God" (19:13). The sword of his mouth functions as a metaphor for the Word of God, which exposes the deceptions of the beast for the lies that they are.[13] In the letters to the seven churches, the means by which the churches conquer is through faithful witness modeled upon that of Christ. John juxtaposes the war in heaven (12:7-9) with the statement that victory was achieved by "the blood of the Lamb and by the word of their testimony" (12:11). John even directly precedes his description of Christ as the warrior king in Revelation 19:11-16 with an admonishment to "hold the testimony of Jesus. . . . For the testimony of Jesus is the spirit of prophecy" (19:10).

The description of the rider also intermingles warfare with witness, though the ambiguity of the imagery makes the identification uncertain. The rider wears a robe dipped in blood (19:13), which may represent the blood of his enemies slain in battle, but may also be either the Lamb's own blood or the blood of the saints who have likewise been slaughtered for their faithful witness. Similarly, the armies of heaven that accompany the rider on the horse and that wear "fine linen, white and pure" (19:14) are most likely the faithful witnesses of God, since just a few verses prior "fine line, bright and pure" is defined as "the righteous deeds of the saints" (19:8). The point here is that an interpretation of the warrior Christ that takes it as antithetical to the image of Christ as slaughtered Lamb does not pay close enough attention to the story.[14] As Miroslav Volf states, the cross of Christ is not about victimization and the refusal to combat violence, but it is about "God's *setting aright the world of injustice and deception*."[15] The righteous judgment of God and the victory of Christ and his followers cannot be defined in isolation from the suffering witness of the Lamb and those who embody that pattern and who, through it, expose the deceptions of the kingdom of the world. Victory in Revelation comes through the faithful witness of Christ and his followers. It is because of such witness that Jesus can be declared "King of kings and Lord of lords" (19:16).

True victory, however, requires the final defeat of the enemy. Consequently, the beast and the false prophet are captured and sentenced to "the lake of fire" (19:20), which represents the final destination for all manifestations of evil in Revelation.[16] Barr argues that the lake of fire "symbolizes what we all know. There are some evils in this world that are beyond hope of repair."[17] With the defeat of the beast and false prophet, the true agent of opposition remains—the dragon. John describes the dragon's defeat with rather ambiguous imagery. The dragon is captured, imprisoned in a pit for a thousand years, and then released for a short time to make his final stand. Then he is cast into the lake of fire (20:1-10). Though the imagery is ambiguous, the message is not. It affirms a spiritual and eschatological truth—that God will defeat all opposition and that the kingdom of God will stand unopposed. The assurance in these scenes is not *when* God will act or even the literal specifics of *what* God will do, but *that* he will establish justice and set things right. It is this assurance that informs the call for endurance and faithfulness on the part of the saints.

Revelation's depiction of this final conflict culminates with a judgment scene centered around "a great white throne and the one who sat on it" (20:11). All are judged "according to their works" (20:12-13), thus fulfilling the *lex talionis* ("measure for measure") theme whereby actions receive their just consequences. Finally, Death and Hades join the beast, false prophet, and dragon in the lake of fire (20:14) as everything that stands opposed to God's plan for his creation (death, suffering, evil, oppression, deception) is destroyed.

Warfare and Opposition

Warfare in Revelation illuminates the nature of the opposition between the kingdom of the world as it exists under the authority of the dragon and the kingdom of God. Saying that warfare language in Revelation is a symbol for a deeper spiritual conflict does not negate its physical consequences. One such consequence is the suffering of God's faithful witnesses (Rev. 1:9; 2:3, 9-10, 13; 6:9-10;11:7-10; 12:11, 17; 13:6-7, 15-17; 16:6; 17:6; 18:24; 19:2; 20:4). Just as Jesus was slaughtered for his faithful witness, so too those who take up his pattern of faithful witness share in his sufferings. It is the kingdom of the world under the authority of the dragon that has waged this war and so war is what they receive. Thus, a second consequence of this war is the suffering of the opposition as a form of divine judgment.

Symbols are a means of expressing truth. In Revelation John presents a symbolic description that reveals the world as it is—in opposition. This is a truth that some in John's audience are deeply aware of, but that others need to wake up to. For those who are aware of it, John calls them to continued endurance in faith (14:12). For those who are not, John calls them to come out of Babylon (18:4).

"ALL THINGS NEW"

REVELATION 21-22

12

Say the word "apocalyptic" to the average person and it evokes images of destruction, gloom, and despair. As perpetuated by countless films, television shows, and novels, "apocalypse" has become synonymous with the end of the world. This common perception, however, misunderstands both the content and rhetorical function of ancient apocalyptic theology. In essence apocalyptic is about creation not destruction. An apocalypse may envision an ending, but when it does, that ending inaugurates a new beginning. Within the apocalyptic worldview destruction is never an end in itself but a prelude to new creation. In this sense the term "post-apocalyptic," which often refers in the popular lexicon to a struggle for survival or for rebuilding civilization in the aftermath of some devastation, becomes a misnomer when applied to a biblical context. This is because apocalyptic itself is as much about what follows destruction as what precedes it. Apocalyptic is about the interplay between despair and hope, pessimism and optimism.[1]

Apocalyptic inaugurates new creation. Rhetorically it effects a new creation by means of the new perspective it affords its audience. Through its use of symbolism and a transcendent perspective, apocalyptic transforms how people experience the world. By granting people a new perspective on the world, the world for them becomes a different place—a new creation. The concept of resurrection lies at the heart of Revelation's apocalyptic theology because resurrection is all about new creation. As with apocalyptic, resurrection involves both an ending and a new beginning. It is death leading to life; the destruction of the body ushering in a new creation body. The resurrection of Christ is also a transcendent event that compels us to experience reality in a new way. In light of the resurrection, old events acquire new meanings. In light of the resurrection, despair turns to hope. In light of the resurrection, suffering and evil do not get the last word.

New Creation

Revelation 21-22 depicts the implications of resurrection for creation. With the demise of the opposition and the destruction of Death and Hades, the old order of things has passed away (Rev. 21:4). Likewise the first heaven and the first earth have passed away (21:1). But these endings are not the final word in Revelation. As with the resurrection of Christ, an ending gives birth to new life. There is a "new heaven and a new earth," complete with a "new Jerusalem" (21:1-2), as the God of creation, the God of resurrection, declares, "I am making all things new" (21:5).

We know who God is by what God does—and God creates. God as Creator frames the main visionary material of Revelation. Revelation 4 extols God's worthiness by describing his creative activity in past tense: "you *created* all things, and by your will they existed and *were created*" (4:11; italics added). Revelation 21 describes the creative activity of God in present tense: "I *am making* all things new" (21:5; italics added). The God who created continues to create. With this vision of a new heaven and a new earth, Revelation asserts that the creative activity of God is not an accomplished fact of the past but very much the basis of our hope for the future because creation is not simply what God once did but a component of who God is.

A second framing device used in Revelation further clarifies this point. Three times Revelation employs the statement "I am the Alpha and the Omega"—once at the beginning of the book and twice at the end. There are a couple of interesting progressive movements with this phrase in Revelation. The first two times it appears, it is God who makes the declaration (1:8; 21:6). The last time it is Jesus who declares himself "the Alpha and the Omega" (22:13). Also, each time the statement appears, an additional explanatory phrase is added to it.

1:8   I am the Alpha and the Omega (God)

21:6   I am the Alpha and the Omega, the beginning and
        the end (God)

22:13   I am the Alpha and the Omega, the first and the last,
        the beginning and the end (Jesus)

The parallel phrases Alpha and Omega, first and last, beginning (*arche*) and end (*telos*) are not simply temporal parameters identifying the beginning and ending point of creation, for there is no end to creation in Revelation. When God declares in 21:6 that "I am the Alpha and the Omega, the beginning and the end," the emphasis is not on the cessation of the old creation but on the dawning of the new one. As the first and last letters of the Greek alphabet, alpha and omega represent the totality of all that comes between them. Essentially these are cosmological, not temporal, titles.[2] They identify the wholeness of God and Christ as they relate to creation. God is all in all. All of creation falls under his sovereignty and divine care. The title "the beginning and the end" affords further insight into the meaning of "the Alpha and the Omega." The word for "beginning" is *arche* and it identifies the origin or first cause of something. The term for "end" is *telos*, which refers to the fulfillment or completion of something. In essence, the *telos* is the goal towards which something is headed. To say that God is the *arche* and the *telos* is to say that God has laid the foundation and has then built upon that foundation for a purpose. The "end" (*telos*) is the proper fulfillment of the "beginning" (*arche*). Revelation 21-22 reveals that the goal towards which God has been working all along is the goal of new creation. This new creation is not a sequel to God's original creation or a "Plan B" as though God is scrapping everything that came before and starting over from scratch. Rather, it is creation's ultimate fulfillment and completion, much like the resurrected body of Christ is the fulfillment and *telos* of his human body. What Revelation 21-22 asserts is that God's new creation is the omega to the alpha, the *telos* of the *arche*.

Since new creation is the ultimate goal and fulfillment of God's original creation, it is not surprising that this "last" creation echoes the "first" and fulfills its promise. Within this new creation is the Garden of Eden, complete with the tree of life (22:1-2). Only this time the curses that marred Adam and Eve's sojourn in the garden and led to their exclusion are no more (22:3). This time God's people experience his presence directly (22:4). There is no longer a need for the sun and the moon for God himself "will be their light" (22:5). Most telling is that in God's new creation suffering and injustice cease to exist. There are no tears, no mourning, no sorrow, no pain, and no death (21:3-4). As we have seen, suffering plays many roles within our world and even though we may not always understand it, living in the tension between faith and experience requires awareness that our suffering and the suffering of those around us is only part of the story. Christ suffered in his human body, yet if the story of Christ ended with the cross there would be no hope. The story of Christ is incomplete without resurrection—a resurrection that gives birth to a new creation without suffering, frailty, or weakness. The story of Christ sets the pattern for the story of creation. As the incarnation with all its attendant suffering found its ultimate fulfillment in the "new creation" of Christ's resurrected body, so also God's creation with all its attendant suffering finds its ultimate fulfillment in "a new heaven and a new earth" where suffering is no more. This is why any attempt to explain or comprehend human suffering that ignores eschatology is insufficient because without eschatology the story of creation is incomplete, just as without the resurrection the story of Christ is incomplete. The good news of Revelation 21-22 is that suffering does not survive resurrection.

Revelation 22:13 culminates the threefold repetition of "the Alpha and the Omega" by presenting Christ rather than God as the one making the declaration. This switch to Christ reaffirms that God's plan for his creation comes to fulfillment in and through Christ. Throughout Revelation the pattern of the Christ has been normative for Christian faithfulness. That pattern is that faithful witness even to the point of death will result in vindication. Prior to Revelation 21-22 the focus has been on the first part of that pattern—faithful witness and the suffering that attends it. Revelation asserts that suffering for one's witness to the kingdom of God is a participation in the pattern of the Christ. The pattern, however, is incomplete without the vindication of God's faithful. In Revelation 14-20 God acted in justice by delivering judgment upon the recalcitrant opposition. For God to be shown as truly just, however, God must also deliver on the promise of vindication and reward for the faithful. Revelation 21-22 brings the pattern of the Christ to fulfillment with its vision of the faithful blessed in the presence of God. But what exactly is the nature of their vindication and exaltation? For that we turn to an examination of the new Jerusalem.

New Jerusalem

John's description of the new Jerusalem that descends from heaven is a symbolic one that reveals the spiritual reality of God's new creation rather than a literal description of final reward. Taken literally, John's description collapses in on itself. How can one have a city that is fifteen hundred miles high (21:16)? What's the point of having gates in the city if the gates are never shut (21:25)? How is it that such massive gates are at the same time a single pearl (21:21)? Recognizing the symbolic nature of John's description is essential because the symbols are the message. The focus of Revelation 21-22 is not reward per se, but the fulfillment of God's divine plan as it is realized in the new creation. The vindication of the saints and their reward for faithfulness is the right to participate in God's new creation. Those who conquer are the ones who "will inherit these things" (21:7). It is through the symbolism of the new Jerusalem that John defines most clearly what participation in that new creation entails.

One common criticism of Revelation and its interpretation derives from this idea of the vindication of the saints. Too many Christians have trumpeted Revelation 21-22 as an announcement of their own glorification at the expense of their enemies. God's reward is that they now get to rule over their oppressors. They, the poor and oppressed, become the new powerbrokers in God's kingdom. It becomes a sort of even trade-off where the wicked get to rule in this world, and the righteous get to rule in the next. The problem with such a view is that it defines "reigning" in the kingdom of God in the same terms as reigning in the kingdom of the world.

Some critics of this Christian triumphalism recognize it as a problem of interpretation, meaning that these ideas arise from a misunderstanding of John's message by certain religious groups. Others, like D. H. Lawrence, blame John himself. For Lawrence, self-glorification represents the entire tone of Revelation as it incorporates John's "grandiose scheme" for annihilating anyone not of his ideological mindset and then "climbing up himself right on to the throne of God."[3] Yet is this the nature of Christian vindication and exaltation in Revelation? Is it lordship over one's enemies or ruling others with a rod of iron? Is it a gleeful power grab or a pseudo-humble celebration of conquest? If the symbols are the message, then the meaning of exaltation in God's new creation is not defined as power or glorification of the saints, but as identity, security, access, and service.

First, the new Jerusalem represents the *identity* of this new creation community. In line with the flexibility of symbolic language, the new Jerusalem is both a place *and* a people, the bride of the Lamb (21:2, 9).[4] The use of the number twelve to characterize the size and structure of the city further elaborates the identity of those who inhabit it. The city measures twelve thousand stadia (approximately fifteen hundred miles) in length, height, and width (21:16). The wall of the city has twelve gates, with twelve angels stationed at the gates, and the names of the twelve tribes of Israel inscribed on the gates (21:12, 21). The wall of the city, which is 144 (twelve x twelve) cubits thick (21:17), has twelve foundations with the names of the twelve apostles inscribed on them (21:14). The presence of the twelve tribes and twelve apostles identifies the city as a composite of patriarchs and apostles, Israel and the church. To be a citizen of the new Jerusalem is to belong to the whole people of God (21:3) united in one covenant community. God's faithful witnesses are declared his children (21:7) and they wear his name on their foreheads (22:4). The vindication of the saints here is their full incorporation into the people of God and their full realization of communion and relationship with God.

A second feature of their vindication is *security*. To be a faithful witness for the kingdom of God in the first-century Roman Empire was a tenuous endeavor fraught with many potential dangers. Unadulterated allegiance to the kingdom of God could result in persecution, economic hardship, or other forms of societal pressure and intimidation. In a world where one is called to be faithful to the point of death (Rev. 2:10), security was a scarce commodity. This accounts for one aspect of the seductive lure of Rome. With its military strength and economic control, Rome offered a sense of security for those willing to align with its concerns. The opposing teachers who are influencing some in John's churches ("Jezebel," the Nicolaitans, the Balaamites, and the false apostles at Ephesus) seemingly advocate for a degree of participation in the religious and cultural life of Roman imperial society. The message that one could be faithful to God and yet enjoy the security, prosperity, and cultural inclusion afforded by Rome would be a powerful temptation. John's counter-argument, however, is that such promises of security and prosperity are as empty and deceptive as the false face that Rome presents to hide its true monstrous and evil nature.

The vision of the new Jerusalem asserts that genuine and lasting security resides only within the kingdom of God realized eschatologically. Only there will there be no death, no pain, no suffering, no oppression, and no deception. The symbolism of the city's walls and gates communicates the security of the city. In the ancient Mediterranean world a city's security was only as strong as its walls and gates. The walls of the new Jerusalem not only measure about fifteen hundred miles in length but in *height* as well (21:16). Furthermore, the walls measure approximately seventy-five yards in width. These are walls that no army could scale or penetrate. Given the emphasis on the impenetrability of the walls, it comes as a bit of a surprise, then, to learn that the gates of the city are never shut (21:25), thus effectively neutralizing the benefit of the walls. The imagery, of course, breaks down when interpreted literally. Interpreted symbolically, however, the massive walls and gates symbolize the security of God's new creation for his faithful witnesses. No harm will come to them here. The presence of the walls and gates communicates security; that the gates are always open simply reveals a different truth about this city and those who inhabit it.

Open gates are a symbol of *access*. The gates allow access to the city and thus access to the very presence of God. The gates are never shut because in this new creation God's people have full and constant access to the presence of God. In the old creation, access to God was tightly controlled by the physical construct of the Jerusalem Temple and by ritualized activity. The presence of God resided within the Most Holy Place (or "Holy of Holies") of the temple, the innermost room of the temple complex. Access to God was then mediated by a series of courts with increasingly restrictive access. The Gentiles (or "nations") could not proceed past the outer Court of the Gentiles. Israelites were unable to venture further than the Court of the Israelites, unless they were priests who could move under proper ritual circumstances into the Court of the Priests and into the Holy Place of the temple building. Only one individual, the High Priest, had access to the Most Holy Place where the presence of God symbolically resided, and that was only on one day a year. The Israelite religion required mediation and barriers that restricted access to the presence and holiness of God.

God's new creation does away with all barriers and mediation. John tells us that God's new Jerusalem has no temple (21:22). With full access to the city comes full access to God. John's statement that the city has no temple, however, receives further symbolic elaboration with the explanation that the reason the city has no temple is because God and the Lamb have themselves become the temple (21:22). In line with this John describes the entire city as the Most Holy Place of God.[5] The city, like the Most Holy Place, is square (21:16) and is a place of purity (21:27) and worship (22:3). The new Jerusalem itself is the Most Holy Place and the throne room of God. To be in the city is to be in the direct, unmediated presence of God and of the Lamb. With all barriers removed, even the nations now have full access to God (21:24). Furthermore, in Revelation 21:3 John says, "See, the tabernacle of God is among mortals. He will tabernacle with them" (my translation). John's use of Greek terminology for the tabernacle here evokes the early days after the exodus event when God formed Israel into a covenant community. The message is that in this new Jerusalem God dwells directly with his people in covenant relationship—and they will see his face (22:4).

A fourth aspect of the vindication of the saints is *service*. The vindication of the righteous in Revelation is not an eschatological power-grab or the self-glorification of the pseudo-humble whereby they now get their long-awaited turn as the overlords. The primary cause of such misinterpretations are the statements that the saints "will reign with Christ" (20:4) or "will reign forever and ever" (22:5). Interpreting this language about reigning within the same framework as the kingdom of the world, in which reigning means power, authority, and oppression, is a grave mistake. What does it mean to "reign" in the kingdom of God? In every instance in Revelation where the saints are either said to reign or are identified as a kingdom, it is *always* connected to priestly service. Revelation 1:6 states that Christ, through his actions on the cross, "made us to be a kingdom, priests serving his God and Father." The way in which "priests" and "kingdom" are set in apposition to each other suggests that one defines the other. In other words, to be a kingdom means to be priests who serve God.[6] John makes a similar statement in 5:10, although there he separates "kingdom" and "priests," stating, "you have made them to be a kingdom and priests serving our God and they will reign on earth." When these two statements are read together, it suggests that the way in which the saints "reign on earth" is through their priestly service to God.

Now, by priestly service, John likely does not mean ritualized activities, but rather that their worship and their faithful witness to the kingdom of God is their priestly service. In Revelation 20, those saints who have been beheaded for their faith come back to life and reign with Christ for a thousand years (20:4, 6). Once again, this reign is not a form of divine payback in which the oppressed get their turn as the oppressors, but is defined as priestly service. These resurrected saints "will be priests of God and of Christ, and they will reign with him a thousand years" (20:6). Finally, within the new Jerusalem the vindicated saints "will reign forever and ever" (22:5). Given the consistent tendency of Revelation to define the reigning of the saints as priestly service, we would expect the same here. Prior to John's announcement of the saints' eternal reign, he declared that the throne of God and of the Lamb will be in the city "and his servants will worship him" (22:3). The term translated here as "worship" is a term commonly used for priestly service.[7] Reigning forever and ever in the new Jerusalem means being a faithful servant of God.[8]

The vindication and reward of the saints is a prominent theme in Revelation 21-22. When one allows the symbolism of the new Jerusalem to define and clarify that reward, one learns that the reward for faithful witness is to be declared the children of God, to have full and unmediated access to the presence of God, to experience complete security with an absence of suffering, and to devote oneself to the worship and service of God.

Overcoming Dualism

In characterizing evil as opposition to the kingdom of God and in defining the nature of that opposition as warfare, Revelation set up several dualistic constructs. The central dualistic structure is the kingdom of

God versus the kingdom of the world. Various representatives of the kingdom of the world have a dualistic counterpart on the opposing side: the beast versus the Lamb, "the great city" (Babylon) versus "the holy city" (Mt. Zion/new Jerusalem), and the dragon versus God. This dualism is not about equality, for the beast is no more the equal of the Lamb than the dragon is of God. Rather, the dualism identifies categories of opposition. The dragon and God are counterparts, the respective leaders of opposing kingdoms. In Revelation 14-20 the war between these opposing forces came to an end and with it the removal of the opposition as the beast and dragon found themselves confined to the lake of fire and "the great city" Babylon fell.

Another dualistic construct in Revelation that represents the opposition between the kingdom of God and the kingdom of the world is the dualism of heaven and earth. The term "earth" does appear in Revelation in a neutral sense as simply a location with no particular value assigned to it (5:3, 6, 13; 6:13; 16:18; 20:11). It also functions to identify an aspect of God's creation (10:6; 14:7) over which he is sovereign as "the Lord of the earth" (11:4). The most common usage of "earth" in Revelation, however, is as a symbol for the kingdom of the world that opposes the kingdom of God. In this sense, "earth" is aligned with evil over against heaven as the representative of God and his kingdom. The use of "earth" as a modifier for the opposition takes many forms in Revelation: "the kings of the earth" (1:5; 6:15; 17:2; 18:3, 9; 19:19), "the tribes of the earth" (1:7), "the merchants of the earth" (18:3, 11), "the magnates of the earth" (18:23), and "the inhabitants of the earth" (3:10; 6:10; 8:13; 11:10; 13:8, 12, 14; 17:2, 8). The "whole earth" follows the beast (13:3), while Babylon corrupts the earth (19:2) and rules over the kings of the earth (17:18).

As representatives of the kingdom of the world and the kingdom of God, earth and heaven are symbolically at odds. Revelation 11:15, however, describes a time when the dualism between these two kingdoms is overcome—not by the destruction of one or the other but by unification. The seventh angel announces: "The kingdom of the world *has become* the kingdom of our Lord" (italics added). As argued earlier, that uniting of the kingdoms in the context of chapter eleven occurs with the prophetic witness of God's people as they embody the pattern of the Christ. That unification of the two kingdoms, however, is preliminary to its full realization within God's new creation. John begins his description of the new creation by announcing the appearance of "a new heaven and a new earth; for the first heaven and the first earth had passed away" (21:1). The passing away of the first heaven and the first earth signifies the removal of opposition. Within the new creation heaven and earth are no longer in opposition, but coexist peacefully. A sign of this peaceful coexistence is the fact that "the nations" and "the kings of the earth"—both of which stood in opposition to the kingdom of God—now enter the city of God and "bring their glory into it" (21:24, 26).

The presence of the kings of the earth here is striking because Revelation 19:19-21 implies that the kings of the earth were all killed by the sword that comes out of the mouth of the rider on the horse. Such apparent contradiction only arises, however, from a too literal reading of the material. The symbolism here is that earth and heaven are no longer opposed in the new creation. "The kingdom of the world has become the kingdom of our Lord" as evidenced by the inclusion of the kings of the earth within the new Jerusalem. The old order of things (evil, opposition, chaos, suffering) has passed away along with the first earth. N. T. Wright says that evil "is the force of anti-creation, anti-life."[9] So evil finds no place in God's new creation since God is one who makes all things new (21:5) and who gives the gift of life (21:6).

Maintaining Dualism

Although John's description of the new Jerusalem effectively removes the dualism of opposition (heaven/earth, Lamb/beast, etc.), John does not fully abandon dualism as a rhetorical strategy. Evil finds no place in the new Jerusalem, yet it persists. Only now John re-frames it as an inside/outside dualistic structure. Those who conquer inherit the city and enter it; those who do evil are kept outside in the lake of fire

(21:7-8). Those whose names are written in the Lamb's book of life are inside the city, while outside is everything "unclean" and "anyone who practices abomination or falsehood" (21:27). Those who wash their robes have the right to enter the city, while "outside" are "the dogs and sorcerers and fornicators and murderers and idolaters, and everyone who loves and practices falsehood" (22:14-15).

The maintenance of this dualism serves John's rhetorical strategy. Apocalyptic is a call to action. Throughout Revelation, John has consistently set before his audience a choice: allegiance to the kingdom of God or allegiance to the kingdom of the world. His final words continue that call to decision. John says that there are two paths—the path of wickedness or the path of righteousness (22:11). These dual paths lead to two different outcomes—inside or outside. When John says that Christ will "repay according to everyone's work" (22:12), he is counseling his audience and all who thereafter read this book to choose their path.

Blessed, John writes, are all those who keep the words of this book of prophecy (22:7, 9). To keep the words of the book is to embody in one's own life the pattern of the Christ. It is a plea to live a life of faithful witness, knowing full-well that such allegiance to the kingdom of God may result in suffering and even death, just as it did with the one who set the pattern. But the resurrection of Christ points us to a vital fact about God and it is that fact that serves as the basis of the apocalyptic hope. Out of death, God brings new life; out of an ending, God brings new beginning; out of destruction, God brings new creation!

13

CONCLUSION

While writing this book, I attended a funeral for a seven-year-old boy who died in a tragic accident. A short time later one of my former students, a young minister with a wife and children who adore him, was diagnosed with terminal cancer. Stories like these could be compounded endlessly. In this study I have focused on the contextual nature of evil and suffering in Revelation, where evil is defined as opposition to the kingdom of God and where the suffering of the righteous is often an outgrowth of that opposition. The primary, though not exclusive, context for suffering in Revelation is the suffering that results from faithful witness. Here, though, I want to explore briefly some of the broader implications of Revelation's message as it relates to the suffering in our world today. What message does Revelation hold for the parents of that seven-year-old boy or my former student as he faces the horror of leaving his family behind? What might Revelation communicate to the rape victim, the refugee, or the abused spouse?

Revelation is one of the most relevant books for the living out of the Christian faith today, not only because of its emphasis on the necessity of faithful witness, but also because of how it encourages faithfulness

in the midst of horrific circumstances. Revelation is *apocalyptic* literature and apocalyptic is an indispensable guide for living faithfully in a
world of evil and suffering. The message of Revelation for all of God's
people who suffer pain and injustice begins with the assertion that the
Creator God is sovereign over his creation. He sits on the throne and
he rules his creation faithfully. As faithful ruler, God has a plan and a
goal for creation. One of the most difficult aspects of faith is the fact
that God's creation is beset by evil and suffering and God seems to be
doing little to stop it. Revelation, however, presents evil and suffering
as an unavoidable component of life. Yet recognizing that God does
not exercise his sovereignty by doing away with all suffering in life is
not the same as saying that God does not respond to it. God responds
loudly and clearly to the presence of evil and suffering in this world.
God's response is to meet us there in the form of the slaughtered Lamb.
Rather than ignore our suffering, he has joined us in it. The image of
the slaughtered Lamb reveals *how* to suffer in faith. The image of the
slaughtered Lamb teaches us that life is about more than the body and
that the suffering and hardship we may face in no way nullifies the love
of God nor his faithful activity on our behalf.

Above all, what the image of the slaughtered Lamb teaches us is that
suffering concludes with resurrection. God's sovereignty over creation
is best expressed through the pattern of the Christ. As Christ suffered
in his life on earth, so do we; but that is only half of the story. The goal
of Christ's story was not death but life! What God in his sovereignty
enacted in the life of Christ, he will also enact within creation itself.
Revelation assures us that the end of the story is only the beginning. In
the midst of our despair and our suffering we can know that God will
bring about new life and new creation. Apocalyptic is indispensable
for living out the Christian faith because apocalyptic is the language
of hope.

ENDNOTES

Notes to Chapter One

[1] All translations, unless otherwise indicated, are from the New Revised Standard Version.

[2] Two of the most common Greek words for "evil" are *kakos* and *ponēros*. Revelation 2:2 identifies the false apostles in Ephesus as *kakous* ("evildoers"). Both *kakos* and *ponēros* occur only one other time in Revelation, but there they are used to describe the foulness of the sores that break out on those who follow the beast (16:2).

[3] Roy F. Baumeister, *Evil: Inside Human Violence and Cruelty* (New York: Henry Holt and Company, 1997), 72-73.

[4] Baumeister, 379.

[5] Luke T. Johnson, *Faith's Freedom: A Classic Spirituality for Contemporary Christians* (Minneapolis: Fortress, 1990), 166.

[6] As quoted in Patrick O'Driscoll, "'BTK' calmly gives horrific details," *USA Today* (June 28, 2005): 3A.

[7] Johnson, *Faith's Freedom*, 172.

[8] David L. Barr, "The Lamb Who Looks Like a Dragon? Characterizing Jesus in John's Apocalypse," in *The Reality of Apocalypse: Rhetoric and Politics in the Book of Revelation*, ed. David L. Barr (Leiden: Brill, 2006), 214.

[9] Ibid., 211, 212, 219-220.

[10] Ibid., 214.

[11] Allan Boesak, *Comfort and Protest: Reflections on the Apocalypse of John of Patmos* (Philadelphia: Westminster Press, 1987), 14.

[12] Ibid., 37-38.

[13] Ibid., 72.

[14] Martin Luther, "Preface to the Revelation of St. John," in *Luther's Works*, vol. 35, trans. Charles M. Jacobs and E. Theodore Bachman (Philadelphia: Fortress, 1960), 398-99.

Notes to Chapter Two

[1] Johnson, *Faith's Freedom*, 152.

[2] John Mark Hicks describes going through a similar process following the death of his first wife. See *Yet Will I Trust Him: Understanding God in a Suffering World* (Joplin, MO: College Press, 1999), 15-23.

[3] C. S. Lewis, *A Grief Observed* (New York: Bantam Books, 1980), 5.

[4] "God Must Be Very Angry," *USA Today* (May 16, 1991), 1A.

5 "Where Was God?" *Detroit Free Press* (January 9, 2005), M1.

6 Jean Améry, *At the Mind's Limits: Contemplations by a Survivor on Auschwitz and It's Realities,* trans. Sidney Rosenfeld and Stella P. Rosenfeld (Bloomington: Indiana University Press, 1980), xi.

7 Frederick Sontag, "Anthropodicy and the Return of God," in *Encountering Evil: Live Options in Theodicy,* ed. Stephen T. Davis (Atlanta: John Knox, 1981), 150.

8 Richard L. Rubinstein, *After Auschwitz: Radical Theology and Contemporary Judaism* (Indianapolis: Bobbs-Merrill, 1966), 46.

9 Irving Greenberg, "Cloud of Smoke, Pillar of Fire: Judaism, Christianity, and Modernity after the Holocaust," in *Auschwitz: Beginning of a New Era? Reflections on the Holocaust,* ed. Eva Fleischner (New York: KTAV Publishing House, 1977), 23.

10 John H. Hick, "An Irenaean Theodicy," in *Encountering Evil,* 42, 48.

11 Hick, 51.

12 Stephen T. Davis, "Free Will and Evil," in *Encountering Evil,* 70.

13 Gregory A. Boyd, *Satan and the Problem of Evil: Constructing a Trinitarian Warfare Theodicy* (Downers Grove, IL: InterVarsity Press, 2001), 16.

14 Ibid., 294-95.

15 David R. Griffin, "Creation Out of Chaos and the Problem of Evil," in *Encountering Evil,* 104.

16 Griffin, 109-110.

17 John K. Roth, "A Theodicy of Protest," in *Encountering Evil,* 10.

18 Ibid., 8, 19.

19 Ibid., 15, 19.

20 Baumeister, 1, 8; Terry D. Cooper, *Dimensions of Evil: Contemporary Perspectives* (Minneapolis: Fortress, 2007), 10.

21 N. T. Wright, *Evil and the Justice of God* (Downers Grove, IL: InterVarsity Press, 2006), 113.

22 Roth, 8.

23 Baumeister, 375; Cooper, 183-192, 259.

24 Didier Pollefeyt, "*Horror Vacui*: God and Evil in/after Auschwitz," in *Fire in the Ashes: God, Evil, and the Holocaust,* eds. David Patterson and John K. Roth (Seattle: University of Washington Press, 2005), 228; see also 224.

25 Arthur McGill, "Human Suffering and the Passion of Christ," in *The Meaning of Human Suffering,* ed. Flavian Doughterty (New York: Human Sciences Press, 1982), 162.

26 Ibid., 172.

27 Kenneth Surin, "Theodicy?" *Harvard Theological Review* 76 (1983): 243.

[28] See Emmanuel Levinas, "Useless Suffering," in *The Provocation of Levinas: Rethinking the Other*, eds. Robert Bernasconi and David Wood; trans. Richard Cohen (London: Routledge, 1988), 157, 160.

[29] Sontag, 149.

[30] Ibid., 141.

[31] Surin, 230-32.

[32] McGill, 160.

[33] Stanley Hauerwas, *God, Medicine, and Suffering* (Grand Rapids: Eerdmans, 1990), 56.

[34] Ibid., 59.

Notes to Chapter Three

[1] Baumeister, 84-87, 181.

[2] Steven Friesen, "Sarcasm in Revelation 2-3: Churches, Christians, True Jews, and Satanic Synagogues," in *The Reality of Apocalypse: Rhetoric and Politics in the Book of Revelation*, ed. David L. Barr (Leiden: Brill, 2006), 127.

[3] Ibid., 128.

[4] Ibid., 136, 142.

[5] Tina Pippin, *Death and Desire: The Rhetoric of Gender in the Apocalypse of John* (Louisville: Westminster/John Knox Press, 1992), 72.

[6] Ibid., 21, 61.

[7] Ibid., 69-70, 80.

[8] Ibid., 80-81.

[9] Barr, "The Lamb," 211.

[10] Ibid.

[11] Greg Carey, *Elusive Apocalypse: Reading Authority in the Revelation to John*, Studies in American Biblical Hermeneutics, 15 (Macon, GA: Mercer University Press, 1999), 162.

[12] Greg Carey, "Symptoms of Resistance in the Book of Revelation," in *The Reality of Apocalypse*, 170-71.

[13] D. H. Lawrence, *Apocalypse*, in *Apocalypse and the Writings on Revelation*, ed. Mara Kalnins (New York: Penguin, 1995), 66.

[14] Ibid., 63.

[15] Ibid., 65.

[16] Ibid., 65, 67.

[17] Ibid.

[18] Friedrich Wilhelm Nietzsche, *A Genealogy of Morals*, in *The Works of Friedrich Nietzsche*, ed. Alexander Tille; trans. William A. Houseman (New York: MacMillan, 1897), 1.15-16 (pp. 52, 56).

[19] Barr, "The Lamb," 209.

[20] Ibid., 207.

[21] Ibid., 210.

[22] Ibid., 214; see also 209.

[23] Pippin, 80.

[24] Barr, "The Lamb," 216, 220.

[25] Ibid., 210.

[26] Robin Wood, *Hollywood from Vietnam to Reagan* (New York: Columbia University Press, 1986), 46-47.

[27] One narrative that employs the principle of incoherence regularly as a rhetorical device is the television series *Buffy the Vampire Slayer*. See Gregory Stevenson, *Televised Morality: The Case of Buffy the Vampire Slayer* (Lanham, MD: Hamilton Books, 2003).

[28] Carey, *Elusive Apocalypse,* 137, 159.

[29] Ibid., 176.

[30] Ibid., 179.

[31] Hauerwas, 43.

Notes to Chapter Four

[1] Tacitus *Annals* 15.44.

[2] For an assessment of the evidence relating to Domitian's reign see Leonard L. Thompson, *The Book of Revelation: Apocalypse and Empire* (New York: Oxford University Press, 1990), 95-115. Thompson also suggests that the portrait of Domitian as a mad tyrant may have been exaggerated by later sources for both personal and political reasons.

[3] Eusebius *Ecclesiastical History* 3.20.

[4] Leonard L. Thompson, "Ordinary Lives: John and His First Readers," in *Reading the Book of Revelation: A Resource for Students*, ed. David L. Barr (Atlanta: Society of Biblical Literature, 2003), 36.

[5] Pliny the Younger *Letters* 10.96. This translation is from Jo-Ann Shelton, *As the Romans Did: A Sourcebook in Roman Social History* (New York: Oxford University Press, 1988), no. 399.

[6] Pliny the Younger *Letters* 10.97.

[7] Harry O. Maier, *Apocalypse Recalled: The Book of Revelation after Christendom* (Minneapolis: Fortress, 2002), xiii.

[8] Ibid., xii.

[9] Ibid., xiii. See also J. P. M Sweet, "Maintaining the Testimony of Jesus: The Suffering of Christians in the Revelation of John," in *Suffering and Martyrdom in the New Testament*, eds. William Horbury and Brian McNeil (Cambridge: Cambridge University Press, 1981), 102; Ian Boxall, *The Revelation of Saint John*, Black's New

Testament Commentary (Peabody, MA: Hendrickson, 2006), 12-13; Wes Howard-
Brook and Anthony Gwyther, *Unveiling Empire: Reading Revelation Then and Now*
(Maryknoll, NY: Orbis Books, 1999), xxii.

[10] Boesak, 38.

[11] Maier, xiv; Richard Bauckham, "Judgment in the Book of Revelation," *Ex Auditu*
20 (2004): 14-15.

[12] Adela Yarbro Collins states that "the crucial element is not so much whether one
is actually oppressed as whether one *feels* oppressed." *Crisis and Catharsis: The Power
of the Apocalypse* (Philadelphia: Westminster Press, 1984), 84.

[13] Ibid., 105-106.

[14] Bauckham, 12.

[15] Ellen T. Charry describes John's apocalyptic response as a double-edged sword
designed "to both bolster the faithful in their precarious situation and to hold their
feet to the fire." "'A Sharp Two-Edged Sword': Pastoral Implications of Apocalyptic,"
Interpretation 53 (1999): 163.

[16] See Robert H. Mounce, *The Book of Revelation*, New International Commentary
on the New Testament, rev. ed (Grand Rapids: Eerdmans, 1998), 71; Boxall, 59-60.

[17] *Supplementum Epigraphicum Graecum* (Leiden: A. W. Sijthoff, 1923-), 26.1817,
LL. 28-39; Judith 4:11-13; 1 Maccabees 9:23-27.

[18] 1 Maccabees 6:7-11.

[19] See for instance, Testament of Benjamin 3:3.

[20] Clement of Alexandria, *The Educator* 3.8.41; Shepherd of Hermas, *Similitudes*
7.1-7.

[21] For a more extensive description of the various roles of temples, see Gregory
Stevenson, *Power and Place: Temple and Identity in the Book of Revelation*, Beihefte
zur Zeitschrift für die neutestamentliche Wissenschaft, 107 (New York: Walter de
Gruyter, 2001), 37-114.

[22] Esther V. Hansen, *The Attalids of Pergamon*, 2nd ed. (Ithaca, NY: Cornell
University Press, 1971), 254-55.

[23] J. Schäfer, "Pergamon," in *The Princeton Encyclopedia of Classical Sites*, ed.
Richard Stillwell (Princeton: Princeton University Press, 1976), 689; Hansen, 263.

[24] *Die Inschriften von Pergamon*, ed. Max Fränkel (Berlin: W. Spemann, 1890,
1895), 8,1.223, 226; 8,2.489-491.

[25] Adolf Hoffmann, "The Roman Remodeling of the Asklepieion," in *Pergamon:
Citadel of the Gods*, ed. Helmut Koester (Harrisburg, PA: Trinity Press International,
1998), 54-57.

[26] Schäfer, 691; Ekrem Akurgal, *Ancient Civilizations and Ruins of Turkey*, trans.
John Whybrow and Molie Emrel, 7th ed. (Istanbul: NET Turistik Yayinlar, 1990), 105.

[27] Hansen, 257-58; Wolfgang Radt, *Pergamon: Geschichte und Bauten, Funde und
Erforschung einer antiken Metropole* (Köln: Dumont, 1988), 149.

[28] Aelius Aristides *Concerning Concord* 18.

[29] Friesen, "Sarcasm," 137.

Notes to Chapter Five

[1] Ernst Käsemann, "The Beginnings of Christian Theology," in *New Testament Questions of Today*, trans. W. J. Montague (Philadelphia: Fortress, 1969), 102.

[2] As related to me by Carl Holladay and used with his permission.

[3] This is a limited definition based on the one created by The Apocalypse Group of the Society of Biblical Literature Genres Project and which is presented by John J. Collins, "Introduction: Towards the Morphology of a Genre," *Semeia* 14 (1979): 9.

[4] David L. Barr, "The Apocalypse as a Symbolic Transformation of the World: A Literary Analysis," *Interpretation* 38 (1984): 49.

[5] Robert Kirschner, "Apocalyptic and Rabbinic Responses to the Destruction of 70," *Harvard Theological Review* 78 (1985): 44.

[6] D. H. Lawrence, "Introduction to *The Dragon of the Apocalypse* by Frederick Carter," in *Apocalypse and the Writings on Revelation*, ed. Mara Kalnins (New York: Penguin, 1995), 47.

[7] Brian Blount offers a helpful survey of such criticisms, *Can I Get a Witness? Reading Revelation through African American Culture* (Louisville: Westminster John Knox Press, 2005), 28-31.

[8] Ibid., 32.

[9] N. T. Wright responds to the idea that we must avoid the dualism of good and evil by arguing that once we jettison the categories of good and evil, it takes us right back to the Holocaust. Wright, 24. L. Russell notes that all moral systems require opposing concepts in some form. "Evil, Monsters and Dualism," *Ethical Theory and Moral Practice* 13 (2010): 49.

[10] Baumeister, 40.

[11] David Aune adds this emphasis on the function of apocalyptic to the earlier definition created by the Apocalypse Group of the Society of Biblical Literature Genres Project; see "The Apocalypse of John and the Problem of Genre," *Semeia* 36 (1986): 89-90.

[12] Wayne A. Meeks, "Apocalyptic Discourse and Strategies of Goodness," *Journal of Religion* 80 (2000): 461-62.

Notes to Chapter Six

[1] Sweet, 104.

[2] Blount, 84.

[3] For an interpretation of being made a pillar in the temple of God as a symbolization of priestly service, see Stevenson, *Power and Place*, 247-250.

[4] Thompson, "Ordinary Lives," 32-33.

⁵ For an image of Helios with radiate crown, see Gisela Marie Richter, *Perspectives in Greek and Roman Art* (London: Phaidon, 1971), fig. 143.

⁶ Suetonius, *Augustus* 94.6; Lucan, *Civil War* 7.457; Harold Mattingly and Edward A. Sydenham, eds., *The Roman Imperial Coinage* (London: Spink and Sons, 1968), 93, nos. 1-10.

⁷ Blount, 82.

⁸ Charry, 163.

⁹ Stephen L. Homcy notes that the two most faithful churches (Smyrna and Philadelphia) are not called to repentance and, considering that the letter to Smyrna alters the common opening of "I know your works" to "I know your afflictions," he asks, "Could it be that the church that suffered the most needed repentance the least?" "'To Him Who Overcomes': A Fresh Look at What 'Victory' Means for the Believer According to the Book of Revelation," *Journal for the Evangelical Theological Society* 38 (1995): 195.

¹⁰ Boesak, 83.

¹¹ Wright, 43.

Notes to Chapter Seven

¹ For more information on the meaning and use of golden crowns, see Gregory Stevenson, "Conceptual Background to Golden Crown Imagery in the Apocalypse of John (4:4, 10:14:14)," *Journal of Biblical Literature* 114 (1995): 257-272.

² As an example, the citizens of Iasos once erected an inscription in honor of the city of Priene after that city sent one of its judges to them in order to help with the adjudication of their court cases. *Inschriften von Priene*, ed. F. FRHR. Hiller von Gaertringen (Berlin: Georg Reimer, 1906), 53I. The conclusion of the inscription reads (with italics added for emphasis): "therefore, in order that the People may be seen showing *gratitude* to its benefactors and that the others who come to judge in our city might seek to complete the cases in a manner *worthy of praise and honors*, knowing that the People both praises and honors noble and good men; be it resolved to praise the People of Priene because of the virtue and goodwill they hold toward our city and to crown them with a *gold wreath* from the amount established by law."

³ David Aune argues that the throne room scene in Revelation 4 may also function as a direct parody of the Roman imperial throne room. See "The Influence of Roman Imperial Court Ceremonial on the Apocalypse of John," *Biblical Research* 28 (1983): 5-26.

⁴ As Johnson notes, God is "the Creator and ruler of all the world, no part of which is simply ruled by Satan." *Faith's Freedom*, 157.

⁵ Boxall, 95; Ben Witherington, *Revelation* (Cambridge: Cambridge University Press, 2003), 120; Robert H. Mounce, *The Book of Revelation*, rev. ed. (Grand Rapids: Eerdmans, 1998), 129-130.

⁶ Bauckham argues that the content of the scroll is not that of the judgments of the seven seals because the scroll is only opened after the seven seals are broken. Therefore, he concludes that the scroll is opened in seven stages and then given to

John only in chapter 10 (thus equating the scroll of Revelation 5 with the "little scroll" of Revelation 10). Consequently, the revelation of the scroll's content occurs only in the chapters following John's ingesting of the little scroll. See "Judgment in the Book of Revelation," 7.

[7] Boesak, 56.

[8] Henry Barclay Swete, *The Apocalypse of St. John* (reprint; Eugene, OR: Wipf and Stock, 1998), 77.

[9] Boesak, 57; Mounce, 132-33; G. R. Beasley-Murray, *The Book of Revelation* (London: Oliphants, 1974), 124-25.

[10] Blount, 70-84.

[11] Ibid., 74.

[12] I agree with Sweet who argues that Revelation's combination of notions of sacrifice, victory, and witness moves us to a "deeper understanding of the atonement than that of the overcoming of sin's defilement by sacrifice." Sweet, 114-115. Witherington notes that the image in Revelation combines aspects of both the sacrificial lamb and the militant ram. 120-21; see also, Boxall, 98-99.

[13] Blount, 86-87

Notes to Chapter Eight

[1] Bauckham, 5.

[2] The same term is also used of the rider on the red horse who takes peace from the earth so that people "slaughter" one another (6:4). Though not necessarily the direct victims of this seal, the souls under the altar are victims of the human tendency to employ violence against whatever is deemed a threat to them.

[3] For a much fuller discussion of altar asylum and the evidence for it, see Stevenson, *Power and Place*, 103-113.

[4] Apuleius, *Metamorphoses* 11.10.

[5] Plutarch, *On Superstition* 166E.

[6] Aeschylus, *Suppliant Maidens* 83-85, 190.

[7] *Lexicon Iconographicum Mythlogiae Classicae*, ed. John Boardman et al. (Zurich: Artemis Verlag, 1981-), 4.2, pp. 338, 340; nos. 266, 272, 274.

[8] Achilles Tatius, *Leucippe and Clitophon* 8.8.9-11. The italicized word is my own translation.

[9] Pausanias, *Description of Greece* 7.25.1.

[10] The altar in the Jerusalem Temple did not function as a place of asylum in the same way, owing to the fact that there was only the one altar with limited access to it. That the Jerusalem altar did not function socially or legally as a place of asylum, however, is not the same as saying that the idea of an altar did not function symbolically as a place of asylum within at least certain segments of Jewish thought, particularly those most influenced by Greek culture. For instance, the first-century Jewish authors Josephus and Philo employ the theme of an altar as a place of asylum.

For a description and examples of such texts in Philo and Josephus, see Stevenson, *Power and Place*, 163-164.

[11] The translation is from James H. Charlesworth, ed., *The Old Testament Pseudepigrapha* (New York: Doubleday, 1983), 1.531.

Notes to Chapter Nine

[1] Aune, *Revelation 6-16*, 541.

[2] David Barr, for instance, writes that in Revelation "One even has the sense that God is willing to engage in torture in an effort to induce humanity to repent." He concludes, however, that suffering does not produce repentance, and therefore "it seems inevitably to lead to destruction," 211.

[3] Johnson, 172-73.

[4] Ibid., 173.

[5] Grant R. Osborne, *Revelation*, Baker Exegetical Commentary on the New Testament (Grand Rapids: Baker, 2002), 404.

[6] The international focus of John's commission differs from Ezekiel's, which is directed at the "house of Israel" (Ezek. 3:1, 4).

[7] Bernard McGinn, *Anti-Christ: Two Thousand Years of the Human Fascination with Evil* (San Francisco: HarperSanFrancisco, 1994), 31.

[8] Ibid.

[9] Witherington, 158-59; Mounce, 217; Boxall, 164.

[10] David E. Aune, *Revelation 6-16*, 628-29. Compare with Revelation 16:9 which equates language of repentance with giving glory to God.

[11] Bauckham, 2-4.

[12] Leo Mildenberg, *The Coinage of the Bar Kokhba War*, ed. Patricia Erhart Mottahedeh (Aarau und Frankfurt am Main: Verlag Sauerländer, 1984), series #1, nos. 1-104; George Francis Hill, *Catalogue of the Greek Coins of Palestine* (Bologna: Arnaldo Forni, 1965), 284-87, nos. 1-20, pls. 32-33.3.

Notes to Chapter Ten

[1] Boxall, 178.

[2] Osborne, 456; Boxall, 178.

[3] Richard Oster, "Numismatic Windows into the Social World of Early Christianity: A Methodological Inquiry," *Journal of Biblical Literature* 101 (1982): 204-208.

[4] Richard Oster, "Christianity and Emperor Veneration in Ephesus: Iconography of a Conflict," *Restoration Quarterly* 25 (1982): 143-149.

[5] Harold Mattingly and Edward Sydenham, *The Roman Imperial Coinage. Vol. II. Vespasian to Hadrian* (reprint; London: Spink and Sons, 1986), 209, coins 440-441.

[6] For instance, see Laura Breglia, *Roman Imperial Coins: Their Art & Technique* (London: Thames and Hudson, 1968), 92-93, #30.

[7] Homer, *Iliad* 2.308; Plutarch, *Isis and Osiris* 359e, 362e, 363b.

[8] Adela Yarbro Collins, *The Combat Myth in the Book of Revelation*, Harvard Dissertations in Religion, 9 (Missoula, MT: Scholars Press, 1976), 57.

[9] Jan Willem van Henten, "Dragon Myth and Imperial Ideology in Revelation 12-13," in *The Reality of Apocalypse: Rhetoric and Politics in the Book of Revelation*, ed. David L. Barr (Leiden: Brill, 2006), 197, 202.

[10] Apollodorus, *The Library* 1.6; Hyginus *Fabulae* 140.

[11] Early Jewish and Christian traditions (1 Enoch; Jude) that attest to the idea of rebellious angels depict them as leaving heaven of their own accord rather than being cast out as a result of battle; see, Aune, *Revelation 6-16*, 698.

[12] In Luke 10:17-20, Jesus uses the language of Satan falling from heaven in response to reports of his disciples casting out demons. This describes the *present* defeat of Satan any time his demons submit to the name of Christ.

[13] Blount, 62.

[14] The early second-century document in which the provincial governor Pliny sought advice from the emperor Trajan provides some interesting parallels to Revelation 13. Pliny asked for help in dealing with trials of Christians. Part of his concern lay with the need to identify exactly who qualifies as a Christian. In order to determine this, Pliny set up the image of the emperor, along with the images of the gods, and ordered those accused to perform an act of worship to the image. The purpose of this "acid test" was simply to discern who was truly a Christian as Pliny had been informed that genuine Christians could not be made to worship any images. For those who refused his command, Pliny ordered their execution; see Pliny the Younger *Letters* 10.96. Considering that worship of the imperial image was not mandated as law in the first century AD, the Pliny-Trajan letter offers one type of context in which a provincial governor might be involved in the execution of Christians over their refusal to worship "the image of the beast" (Rev. 13:15).

[15] Steven Friesen, *Imperial Cults and the Apocalypse of John: Reading Revelation in the Ruins* (New York: Oxford University Press, 2001), 203.

[16] Bauckham, 11.

[17] Boesak, 27.

[18] Aune, *Revelation 6-16*, 749-750; Boxall, 192.

[19] Boesak, 106-107.

Notes to Chapter Eleven

[1] George Lakoff and Mark Johnson, *Metaphors We Live By* (Chicago: University of Chicago Press, 1980), ix, 3; Max Black, "More About Metaphor," in *Metaphor and Thought*, ed. Andrew Ortony, 2nd ed. (Cambridge: Cambridge University Press, 1993), 38-39.

[2] Some would argue that all of the females in Revelation are negative stereotypes because they are subordinate to males (a debated accusation). This, however, involves holding Revelation accountable to very specific modern feminist standards (for